NEW GOD, NEW NATION

NEW GOD, NEW NATION
Protestants and Self-Reconstruction
Nationalism in Korea
1896–1937

Kenneth M. Wells

UNIVERSITY OF HAWAII PRESS
HONOLULU

To Young-Oak and our children

Acknowledgement is made to Cambridge University Press for permission to reproduce much of the material from chapter 7, originally published in *Modern Asian Studies*, Number 19, Volume 4, 1985.

Published in North America by
University of Hawaii Press
2840 Kolowalu Street
Honolulu, Hawaii 96822

Published in Australia by
Allen & Unwin Pty Ltd
8 Napier Street, North Sydney, NSW 2059 Australia

Library of Congress Cataloging-in-Publication Data

Wells, Kenneth M., 1953–
    New God, new nation : Protestants and self-reconstruction
nationalism in Korea, 1896–1937 / Kenneth M. Wells.
    p. cm.
    Includes bibliographical references and index.
    ISBN 0-8248-1338-3
    1. Nationalism—Korea—History. 2. Protestants—Korea—
Intellectual life. 3. Korea—Civilization—20th century.
I. Title.
DS916.25.W45 1991   90-21320
951.9′03—dc20   CIP

Printed by SRM Production Services SDN BHD, Malaysia

Contents

Abbreviations

CDU   Chōsen dokuritsu undō
CMSS   Chōsen mondai shiryō sōsho
CTS   Chōsen tōchi shiryō
GGPAB   Government-General Police Affairs Bureau
GSC   Gendaishi shiryō: Chōsen
USPM   United States Presbyterian Mission Archives
YUL   Yonsei University Library

Preface

This book is a cultural history of the development of a Protestant
form of nationalism in Korea, a type of ethical nationalism which I
have termed self-reconstruction nationalism. Its objective was to
build a modern nation-state whose identity centred on the attainment
of a democratic, self-reliant, 'Christian' society through spiritual renewal, moral reformation and purposeful action. This stream of
nationalism was not in the end the largest or most influential among
the several competing forms of nationalism the Korean nation would
adopt. But from its first strong appearance in the Independence Club
in 1896 to its final suppression along with other streams when Japan
invaded China in 1937, Protestant self-reconstruction nationalism remained remarkably true to its original inspiration. It also constantly
either contributed to or became the object of serious debate over
issues of tradition, ethnicity, culture, politics, class and collaboration.

A study of Protestant self-reconstruction nationalism is important
for several reasons. First, it brings into sharp relief some of the thor-
niest and most emotional issues of nationalism of the oppressed—
in this case of Koreans under a rather heavy-handed, militaristic
Japanese colonial administration. The specific charges of collaboration in which self-reconstruction nationalists were at times embroiled
highlight the general difficulty of attaining unity over means, let alone
ends, among people who have been robbed of political power. I have
endeavoured to describe the Protestant movement in terms of its dissatisfaction with much of the more explicit nationalism of the colonial
era. Apart from the Korean 'conservative' scholars, whose influence
waned dramatically in the early twentieth century, the Protestant
self-reconstruction nationalists were virtually the only group to raise

serious questions about the assumptions of the anti-Japanese
nationalist movements. With certain changes, such debate continues
today, and the importance of the Protestant contribution to it is far
from negligible.

Secondly, the tensions experienced by many of the Protestants engaged in nationalism—tensions between the universalistic nature of
their faith and the particular demands of nationalism—remind us of
what nationalism essentially is: a creed or movement that demands
exclusive allegiance, often on the basis of race, and of the culture
which it is asserted belongs to that race, or vice-versa. Under the rule
of a different race with a different culture, the tensions became acute.
These tensions raise questions about the nature of a religious alliance
with nationalism. The experiences of the Protestants who experience
this tension also shed some light on why it is that nationalism is so
ambiguous, appearing at times to be intellectually barren, narrow
and even dangerous, and at other times culturally rich and even liber-
ating.

Thirdly, the fact that Protestantism was a new and 'foreign' religion
throws into relief the whole question of national identity: its sources,
its relation to tradition versus the nationalist drive to create something new, and its often explicit demand for cultural homogeneity.
The Korean self-reconstruction movement, at least in terms of its
rhetoric, looked forward to an almost total reformation of national
culture. Consequently, it was involved in a profound cultural struggle
over the nation, in which each of the other streams, including socialist
nationalists, campaigned to unite the people under one cultural form.
In its nationalist form, cultural struggle appears to require a statist
resolution of conflict.

Fourthly, the foregoing illustrates another characteristic of
nationalism, namely, that it operates by excluding or minimalising
divisions within society. Related directly to this is its avoidance of any
analysis of society in terms of differences of interests, background
and so forth within it. Almost by definition, 'national society' refers
to unity. Nationalism therefore is considered to be something generic: it is everyone's business and everyone stands to gain from the
success of the nationalist enterprise. Sectional interests either do not
exist or, where they cannot be ignored, must be suppressed. The Korean Protestant nationalists regarded the nation as they did their
church: as a community of shared values. As each church member
was equal before God, so each citizen was equal before the nation.
They were interested in class and gender as part of their attack on
Confucianism, and there is no reason to believe they were not fully
sincere in this, but self-reconstruction was not a program of liberation
of classes or women. Externally, liberation from foreign interference
was wanted, but internally the people were to be trained to recon-

struct the nation. The movement was pioneered by high-class males, with few exceptions; the lower classes and the women were to be freed from ignorance and indolence for the sake of the nation. They were to be nationalised.

Finally, a study of Korean Protestant self-reconstruction nationalism underlines the variety of nationalisms in existence and the difficulty of defining each. Within the general definition of nationalism as a movement to possess and advance one's nation in the form of a strong, fully independent state, there is something quite unique in each instance of nationalism which seems at times to be far more important and certainly more engaging than the broader concept of nationalism. The more one studies a specific nationalist creed and movement, the more a general definition recedes from one's sights. This, I suspect, is the meaning of Pascal's observation that the more the mind is at work the more it discovers the original. Yet after close examination of a specific nationalism, one is pleasantly surprised to discover a deeper sense of nationalism as a general reality of our modern world—as if to confirm that it is, after all, only through attention to a particular case that we grasp some inkling of the general. This I suppose is a justification of history, and it is in the hope of promoting a greater understanding of both Korea and ourselves that I have written this book.

I have used the McCune–Reischauer system of romanisation of Korean *han'gŭl* strictly throughout this book, even for terms which have traditionally been written otherwise, in the belief that it is time to standardise transliteration of Korean in scholarly works. The only concession made here is to Syngman Rhee, whose name is virtually a household term. In addition, the romanisation of names of Korean authors of English-language works in reference notes and the bibliography follows the preferences of the authors concerned.

A book is seldom the work of one person, and in this case there are more people who have contributed to it than I can possibly acknowledge. Over the course of the years I have devoted to this book I have met numerous kind people who have generously encouraged, advised or actively supported my labours. There are many whose comments have sparked an insight or prompted a train of thought which then became part of this study.

My lifelong gratitude goes to Professor Wang Gungwu, now Vice-Chancellor of the University of Hong Kong, for inspiring me at a crucial time to undertake serious study of Korean history and culture and for his continued interest in my progress and support for my endeavours. To Andrew Fraser and John Fincher of the Department of Far Eastern History at the Australian National University, I owe a great deal for their efforts to expedite publication of this work. I have especially appreciated the supportive environment at

Indiana University and count it a privilege to work amongst colleagues who show a genuine interest in one's field of research. My thanks go to Charles Greer for reading over part of the manuscript, to Robert Eno for much welcomed moral support, to Sue Tuohy for helpful insights on the culture of nationalism, to Jody Ferguson for patiently solving glitches in my computer and to George Elison and George Wilson for constant encouragement, advice and assistance over the past three years. Horace G. Underwood and Samuel Moffett both showed great patience in allowing me to work through their valuable private collections in their own homes. Finally, my discussion of Korean nationalism has been aided greatly by the recently published studies in the field of modern Korean nationalism by Vipan Chandra and Michael Robinson.

In the final stages of preparing a manuscript it seems only too true that 'of the making of books there is no end'. I cannot adequately express my gratitude and respect to my wife, Young-Oak, for her patient support despite her own busy life. I also thank my children, Natalya, Jaeson, Jeremy and Maurice, for accepting so graciously my rather too frequent absences on weekends and holidays.

Bloomington, Indiana
March 1990

Introduction

The concept of the nation-state is one of the most powerful political concepts of modern times. The sheer strength of the nationalist movements of the past century and a half is startling, and yet, as Isaiah Berlin has observed, this global phenomenon was unforeseen by the political and social thinkers who lived immediately before its appearance.[1] Nor, with few exceptions, did they desire it. To the great minds of the nineteenth century, excited (or troubled) by the deep changes taking place in intellectual and material culture, it was inconceivable that something as intellectually barren or even irrational as nationalism should take centre stage in the development of human history. In nationalism, history has handed us a paradox.

The paradox is only deepened by the frequent fusion of inherently particularistic nationalisms with universalistic religions. Ever since Carlton Hayes' ground-breaking study of 1933, historians have tried to dispel at least the paradox by attributing the rise of 'state churches' to the decline of sacred or international languages and the accompanying disruption of Christendom and its counterparts.[2] By identifying itself with something limited like a state, religion presumably became open to serving something particularistic like nationalism. But the precise nature of this unlooked-for alliance remains a puzzle. In the West, one may trace this development back to the Reformation period. In Korea, however, the alliance between Protestantism and nationalism occurred extremely rapidly. To Korea's traditional scholars, the prospect of an age-old order based on supposedly universal norms of civilisation being replaced by a fragmentary system of nation-states was a baleful one. Although the decline of their own tradition and its sacred writings opened the way for it, they regarded the new system not as a development but as an imposition. Nor were the ready-made conclusions of the new political philosophy that gained entry with the new faith without difficulties and tensions for Korea's Protestant intellectuals.

Nation, state and religion: Concepts in tension

Large and significant events in the lives of groups appear at times to stimulate deep reflection on their identity. Where the situation is insecure, threatening or in some other way critical, the people tend to develop a heightened awareness of 'history'. This awareness has inspired inquiries of considerable influence into the meaning of history. An example is Augustine's *City of God,* in which he searched for an understanding of human life that both made sense of the impending collapse of the Roman system and defined the cosmic role of the community of belief to which he belonged.

In the case of Augustine, the community concerned had the advantage of a strong identity as a growing Christian church. But as an expanding community it had cosmic ambitions and therefore it set itself no racial, ethnic or geographical boundaries. In this respect the contrast with the narrow exclusiveness of modern nationalism could hardly be more complete. Augustine did not produce an argument for nation-states and no nationalism arose in response to the crisis of his time. Yet nationalism in recent times has arisen in part out of reflections on identity at a critical historical juncture,[3] and in the West has involved exactly the same religion. While co-operation between a universalistic religion like Christianity and the particularistic concept of the nation-state may indicate the strength of modern nationalism, it is thus not self-explanatory.

Many Christian thinkers have strongly condemned the identification of nation and state and the churches' patronage of it. Though the Protestant social scientist Jacques Ellul and the Catholic philosopher Jacques Maritain seem to have little else in common, they are united in their opposition to nationalism. Ellul considers it idolatrous,[4] while Maritain brands nationalism as a plague and describes the 'myth of the National State . . . the so-called principle of nationalities . . . that each group must set itself up as a separate State' as the demon of modern history.[5] He accuses the 'systematic identification of . . . *Nation* and *State*,'[6] and of nation and race, of betraying universal human priorities. The nation had become 'an earthly divinity whose absolute selfishness is sacred'.[7] Nationalism, the particularistic commitment to ties of blood, tribe or clan, was the antithesis of Christianity.

The catastrophe of World War I also prompted Christian censure of the identification of churches with nation-states, if not the concept of the nation-state itself. The Swiss theologian Karl Barth was a prominent leader in this movement from the 1930s, and the German Barmen Declaration of 1934 became its definitive document. Both the creation, at this time, of the Confessing Church in opposition to the German *National* Church and the co-operation between Dietrich Bonhoeffer and Bishop Bell of Chichester were attempts to retrieve and reaffirm the universality of the Christian faith. That this should have been necessary and that it should have encountered such resistance is a measure of Protestant servitude to nationalistic demands.

This phenomenon of the nation-state concept overcoming universalistic systems has recently come under scrutiny by a number of different scholars. In 1983 the philosopher Ernest Gellner argued that the political principle of the absolute congruence of nation and state is simply a realistic and even necessary response to gathering changes in the international order. What we call nationalistic sentiment, described by Lord Acton as the idea 'that nations would not be governed by foreigners',[8] is simply an emotional adjustment to the new realities—one which mistakes itself for the cause.[9] Although nationalist sentiment has thereby become one of the most powerful sentiments of modern times, this emotional aspect is relevant only as a means of mobilisation. It has no great determinative importance, because the global socio-economic developments of recent centuries have created an international environment in which nation-states are the only viable arrangement.[10] Since nationalism is sufficiently explained by these socio-economic developments, Gellner concludes, the 'ideological or doctrinal history of nationalism is largely irrelevant to the understanding of it'.[11]

In a more historically minded study published the same year, Benedict Anderson provides an interpretation which in some ways resembles Gellner's but which pays more attention to the emotional content and strength of nationalism. In order to make sense of the complex and discrete historical phenomena from which nationalisms have emerged, Anderson identifies two broad categories: the technological–economic developments and the anthropological–psychological changes which were perhaps attendant features of the former. The first category is similar to Gellner's socio-economic thesis, only the lynchpin in the whole process is 'print-capitalism,' which forms consciousness of horizontal communities of 'citizens' within specific geographical and linguistic boundaries. The second category encompasses intellectual, psychological and emotional factors.

The erosion of religious cosmologies in Europe gave rise to the emotional and intellectual climate in which particularistic nationalism thrives, as the loss of the religious viewpoint left a 'gaping emotional vacuum' which nationalism filled.[12] The emotional appeal of nationalism, according to Anderson, is therefore derived from its function as *ersatz* religion. It is in fact this emotional appeal which frustrates the more universalistic ideologies of our times. It explains in part why nationalism has become the great stumbling-block of Marxism, why even genuine socialist revolutions are defined in national terms,[13] and presumably why state allegiances are often more fundamental than religious beliefs.

The kinship Anderson posits between religion and nationalist sentiment is suggestive. Nevertheless there is something missing from his treatment of the subject. It does not recognise the strangeness of 'Christian nationalism,' which logically appears to be a self-contradiction, nor does it address the fervent opposition to 'Christian nationalism' by most serious theologians and Christian thinkers. The decline of religious cosmologies represents the loss of their cosmic vision, of their universalistic mode of thought. Thus the loss is primarily an intellectual one and the emotional vacuum only gapes as a consequence of this loss; it cannot be fundamental. To serve as *ersatz* religion, nationalism must compensate for the intellectual loss. Certainly, one can claim that nationalism gives a sense of meaning to human existence and that, by borrowing religious symbolism, nationalism wields an emotional power that supposedly 'scientific' ideologies are hard put to match.[14] But meaning in religious cosmologies is not exclusively an emotional matter; it is also very much an intellectual quest.

Gellner and Anderson agree that nationalism boasts no great thinkers. But this can hardly be said of religions, which do boast a good number of very profound thinkers. In this connection it must be noted that ideology, too, dates its rise from the decline of religious cosmologies. The non-nationalistic ideologies, particularly those that claim an all-embracing wisdom, reveal greater kinship with religion in this respect. It is hardly accidental that religions perceive in the modern rise of ideologies their greatest rival and threat—for instance, that the historian Herbert Butterfield should judge that Marxism poses the greatest challenge to Christianity because, like Christianity, it bases itself on a cosmic doctrine of history. At any rate, it was not because of its beguiling kinship to Christianity that Maritain denounced nationalism, but because he saw it as a negation of the Christian vision. Nationalism erects and justifies barriers between peoples; Christianity has to work in the opposite direction. What in nationalism is virtue becomes vice in Christianity.

But is there not perhaps some degree of kinship between nationalism and religious cosmologies in the sense of meeting the same human needs? Nationalism does appear to direct the ego towards an objective larger than itself. However, in a religion like Christianity, the service of God creates meaning in every conceivable contingency of life. Nor is any death meaningless, however it occurs, for all days are appointed and one is in God's knowledge after as before physical death. In nationalism, on the other hand, where meaning is related to national ends, only dying for the nation is comprehensible. There is no provision in nationalism for the comfort of parents whose infant dies of snake's venom or chance disease. Nationalism's design, if there is one, is to provide a secular form of religion's 'man-in-the-cosmos' and continuity beyond death; as such, it is transparently limited. Nor is its promise of relief from egotism genuine. To return to Maritain, the nation 'is an earthly divinity whose absolute selfishness is sacred'.

It may yet be argued that there is a *prima facie* case for divining kinship between religion and nationalism in another respect: both Islamic nationalism and the Catholic–nationalist connection in contemporary Poland indicate that the two *can* thrive together, and in Asia, nationalist movements which identify with religious movements are not uncommon. It has even been claimed that an 'understanding of the religious environment within which the politics of Asian States operate is essential to a comprehension of the role of nationalism in these politics'[15] The Aglipayan, or Philippine Independent Church, for example, enjoyed a symbiotic relationship with nationalism whereby both grew in strength. This suggests the possibility of a kinship, not where one fills the vacuum the other has left, but where the two discover common aims.

It is not difficult to imagine or find situations where common aims exist. Religious groups under colonial regimes have moral grounds for sharing the nationalists' objectives, especially where brutality and exploitation are rife. This does serve as a partial explanation of religious alliances with nationalism. Yet one would expect to find differences not only between the reasons advanced for opposing colonialism, but also between the methods adopted. And here the religion–nationalism alliance becomes problematic. Who ultimately calls the tune and who dances to it? It would seem that either the religion must adopt the principle of the nation-state, with its mythical rationale, as part of its creed and thereby become an expression of nationalism, or present an agenda of its own which will involve increasing tension with nationalism. The attempt to fuse nationalism and religion in the Russian literary tradition from Dostoevsky to Solzhenitsyn illustrates this problem. Dostoevsky's claim that the 'Russian Christ' is the true universal is designed to get the best of both worlds, but leads to imperialism. And when Solzhenitsyn implied that the proper duty of a Russian Orthodox priest is to serve the restoration of the 'real' Russia, he invited the reproof that serving God and serving this Russia are not the same thing.[16]

The attempt to fuse the two does not prove any essential likeness between religion and nationalism. There are and have been nationalist–Marxist alliances also, as shown by the numerous united front movements of this century. But these alliances, too, involve considerable tension, and Anderson's observation that all successful socialist revolutions have been defined nationalistically indicates that here also nationalism is capable of calling the tune. Further, genuine attempts at fusion at the level of ideas also take place between religion and ideology, as in the attempt to combine Marxian social analysis with Christian theology in recent 'liberation theology'.

A more satisfactory way of accounting for the fusion of religion and nationalism is to regard both as similar modes of cultural expression. Both sanctify culture and place it above everything else. The culture of a religion, because it is thought to derive from sacred ideas, is also sacred. The culture which nationalism projects is exalted above political ideologies, gender and class differences, and called the 'nation'. Both in this way make devotion and service of their cultural constructs the condition and content of unity.

This formulation comes very close to Benedict Anderson's view, since it implies that nationalism is a form of religion. Viewed as a cultural expression, it is difficult not to notice how nationalism deifies the nation and turns political activity into religious service. Culture and nation become one, and each reinforces the sacred character of the other. A recent study on Australian and Sri Lankan nationalism by Bruce Kapferer takes this approach, and in a sense develops Anderson's position to the point where nationalism is no longer *ersatz* religion, but authentic religion.[17] On this cultural basis Kapferer succeeds in attributing much greater depth to the religious mode of cultural expression than Anderson. Nationalism becomes a rather sophisticated phenomenon with carefully worked-out beliefs and well-planned institutions and programs which constitute its power. This, in addition to the emotional properties Anderson observes, is responsible for the achievements for good or ill of many nationalisms.

My own approach is similar to that employed by Kapferer and several others in the field of 'cultural history.'[18] However, some distinctions need to be made. There is an element of reductionism in recent cultural studies which I wish to avoid. In particular, I do not wish to reduce religion to culture, as if culture were primary. It seems just as possible and at least as intelligent to argue that culture is a religious expression rather than vice versa, though I fail to see that either is reducible to the other. Nor do I subscribe to the notion that this or any cultural struggle is the single principle of cause and effect in history—in other words, I am not advancing a materialist or monocausal point of view. Culture is not the whole story.

Nevertheless, it is a very important part of the whole story, and the value of the cultural approach is that it gives a more active, less secondary role in the making of history to beliefs, mental structures and their material expression than has often been the case. The 'discovery', (which though not new has some new twists) that these cultural ingredients create and invest power as much as, and often before, the reverse, has been very helpful in analysing such thorny issues as change in history. Nothing perhaps has contributed more in this respect than recent feminist studies of history.[19] In gender relations more than any other, cultural constructs are central, and nowhere else has it been so persuasively argued that power is not something simply imposed through institutions by one group over another or determined solely by economic forces, but is invested by the representations people share of their social world and by which they undertake the creation of that world. This approach I find fruitful in analysing the intense cultural struggle over the sources and content of nationhood which began in earnest in Korea from at least the mid-nineteenth century, although some further observations are necessary.

However we might understand both nationalism and religion as cultural expressions in history, it is still advisable to maintain a distinction between them. Only in their mode of expression are they at times indistinguishable. At least in regard to universal religions, religion and nationalism do not occupy exactly the same historical space, and there is no justification for having them occupy exactly the same analytical space. Universal religions have not derived from the same sources as nationalisms; they do not address entirely the same questions; and they do not have the same ultimate goals. There is, therefore, always active or latent tension, and so cultural struggle also takes place between religion and nationalism. Further, a religion like Protestantism has a rather less intense connection with culture than nationalism, for which culture and nation are one and the same thing. These issues are especially important in Korea, where Protestantism began as a foreign import and is still regarded by many as such.

My reference to universal religion can be questioned, for in a cultural analysis a religion does not exist as an essential system. Therefore, comparing the actual beliefs and practices of a religion's adherents with a scheme of what the religion 'really' is is out of court and can add nothing to the analysis. If no universalist principle was active in the minds or activities of Korea's Protestant nationalists, my use of the term 'universal religion' would have no point. However, I find evidence in their position of universalism which, though often latent, surfaced enough to raise questions about the depth or propriety of the Protestants' involvement in nationalism. Nationalism, of course, works to exclude anything disagreeable from religions it co-opts, and so it is difficult to see how universalism might surface within nationalist discourse itself. But Korean Protestantism did exist empirically outside of Korean nationalisms, including the nationalism it helped to fashion, and Protestant nationalists did not live exclusively within a nationalist world. The 'texts' of Christianity, the Bible and the secondary canon, also existed empirically as sources which were appealed to for a critical appraisal of nationalist dogma.[20]

Protestants and the Korean nation

It is not surprising that Tonghak (Eastern learning), later Ch'ŏndogyo (the religion of the Heavenly Way), should have become deeply involved in Korean nationalism. It was founded in 1860 by a politically unsuccessful scholar who believed it was the peculiar mission of Korea to revive Eastern wisdom and set it uncompromisingly against the West. Its objective was the exultation of Eastern culture according to the Korean genius. But first it was necessary to reform the Korean nation and state, and for this it engaged in chiliastic rebellions, prophesying the advent of a new dynastic millennium. It was natural that it should become a force in nationalism in the twentieth century, for it is an example of a religion founded within a nationalistic context, and its pantheistic scheme adapted well to the nationalist requirement of unity.

Nor is it surprising that, amidst the contemporary search for the authentic, indigenous origins of Korean nationhood, current historiography in Korea pays a great deal of attention to the Tonghak movement. It is assumed that the central religious motif that 'Heaven and humanity are one' (*In nae ch'ŏn*) pointed to a Korean type of egalitarian society which the Japanese invasion and subsequent national division and neo-colonialism have forestalled. But while this focus on Tonghak is understandable, it is as well to remember the existence of not one Korean nationalism, but several competing nationalisms, all with their views on the origin and content of nationhood. An exclusive concentration on Tonghak and its related movements would amount to a suppression of evidence concerning the contribution to Korean nationalism of, among others, Protestants, whose influence was disproportionate to their numbers and whose activism is unusual in East Asia.

From the foundation of the Independence Club in April 1896 to the Japanese invasion of China in July 1937, Protestants were involved in most phases and streams of the nationalistic movement in Korea and abroad. Those who counted themselves Protestants included Syngman Rhee, leader of the American-based democrats, president of the Shanghai Provisional Government and later of South Korea, Yi Tonghxi, Prime Minister of the Provisional Government, guerilla leader and a founder of the Korean communist movement, Yun Ch'iho, politician, educator and president of the Independence Club and

Self-Strengthening Society, An Ch'angho, leader of the 'gradualist' movement, ten of the eleven organisers of the Tokyo students' Declaration of Independence of 8 February 1919, sixteen of the 33 signatories to the March First Declaration of 1919, Ch'oe Hyŏnbae, a leader in the Han'gŭl literacy movement, Kim Kyusik and Yŏ Unhyŏng, proponents of socialism, Kim Maria and Yim Louise, organisers of national women's movements and education, and Cho Mansik, champion of economic nationalism and head of the Interim Government in North Korea from August 1945 until January 1946. Even Kim Ku, organiser of assassination and sabotage squads, was a Protestant.

This distribution of Protestants among such a wide range of approaches, some of which were mutually antagonistic, makes it difficult to identify any specific Protestant contribution to Korean nationalism. What reasons for participating in nationalism did Protestants have which distinguished them from non-Protestants? Was it simply that, being among the first to receive a Western education, the Protestants were among the first to imbibe Western political ideas? Or were they persuaded that because the 'Christian' nations were so ordered, the nation-state principle was therefore Christian, just as eighteenth century Korean Catholics believed a feudal order was Christian? For many Protestant nationalists the answer to both questions seems to be 'yes'. However, the writings and activities of one group of Protestants indicate that Protestants did directly influence the formation of at least one stream of nationalism: self-reconstruction, or 'ethical' nationalism. Insofar as it attempted to shape nationalism according to the faith of its members, this group also experienced the most tension with nationalist sentiment which focused on the expulsion of Japan.

In the late nineteenth century a self-strengthening movement arose among members of the Reform Party (Kaewha Tang). This initially meant strengthening the army and economy through modernisation in the same way as Meiji Japan, which was supposed to have adapted Western learning to its own needs. But among Protestant reformers the idea gained currency that inward, spiritual and ethical strengthening was required before outward, material strength could be achieved. In the 1890s Sŏ Chaep'il and Yun Ch'iho developed an ethico-spiritual critique of Korean society, beliefs and politics on the basis of their recently acquired Protestant faith. Korea's material weaknesses were regarded as symptoms of moral and spiritual decline, and self-strengthening was reinterpreted as the religious and ethical renewal of individual and society. In addition to, or rather as an extension of, Christian faith, this required modern education, training in civic virtues and unity among all classes. The perceived result was the institution of a liberal democracy.

After Japan annexed Korea in 1910, this view was developed into a self-reconstruction theory which was supported by some Buddhists and Ch'ŏndogyo adherents as well as Protestants. The basic outline of the theory can be stated simply enough. Korea's colonial fate was a result of the lack of the material requisites of a modern state. This material lack was a result of an absence of moral fortitude and spiritual integrity which was manifested in factionalism, a lack of public morality and a fatal tendency to rely on larger powers in times of both peace and crisis. Japan herself was certainly a problem, but she was also part of a deeper and more pressing problem: if Japan were to leave one day, she or another power would be back the next. Hence any independence which bypassed spiritual self-reconstruction would depend constantly on outside protection. Self-reconstruction involved reform of the national character, to be pursued within the supportive structures of model communities. These pilot communities were to be the future form of Korea in embryo; as they matured, they would render foreign rule unnecessary and ultimately impossible.

Protestants naturally took an ethical view of nationalistic activity. The value of any action was based on its relation to universal and eternal ethical standards. History acquired meaning insofar as it was oriented towards the 'Kingdom of God', just as individual life had to be directed towards the perfection promised to it through the resurrection. Conversely, all action contrary to truth and holiness would be eternally condemned, regardless of the end it served. The solution to the tension between nationalistic ends and transcendental claims was *ethical nationalism,* a nationalism which would align the people with the values of the 'Kingdom of God'. Self-reconstruction of individual and national character was more than a nationalist strategy; it was the spiritual task of any nation, whether independent or not.

The inflexible opposition of the Japanese Government-General to any political movement among Koreans after 1905 encouraged self-reconstruction Protestants to separate the concepts of 'nation' and 'state' in order to emphasise the priority of cultural reconstruction over political action. This was not a denial of the nation-state formula: it was meant to establish national culture as the only valid basis of the state and also to argue the meaningfulness of ethical nationalism, especially when political nationalism was blocked. In the 1920s this became the basis of the self-reconstruction Protestants' call to reconstruct the nation as a 'Christian' civilisation, and ensured their participation in the culturalism of the time.[21]

This raises the issue of the Korean Protestants' view of culture. The New Testament contains no mention of 'culture', which suggests that the concept was considered irrelevant to spirituality. While this does not mean that spirituality is irrelevant to culture, it strongly implies that culture and civilisation are not ends in themselves, and indicates a hostility to the adoption of the faith for its cultural potential. Many Protestants in the West have therefore tended not to value culture or civilisation very highly. The Reformation view (to simplify matters) is that faith so transcends culture that 'it makes civilisation, as such, questionable'.[22] Wherever it competes with faith as a solution to the human condition, it has to be rejected. The idea that Christ stands above cultures, judging them all, is a powerful current in Reformation theology.[23] Nevertheless, many Protestants have sought to mitigate the tension between civilisation and faith. Even Kierkegaard, who developed the Lutheran doctrine of salvation by divine grace alone into his principle of the 'absolute qualitative distinction' between God and humankind, combined aesthetics, ethics and the spiritual life as interdependent components of human civilisation.

Korea's Protestants, however, divined no tension between faith and civilisation. Even T. S. Eliot, who argued that there was an intimate and necessary relationship between the two, is set apart from Korean Protestant intellectuals by his denial that a people can deliberately construct a civilisation according to conscious design.[24] Perhaps their closest ally in the West is Karl Mannheim, founder of the International Library of Sociology and Social Reconstruction.[25] Korean Protestant leaders did not bother with the question of whether civilisation belonged to 'nature' or 'grace'. Although they recognised that the separation of knowledge and virtue was possible, they regarded it as an aberration, and for that reason defined the civilised person as one who was spiritually refined. Their iconoclasm was directed against specific 'idols' in Korean culture, not against a high view of civilisation; they had no argument with the highly positive Chinese concept of civilisation (*munmyŏng*).[26] They were not, after all, Western Protestants, but Korean intellectuals with a cultural heritage of their own. The distance between belief in the new God and the expectation of a strong new Nation was spanned by the assumption that true nations derive from civilisation which is founded on an ethico-spiritual ideal.

This brings us to a consideration of the Confucian background of the majority of Protestant nationalist leaders. When the Chosŏn dynasty was founded in 1392, neo-Confucianism was proclaimed as the state ideology and, with one or two exceptional periods of tolerance of Buddhism, it was given pride of place and exclusive privileges until the end of the nineteenth century.[27] Strong emphasis was placed on moral development, or 'polishing' one's moral nature, in which loyalty (*ch'ungsŏng*) and filial piety (*hyodo*) especially were to shine forth. The profounder one's scholarship, the greater one's moral rectitude, or conformity to the way of Heaven (*ch'ŏn*), was believed to be. Through their moral wisdom and example, the rulers from king down to bureaucrat were to lead the common people in a paternal, authoritarian manner, and so bring harmony and prosperity to the land. The means of this moral development was thorough schooling in the Chinese Confucian classics. This course was available only to the higher classes, known in Korea as the *yangban*. Advanced literary training in the Confucian texts was the key to civilisation.

Korea's cultural nationalists, among whom we must include Protestant self-reconstruction nationalists, carried over neo-Confucianism's faith in the civilising function of education and moral self-improvement. They believed in the force of ideas, even imported ideas, to change national character and thereby the national state. Essentially, political change had to go hand in hand with cultural change, a change which could be planned and effected only by intellectuals. The traditional view of human nature, that it was distinguished by a capacity for moral understanding and was therefore morally educable, was applied more democratically than before to include the lower classes. But the people continued to be regarded as a moral 'category', and the nation was seen to depend on their 'enlightenment' by the cultural élites.

The Protestant self-reconstruction principle of the ethico-spiritual foundation of the nation-state, the intensity of the Protestants' educational campaigns and their preoccupation with civilisation may all be understood in the light of the Confucian background of the movement. The 'self-cultivation' societies (*suyanghoe*), established by An Ch'angho and Yi Kwangsu to train the new citizenry, appear to have stemmed from the neo-Confucian concept of polishing one's moral nature. Not only does the cultural *modus operandi* of the self-reconstruction movement reflect this tradition, but the very idea of adopting a new religion to form the people into a new nation fits the neo-Confucian understanding of civilisation perfectly. (Naturally the choice of Christianity or anything other than the Confucian tradition was unacceptable, but the principle behind it was the same.)

Granted these neo-Confucian legacies, it would nevertheless be extremely misleading to conclude that Korean Protestant self-reconstruction nationalism was essentially an extension of the traditional background of its protagonists. For in a real sense, it was a very iconoclastic movement, dedicated to the eradication of the neo-Confucian mentality, culture and political system of the time. Obviously this was not 'pure' Confucianism, but the Protestants had to attack the form that existed and did not appeal to pristine Confucianism in order to do so. Neither the content of the new civilisation, nor the grounds of its desired unity was envisioned as neo-Confucian. Where certain traditional ideas or moral precepts overlapped with the actual form of Protestantism brought into Korea, the traditional views were reinforced, and they certainly influenced the

way in which the new ideas were adopted. But even this is misleading, for the traditional ideas were frequently reinterpreted by Protestants in a way which was inconceivable within the tradition, then used
as weapons with which to overthrow neo-Confucianism.

There is nevertheless a strong tendency to overestimate the degree
to which a new system is fashioned by the existing tradition, for
reasons which do not appear particularly valid. It is often assumed
that a tradition has extraordinary inertia and that the longer its history, the stronger its grip on a people. One almost gains the impression that tradition becomes part of the genetic make-up of a people
and travels in the bloodstream. But tradition exists in the people's
minds and operates through structures and institutions, such as government, religion and family, which socialise the people. A long
tradition appears to have such a hold because these institutions have
had longer to perfect themselves and to eliminate alternatives. But no
socialisation is ever complete, since discontinuities occur through
war, economic crises and so forth, and alternatives arise through contacts with other societies. Faced with such crises and contacts, people
can change their minds and set about changing the socialising structures. Whether they succeed or not depends on how many people
change their minds, how comprehensive the traditional institutions
are and how politically strong their defenders may be.

It is also argued that the advocates of a supposedly new ideal are so
involved in traditional terminology that they are themselves unaware
of the power tradition wields over them. It is certainly proper to point
to the seemingly intractable difficulties of extricating oneself from
language and symbolism, but it easily leads to the paradox that the
more fiercely the Korean Protestants, say, engaged tradition, the
more enmeshed they were in neo-Confucianism. On this showing,
Spinoza was really a traditional Jewish monotheist and Marx was
really a bourgeois moralist. There is something a little patronising
about this, and it would be better in our case to find out how aware
the Korean Protestants were of the differences between their own
and the traditional position before assuming they were basically neo-
Confucian.

With regard to filial piety, Protestantism certainly enjoins believers
to honour their parents and teaches a high view of the family. There
was therefore an overlap with Confucian ethics. But Korea's Protestant nationalists did not retain filial piety as the pattern for all social
relationships. On the contrary, when Syngman Rhee, Sŏ Chaep'il,
Yun Ch'iho and An Ch'angho all taught that officials were servants of
the people, this was a deliberate repudiation of the tradition of filial
piety. It is likely that the self-cultivation societies owe something to
neo-Confucianism, but again, when An Ch'angho established his
Hŭngsadan organisation, it was designed to encourage the practice of

democratic principles and its training method closely imitated the catechism classes of the Presbyterian denomination to which he belonged. His own inspiration was the local association system he (and de Tocqueville) observed during his exile in the United States. The content and objectives of the Protestant education endeavour, however it was expedited by the traditional regard for education, were also contrary to neo-Confucianism. In particular, the idea that the humblest person, male or female, could attain moral stature ahead of the highest élites flew in the face of neo-Confucian wisdom/ morality teaching.

Hence, although Protestant self-reconstruction nationalists carried over some key emphases and methods from their neo-Confucian background, they were advocating something genuinely new. They accepted the nation-state system as the natural and proper order for the world, and hoped to remould national identity around Protestant values. They regarded the spirit of Protestantism as a spirit of self-reliance and public altruism, in opposition to the 'toadyism' and corrupt self-seeking of the neo-Confucian establishment. The new nation was to be organised essentially as a liberal democracy, with modernisation of commerce and industry taking place along capitalist lines. Given that Protestants accounted for less than 2 per cent of the population by 1910, and not quite 3 per cent by the 1930s, it is remarkable that their views should have enjoyed the currency they did. This, however, has to be understood within the context of a wider nationalist impulse to modernise the nation through adaptation of Western civilisation.

What the Protestant nationalists retained from their tradition was a strong emphasis on the importance of culture both as an end and as a means, and a consequent reluctance to base national identity simply on race. Protestantism, also a universalist creed, served to confirm the tradition in this respect and to encourage the adoption of a culturalist form of nationalism. As a consequence, self-reconstruction nationalists tended to separate national culture from the state and concentrate their energies on the former. The exaltation of cultural reconstruction over political action exposed them to charges, from both the nationalist left and right, of compromise, opportunism and even passive collaboration in the 1920s and 1930s.

Incipient collaboration: A question of definition

Since the removal of Japan by non-Korean forces in August 1945, it has become commonplace to regard national figures such as Yi Kwangsu and Yun Ch'iho as failures; even Cho Mansik has not escaped unscathed.[28] The standard against which such figures are judged is simple and clear: it is overt, political resistance to the Japanese colonial regime; the benchmark is the type of national hero whose features adorn frescoes or are moulded into statues.

Somewhere in his writings, Karl Popper warns against over-subtle arguments which 'elaborately and solemnly' miss the point. On occasion it does happen that the intricacy of an argument becomes its undoing: the less straightforward, the less conviction it carries. Yet in historical writings, arguments are often dismissed on the basis of certain emotional commitments which refuse to admit any complexity into the problem. Few subjects are more prey to this emotional impatience than the problem of 'collaboration' under colonial regimes. Yet few subjects require so much emotional distance, for the intrusion into one's argument of the same partisan spirit that is under scrutiny is extraordinarily unhelpful. Here it is not subtlety, but the lack of it, which is unconvincing.

A thorough examination of the problem would require consideration of three aspects:

1. what the alleged collaborators claimed they were doing;
2. what other Koreans and the Japanese believed they were doing; and
3. what the historian with hindsight interprets them as having done.

In this book I deal more with the first than the second aspect, since the former has been neglected in favour of the latter. But I also offer an historical interpretation. My argument is that the issue in the debate over collaboration was essentially a question of political versus nonpolitical resistance, and that it was the tendency of the self-reconstruction group to give the 'nation' both logical and historical priority over the 'state' that brought upon them charges of compromise. Deeply involved in this issue is the tension between Christian universalism and an increasingly particularistic, race-based nationalism.

This tension is crucial to an understanding of Yun Ch'iho, who was the architect of self-reconstruction nationalism and, from the point of view of Christianity, one of the most eminent figures in Korea. But for most nationalists he was, after 1918, a disappointment. Yun is usually seen as an example of the vulnerability of highly educated aristocratic culturalists to the Japanese cultural offensive. But it is also very important to understand his alleged compromise in terms of his explicit Christian universalism. On his own terms he was a nationalist, deeply concerned over improving the lot of his compatriots, but he cast the struggle within his Christian understanding of society, of the behaviour of people in a fallen world. Though he was conscious enough of race, race was not a proper starting point, and a nationalism fuelled by hatred was dangerous. He began with individual corruption and transposed it on to the national and international arenas. Reconstruction of the nation was a necessity on several levels, but essentially it was a moral imperative that required prior spiritual renewal. Whether or not he later lacked will or courage, he remained consistent in his views.

A more pertinent criticism of the self-reconstruction ideal may be that it was naive. The philosophy of change which self-reconstruction nationalists held, that improvement of individual morality, knowledge and expertise would inevitably transform society and finally secure independent statehood, neglected the possibility of autonomous social 'laws' and appeared unmindful of the fact that, even in democratic nations free of foreign rule, social change demands considerable struggle. The notion that the militarily powerful Japanese empire would withdraw from the strategic Korean peninsula in recognition of its inhabitants having acquired the attributes of nationhood seems absurd. But then any self-assertion by Koreans, including political and military action, was on this view hopeless.

Again, the whole question requires closer examination. The debate between the Protestants and the radical left over the issue of feasibility suggests that the former were not so naive and that the idea that there were hard and fast divisions between socialists and non-socialists on this point needs modification. There were 'ethical' socialists (those who based an argument against treating human beings as commodities on Kantian ethics) involved in Cho Mansik's program for economic reconstruction and in An Ch'angho's gradualist approach. There was also prolonged debate among self-reconstruction leaders over the means of change and the relation between their ideals and independence. On the historical level, many Koreans appear to have adopted Christianity and socialism for the same reason—and many embraced both. Christianity offered relief from the degradation suffered at the hands of a non-Christian, non-Western power, but insisted also on overcoming the evils within Korean society; socialism promised the liberation of the oppressed colonial 'class', but was also concerned with attending to the class struggle within that 'class'.

The scheme of the study

This study begins with the creation of the Independence Club by Sŏ Chaep'il in 1896 and concludes with the invasion of China by Japan in 1937. The Independence Club is widely regarded as the first modern nationalist organisation in Korea, and was also the first opportunity for Korea's new Protestant intellectuals to present their self-reconstruction ideology to the nation. The Japanese invasion of China marked the end of all legal nationalist organisations and most illegal nationalist activities inside Korea. For the Protestant Church, it marked the beginning of a new period of intense suppression as the whole peninsula became pressed into the service of Japan's war effort.

Chapter 1 describes the expansion of Protestantism in Korea from its beginnings in 1884 up to the Great Revival of 1907–08 and the Japanese annexation of Korea in 1910. During this period Koreans experienced an attempted coup d'état (1884), the Tonghak Rebellion (1894), two major wars fought on their soil by Japan against China (1894–95) and Russia (1904–1905), the establishment of a Japanese Protectorate in 1905 and the final loss of independence in 1910. It was a period which saw the rise of competing nationalisms represented by the Reform Party (Kaehwa Tang), the Independence Club (Tae-han hyŏphoe), the politics of the Regent, known as the Taewŏn'gun, the self-strengthening and enlightenment campaigns and guerilla resistance to Japan. Within this context, Protestantism grew rather rapidly, expanding among the rural and lower classes as well as gaining the allegiance of a number of talented and energetic *yangban*, or élites. As the latter became prominent in nationalist organisations, the presence of a far larger number of Protestant commoners encouraged them to regard the new faith as the source of a new national unity and form.

Chapter 2 examines the same period, but focuses on Yun Ch'iho's development of self-reconstruction nationalism. A renowned polyglot, Yun was educated in Korea, Japan, China, the United States and France. In Korea he received a classical Confucian education, and in America a Protestant theological training at Emory College and Vanderbilt University. He became an active nationalist through his leadership of the Independence Club, as a founding member of the Korean YMCA and as the advocate of a new Christian-based education system. Yun became a harsh critic of neo-Confucianism as it was practised at the end of the Chosŏn dynasty and laid the groundwork for the succeeding self-reconstruction movement.

Chapters 3 and 4 concern what is known among Koreans as the 'Dark Ages', the first decade of Japanese military rule over the nation. The annexation deeply affected the nature of Korean nationalism. The Japanese suppressed all national organisations and began their ill-fated attempt to assimilate Koreans into the growing Japanese empire. Nationalism, previously more concerned with reforming or transforming the nation, now focused almost exclusively on independence from Japan. But by 1913 guerilla resistance inside Korea was crushed, and thereafter any direct political defiance had to be staged in Manchuria in the border regions. Protestants endeavoured to preserve a sense of Korean identity through churches and schools, but were subjected to sustained attacks by the

Government-General. With the arrest in 1911 of Yun Ch'iho and scores of other nationalist leaders, mostly Protestants, the scope for activism on the peninsula was severely curtailed.

The sufferings of this period encouraged the Protestants to regard their community of faith as a type of ancient Israel under bondage. As a remnant community, it was their mission to restore the nation and recreate it according to an ideal of Christian civilisation. Many Protestants who had fled abroad as annexation became imminent assumed positions of leadership in the exile communities through which they also popularised the identification of the Korean church with ancient Israel (in exile in this case). This symbolism was especially potent among Koreans in the United States, which as a 'Christian' nation was presumed to be a natural ally. It was in America that An Ch'angho, Yun Ch'iho's younger colleague, established the Hŭngsadan and further refined Protestant reconstruction ideology.

Chapter 5 examines the response of the Protestant self-reconstruction nationalists to the apparent opportunity for cultural nationalism afforded by changes in colonial policy in the wake of the March First Movement of 1919. This nationwide mass uprising for independence, designed in part to gain the support of the Western democracies gathered in Versailles at the conclusion of World War I, prompted the Japanese to allow the Koreans some limited expression through carefully scrutinised newspapers, journals and national organisations. But the failure and tremendous human cost of the movement, though itself a startling demonstration of unity, rent nationalism apart. Some saw in it proof of the need to organise military forces in Manchuria, some concluded that greater efforts must be put into the diplomatic offensive, while others forsook the Western democracies in disgust and embraced socialism. But the lesson drawn by self-reconstruction nationalists from the movement's failure was that it underlined their contention that politics without substance was counterproductive. Drawing upon their axiom that nationhood rested on an ethical and spiritual foundation, they proposed a separation of nation (i.e. culture) from the state (i.e. politics) and concentrated their efforts on education. This immediately embroiled them in a debate with socialists and right-wing nationalists, who charged them with compromise and collaboration.

From the mid-1920s, beleaguered nationalists from both left and right began to negotiate a united front movement, which materialised in 1927 as the Sin'ganhoe. In 1931, however, the front dissolved. In the same year the Japanese made their final preparations for the annexation of Manchuria, which heralded a period of intensified industrial development in northern Korea and of markedly increased suppression of Korean national movements. The self-reconstruction camp was not uninvolved in the united front, but its main focus was the Tonguhoe, the self-cultivation society which Yi Kwangsu had established in Seoul in 1923 as the Korean arm of An Ch'angho's Hŭngsadan. Its journal, the *Tonggwang*, became a forum for debate on the definition of national culture. This debate is the focus of Chapter 6.

The final chapter turns to the major test of the feasibility of self-reconstruction principles under colonial rule, namely, its application to economics. In 1922 the Presbyterian Cho Mansik established the Korean Products Promotion Society (Chosŏn mulsan changnyŏhoe) with the object of achieving economic self-sufficiency among Koreans. It initially attracted support also from Buddhists, Ch'ŏndogyo adherents and even some socialists, but soon ran into strife with the Japanese and came under fire as a bourgeois movement from socialists. Though not a resounding success, it was one of the most sustained movements in the 1920s and 1930s and, together with the Tonguhoe, ensured for the self-reconstruction movement a visible place in the nationalist debate.

Under the prohibitive conditions imposed by Japan, the self-reconstruction Protestants were unable to transpose their beliefs satisfactorily into action. In 1937 the Government-General ordered all national organisations to disband, began arresting self-reconstruction nationalists among others, and in 1938 forced the major Protestant denominations to bow to Japanese supervision. The experiment ended, for the meantime. The significance of this Protestant contribution to Korean nationalism lay in its creative 'solution' of the tension between faith and nationalism, its refusal to define nationalism in terms of the 'enemy', and its provision of a positive alternative. The extent to which it thus gave meaning to the everyday existence of the politically powerless Koreans on the peninsula is a subject for future social histories of the period.

The Protestant self-reconstruction movement was only one among many streams of nationalism active in Korea in the late nineteenth and early twentieth centuries. This study therefore does not pretend to be an interpretation of Korean nationalism as a whole. There is not one nationalism in Korea, but a number of competing nationalisms, and no definition of nationalism in terms of its content can draw them all together. Apart from desiring an independent nation-state and apart from believing in a historic mission to unite the whole nation under one state, Korean nationalists of different streams did not share the same views on what makes a nation and a state. Since there was no one view of what Korean culture was, there was no agreement on how to define the nation and consequently no common principle of unity or method. Among these competing streams, and in a time of discontinuities, Protestant self-reconstruction nationalism was a very consistent nationalist philosophy.

If anything draws Korean nationalisms together, it is that all were engaged in a cultural struggle over the form and content of the nation, a struggle which continues and which is still not resolved. Given the present division of the nation into two states, the tenacity of competing streams of nationalism, the growing revival of folk culture and the continuing engagement of Christianity in Korean national affairs, resolution of this struggle may have to await mutual recognition of the fact that, in any case, the imposition of a hegemonic culture will be no sound solution.

1 The introduction of Protestantism

In Chosŏn Korea, as in with many traditional civilisations, the boundaries between philosophy, religion and state ideology were indistinct. Non-Confucian religions had to be regulated or suppressed, not because of any anti-religious fervour, but lest they usurp neo-Confucian dominance of the national polity. Thus the presence of religious interpretations of the domestic and international crises facing the Chosŏn dynasty in the late eighteenth to early twentieth centuries, and the religious rivalry over the nation, were not exceptional. Korean nationalism, even in its modernising forms, was not a secularising force, but rather sanctified the nation, thus heightening the sense that the issues of a nation's origins, cultural values and political content were inherently religious. Although Protestantism had much to say on each issue, it entered a longstanding debate, the terms of which it often did not establish.

Traditional religious background

In the eighteenth century, deteriorating rural conditions were accompanied by growing peasant unrest. Partly in response to this strain on the feudal structure, there arose a group of scholars who promoted Silhak, empirical study, in opposition to what they believed was the excessive metaphysical speculation of the official neo-Confucian orthodoxy. The most renowned Silhak proponent, Chŏng Yag'yong ('Tasan': 1762–1836), was a Catholic, and the Namin faction with which he was associated had partially adopted the Catholic view of the world by the nineteenth century. Tasan attempted to synthesise the new Catholic doctrines and science with his version of pristine Confucianism and apply them to feudal economic and political structures as an alternative to the neo-Confucian orthodoxy.[1] However, he and his colleagues failed to muster enough support to win tolerance at the court, and early in the nineteenth century the orthodox Noron (Elders) faction was able to suppress Silhak, proscribe Catholicism, and adopt the inflexible position which disabled it in the face of subsequent upheavals.

After a major peasant insurrection in 1862, which Tasan had anticipated, Silhak philosophy seemed about to fulfil itself when certain young noblemen, who were open-minded on Western ideas, formed a reformist lobby. But their adoption of Silhak was selective, and the genuine presence of its principles in the reformers' political and economic programs has been questioned.[2] When their December 1884 coup d'état failed, many reformers with religious leanings turned to Christianity. Even reformist Confucianism lost prestige after Japan routed China in 1895, and the fall of the Chosŏn dynasty a decade later deprived it of institutional support.

In the nineteenth century, Buddhism, too, was suffering a serious loss of morale. As neo-Confucian orthodoxy was threatened both from within and without, it clamped down even more heavily on unofficial, 'voluntary' religion.[3] Given the opportunity and conditions to develop an integrated, nationwide organisation, Buddhism might have posed a challenge to the existing political order during the turbulent nineteenth century. But the Korean ruling élite had systematically denied it this opportunity during the Chosŏn dynasty,[4] while the institutional weakness of Buddhism in Ch'ing China deprived it of outside support. Buddhism was pushed into a position largely divorced from the major social and political institutions, leading an early Christian missionary to observe, a little ingenuously, that 'Buddha's sun seems to be setting over Korea.'[5] Added to this political disadvantage was the loss of respect for Buddhism among the people: rumours and allegations of sexual immorality and financial misconduct by monks and nuns were rife at this time.[6]

Underlying the Confucian and Buddhist traditions was Korea's indigenous, or 'classical', religion—an animist tradition connected with Shamanism and the cult of Tan'gun, who was revered as the founder of Korea and ancestor of the Korean race. Regardless of any other religious profession, the people generally believed that in all natural, material and animate phenomena such as thunderstorms, rivers, rocks, beasts and humans, dwelt conscious, individual spirits. Human spirits in particular continued to exist after death or physical destruction. The classical tradition was all-pervasive and amounted to a native cosmology: the perception of the visible universe was as something spiritually animated, where there were no natural causes, only

natural effects of supernatural activity, and where remarkable occur-
rences in the natural realm were expected to correspond with noteworthy events in the realm of human affairs. However broadly the
spirit of this classical religion may be defined, its focus was clearly its
'spirits'. This belief in spirit realms and activities provided an interpretation of life's vicissitudes which gave the people a sense of nume-
nous reality outside and beyond the material order of the Confucian
state.

Throughout the Chosŏn dynasty, the high officials and educated
élites scorned the animist–shamanist beliefs as superstitions born of
ignorance. (Despite superficial similarities with selected elements of
Yi T'oegye's neo-Confucianism, the classical tradition of the spiritual
structure of the universe did not entail any idea of a hidden spiritual
principle lying behind everything. Rather, the actual visible universe
itself was spiritual. Although a deity might cause rain to fall, neither
it nor any principle produced raindrops.) In 1392, the foundation
date of the Chosŏn dynasty, all shamanic rituals were forbidden except selected ones approved by the state. An Altar of Grain and Millet and one shrine were permitted in each village so that they could be
linked to national ceremonies, while popular deities were given state-
serving titles such as 'Duke of Pacification of the Realm'. Eventually
even these official titles were withdrawn when the rulers felt their
position was secure enough to do so.[7] Had Tertullian been present to
hear King Sejo's (r. 1455–68) sacrificial ode at the Temple of Heaven
endowing Tan'gun with the title of 'Son of Heaven', he would doubtless have claimed, as he did of Rome, that the gods were admitted
only if they served state interests.

Although this tradition became absorbed and diffused among neo-
Confucian institutions with a view to its reinforcing the state, the fall
of the Chosŏn dynasty did not damage it. On the contrary, it freed it
for development, particularly after the Japanese annexation in 1910,
when it became a source of national unity and resistance to Japanese
assimilation policies.[8] This was important to the relationship between
indigenous belief and Protestantism. Its lack of an institutional superstructure may have eased the way for early Protestant missions, but it
was also its strength. For, despite clashes between shamans and missionaries or their converts (which could also be interpreted as power
struggles), the traditional religious outlook of the common people
quickly coloured the new faith as it spread among them, unhindered
by any sense of burning institutional bridges.

A consequence of this 'indigenisation' of Protestantism was the re-
plication in Korean Christianity of the erstwhile division between folk
and élite cultures in Korea. As we shall see below, the great Protestant revival of 1907–1908 brought this issue to a head, at least for the
educated, nationalistic Christian leaders such as An Ch'angho, who

deplored the reversion of the new, reformist faith to traditional folk practices. But the educated Protestant leaders could equally be charged with imbuing Christianity with neo-Confucian values and methods. Thus the old cultural struggle apparently proceeded under a new guise. This formulation is too straightforward, however, and requires a good deal of qualification, as we shall discuss later. Here, we may note that Christianity was partially successful in overcoming the division, since both commoner and élite shared certain basic beliefs which Confucians rejected as superstitious and certain social ideals which traditional élites branded as subversive.

Before Protestantism could take advantage of the weakening state institutions, a revolutionary, but decidedly conservative, new faith called Tonghak, meaning Eastern Learning, arose in Korea. Launched by Ch'oe Cheu in the 1860s, Tonghak was a syncretic religion which claimed to be the champion of agrarian reform, the enemy of corruption, the protector of Eastern Culture and the true religion of the people. As a chiliastic movement it resembled the Chinese Taip'ing movement, but was more xenophobic and harboured bitter hatred of Catholics (elements of whose doctrines it nevertheless had borrowed).

The central doctrine of Tonghak is *In nae Ch'ŏn*, the principle that Heaven and humanity are one. On this basis, all Koreans of every class and station were to be regarded with equal respect and society was to be organised as a harmony of interests. Whether this meant removal of hierarchies, the complete abolition of classes and representative politics is yet to be demonstrated. It is by no means certain that, beyond providing for some local economic autonomy, the village councils (chipgangsŏ) established during the 1894 rebellion were as egalitarian as some claim, and there is little to suggest that the restrictions on women were to be lifted. Such questions must await detailed analysis of the councils and the *ture*, or traditional farmers' co-operatives.

Tonghak had been involved in the 1862 peasant rebellion and also flourished among the dissident and unemployed *yangban* (the Korean aristocracy). In the 1890s, Tonghak forces spearheaded a major rebellion directed against corruption and fuelled by famine. When, in May 1894, the Tonghak Rebellion threatened the capital, King Kojong was persuaded by his wife, Queen Min, to petition China for troops, and thus helped to precipitate the Sino-Japanese War.

The Tonghak Rebellion was crushed in the course of the war, but the movement survived as a reformist, patriotic ideology dedicated to national independence. Renamed Ch'ŏndogyo (Religion of the Heavenly Way) in 1905, the religion established schools, managed a patriotic newspaper and by 1910 claimed a membership of some

300 000 Koreans. Under the banner of '*Poguk Anmin*'—Protect the Nation and the People's Welfare—Ch'ŏndogyo provided leadership and hope to a suffering populace.[9] With its particularly strong roots in rural society, Ch'ŏndogyo became a major religious force in Korean nationalism, augmented by a number of related chiliastic religions such as Hŭmch'igyo, Chŭngsan'gyo and Poch'ŏn'gyo. The Tonghak movement has, in fact, become a major focus of purposeful research by contemporary Korean historians searching for a genuine national basis for reunification of the peninsula.[10]

The entry of Protestantism, 1884–1895

The process by which Protestantism entered Korea under unlikely and even hostile conditions and thrived among the populace until Korea became the exception in East Asia has teased a number of minds.[11] The puzzle can be approached from both a psychological and a historical standpoint. The former asks why Christianity appealed, while the latter examines how it took root. However, a strict distinction is difficult to maintain in practice, for unless one dogmatically asserts that the socio-political functions of religion are its only cause, the internal dynamics of religion must also be admitted as an historical factor. The early missionaries noted that there were aspects of the Korean religious traditions which facilitated acceptance of Christianity; they attributed this to Providence. More recently, a scholar has judged that it 'was an unequivocal advantage for the Christian religion to be rather easily linked with old Korean conceptions',[12] which suggests there was some psychological 'preparation' for Christian growth in Korea.[13]

The most popular religious explanation of the Korean reception of the new faith is the existence of a current of monotheism in Korean classical religion, related to the Tan'gun cult. In this there is a tradition of a divine being known as Hwanin or as Hanŭnim, the Heavenly One. An early missionary, Charles Clark, commented that many of Korea's Christians 'first had their interest in the Christian Gospel aroused through their knowledge of Tan'gun and his God, and they have recognised that He is one and the same as the God of their Bible'.[14] Some Korean nationalists later took pains to emphasise this monotheistic current to explain the 'naturalness' of Koreans embracing Christianity. Ch'oe Namsŏn, nationalist and historian, published a finely argued exposition about Korea's Hanŭnim, the god who was the actual sun, the patron of Tan'gun and the creator of all existing things. Ch'oe claimed this monotheism was an unbroken tradition reaching into Korea's deepest past and embedded in the Korean

psyche as the locus of all ideals.[15] Another construed the tradition of
ch'ŏnbu samin—the three deities of the past, present and future—as
identical to the Christian Trinity.[16]
   There are difficulties inherent in this explanation. The monotheistic current was largely inoperative and submerged under both
polytheism and pantheism when the Protestant missions arrived. For
all practical purposes, the classical tradition involved 'apathy about
the supreme being' and a 'concentration of intellectual and emotional energies on the figures of the lesser spirits'.[17] Charles Clark's
observations reflect an optimistic view of the compatibility of indigenous Korean and Protestant spirituality. A less sanguine view was
that folk traditions were stealing the raiments of Christianity to re-
clothe beliefs and practices ultimately at variance with the new faith.
A choice between these positions is not relevant to our purpose.
More to the point is the use which was later made of supposed affinities by Christian nationalist intellectuals. Their identification of
Christian and classical conceptions of God had a clear nationalistic
intent: to convince Koreans that becoming a Christian did not entail
any loss of Koreanness and to demonstrate that Korean tradition had
always been implicitly Christian and that Christianity would therefore
be the means of Korea's national salvation. However, this argument
was only advanced after the annexation, when Korean nationalists
needed to promote a strong sense of national identity in opposition to
Japan's assimilative colonial policies. In terms of the national structures, social organisation and political values of the late nineteenth
century, the question remains of how an imported, heterodox belief
made any headway against a hostile Confucian orthodoxy.
   The Korean political climate in the 1880s was unfavourable to
Christianity. The insecurity of neo-Confucian orthodoxy had only intensified official persecution of heterodoxy. The court not only suppressed indigenous movements—Silhak and Tonghak—but had also
periodically subjected Catholicism to bloody purges since its establishment in 1784, culminating in the Taewŏn'gun's massacre of native
and foreign Catholics alike in 1866. Thus the chances of Protestantism gaining a legal foothold were slim, and Protestant missions only
won tolerance when the court no longer had any real choice.
   In order to appreciate the Protestant challenge to the late Chosŏn
dynasty, it is important to grasp that the Korean rulers had not been
simply wilful or irrational in suppressing Catholicism. Although tensions certainly exist in pluralist societies, religion is generally respected by the state rulers as the domain of the various churches. But
Korean neo-Confucianism held that the highest bond of society was
the state, on which all other societal relationships necessarily depended. The Chosŏn state therefore claimed to be the sole authority
in ordering, maintaining and enforcing the Korean social system, and

indeed in putting forward the ideal pattern to which all social, economic and ethical systems should conform. To deny this priority was to attack the state; to follow ethical systems or gods independently of the state was subversive. This is why, if it could not actually be eliminated, Korean classical religion was also expected to sanctify the state. Quite apart from its teachings and origin, Christianity— Catholic and Protestant—was subversive insofar as it resisted being absorbed by the state. Since its contemporary connection with Western learning and politics made it doubly suspect, acceptance required either a certain weakness in the state or a radical change in the concept of the state. At the end of the nineteenth century it was largely weakness which allowed the necessary changes, while it was the involvement of Protestants in these changes which allowed their participation in nationalism.

Official opposition to Christianity remained explicit at least up to 1884 and was actively encouraged by China and Japan. In 1860 Japan intimated to Korea that, whereas she had agreed to open trading relations with Western powers, she 'regarded the continued proscription of Christianity as essential'.[18] The Ch'ing were less forthright, although in his draft for the Korean–American Treaty of Amity and Commerce of 1882, Viceroy Li Hung-chang stipulated the exclusion of Christian mission work on the peninsula.[19] Most Korean officials needed little such encouragement. The isolationists deeply mistrusted anything Western, and in 1876 the influential scholar, Ch'oe Ikhyŏn, stated in a memorial to the throne that opening the country 'would amount to a total destruction of traditional values and national identity'.[20] Even the moderate reformers, who separated techniques from values in Western civilisation, wished to insert an anti-Christian clause in the 1882 treaty.[21] In the end the clause was not inserted, but nor was the Taewŏn'gun's anti-foreign edict annulled.

Yet by opening up diplomatic relations, the 1882 treaty did break some ice. Even prior to the treaty, suspicions about Christianity had been allayed a little by a book written in China in the 1840s and called *Haejok Toji* in Korean, in which the European Reformation was explained. This was followed by a booklet titled *Chosŏn Ch'aengnyak* from which some learned Koreans adopted a generous view of Protestantism.[22] Under such influences, the more radical reformers began to regard Western beliefs as the source of Western science and institutions. The Buddhist Kim Okkyun accordingly befriended Robert S. Maclay of the Methodist Mission in Japan and in July 1884 obtained King Kojong's permission for Maclay to open educational and medical facilities in Seoul.[23] In September of the same year, a medical missionary from Ohio, Horace Allen, who (to use his own expression) 'sneaked in by a ruse',[24] noted that the King had assured Maclay that 'no objection would be made to the introduction of Protestant Christianity into his kingdom.'[25] Upon successfully treating Prince Min Yŏngik for serious injuries sustained during the radical reformers' abortive coup d'état in December 1884, Dr Allen was welcomed at court and soon became the king's trusted advisor. Allen used his new-found prestige to introduce medical and educational work by 'unofficial' missionaries. As secretary of the United States' Legation from 1890 to 1897, Allen pursued a policy of introducing Protestantism cautiously to the nation through its ruling stratum.[26]

Christianity was nevertheless still illegal, its position anomalous and precarious. A virile anti-foreign movement known as *wijŏng chŏksa* was still robust in the 1880s and, at least in respect to its hostility towards Christianity, it conjoined Tonghak rebel and neo-Confucian scholar-official. While Tonghak leaders called for a purification of the nation from foreign contamination and placed threatening placards against missionary dwellings,[27] neo-Confucianists like Ch'oe Ikhyŏn and the disciples of the deceased Yi Hangno branded Protestantism a religion of beasts and a cover for spies.[28] Naturally enough, Dr Allen chose to tread softly and discouraged missionaries from testing their reception outside the capital. On his own terms this caution paid off: 'By 1890 the anti-foreign law had by common consent become a dead letter and was superseded by a general goodwill.'[29]

The missionaries, especially the Methodists, who favoured opening doors through education and medicine, at first fell in line with Allen's strategy. 'The present social and political condition of Korea,' remarked the Rev. Henry Appenzeller in 1886, 'is such that it is the unanimous judgment of all the missionaries here not to attempt open evangelistic work.'[30] The Presbyterians, whose explicit primary objective was the conversion of the working classes before the aristocracy, were in fact less cautious. The Presbyterian, Dr H. G. Underwood, secretly baptised a Korean in Seoul in July 1886, travelled north to baptise 20 more the following year, and baptised a further 33 Koreans in April 1889. By this time, the Methodist Appenzeller had begun to undertake similar forays with like results.

Although by 1890 the Korean government tended to turn a blind eye to such activities, this practice of taking Christianity directly to the villagers marked a departure from Allen's position of which he disapproved. The historical importance, as well as the cost, of this departure are hinted at in the diary of Australia's first missionary to Korea, the Rev. Henry Davis. Henry Davis arrived in Korea in October 1889 and after a few months' language training set off southwards. He travelled alone on foot and on horseback from village to village, carrying books and quinine. Davis noted the Koreans' eagerness for books, whose contents he was constantly asked to explain, and found them 'a very studious lot'.[31] He was, however, harassed by officials and after only six months in Korea became ill and died.

The cumulative effect of this type of evangelism was to enable Protestantism to take root among the rural commoners and merchant class before noticeable interest arose in urban centres and among the higher classes. The few nobles who were converted before 1895 were of high calibre, but were mostly reached abroad. Nevertheless, their day was soon to come. When it did, Dr Allen's strategy and the grassroots emphasis of the Presbyterian missions worked together to produce in Korea a Christian growth and socio-political influence unparalleled in East Asia.

Growth and social involvement, 1895–1905

The decade 1895 to 1905 has been described as being 'like a chapter from the Acts of the Apostles'.[32] During this decade the Korean Protestant movement expanded from 528 to at least 12500 baptised members.[33] The same period, from the Sino-Japanese to the Russo-Japanese wars, spans the final loss of Korean independence to Japan in all but name. The political and religious aspects are interrelated: the troubles of the one were the fortunes of the other.

The political disarray of China created by its defeat by Japan in 1895 had far-reaching effects in Korea. It marked the end of Korea's semi-vassalage to the Middle Kingdom and, together with the social and economic deterioration in Korea, hastened the decline of neo-Confucian legitimacy. Since the Tonghak movement, too, was a casualty of the war, Christianity at this juncture offered a new ideology and symbolism around which to rally and by which to interpret the nation's woes. Though Russia loomed large as a competitor from 1897 to 1899, China's elimination enhanced Japan's overall power on the peninsula. Since Japan's success was widely attributed to its adoption of Western learning, the number of Koreans who sought in Western civilisation a basis for independence increased sharply. Some influential *yangban* and former Reform Party politicians began to promote Christianity as the path to national salvation.

Meanwhile, the Chosŏn monarchy began to fall back on religious sanctions of its rule. The readiness with which the last reigning monarch, Kojong (r. 1864–1907), turned to classical tutelary deities may well have vexed the literati, but much more seriously, it exposed orthodoxy's weakness and suggested the state was responsible to a religious authority beyond itself. The Protestant reformers were quick to capitalise on this situation. Firstly they contrasted the weakness of Korean orthodoxy with the vibrancy of the Western 'Christian' nations. Secondly, they affirmed that there was indeed a

transcendent and normative religious authority—the Christian God
—to which the state and its laws were responsible. What Korea
needed, then, was an entirely new education, and the Protestants
duly embarked on a vigorous enlightenment campaign through
schools, churches and newspapers.

Missionaries had established schools before 1895, but now Protestantism began seriously to supplant Confucianism in education, its
traditional pride and domain. The idea that Western religion and
education were separable lost ground as the new education was advanced as the key to enlightenment, progress and national strength.
Editorials of the *Tongnip Sinmun* (1896–99), under the direction of
the Christian triumvirate, Sŏ Chaep'il, Yun Ch'iho and Namgung
Ŏk, maintained in concert with explicitly Christian newspapers that
there was an intrinsic connection between Christianity, modern
education and national revival.[34] Besides this invasion of an en-
trenched Confucian preserve, missionaries and Korean Christians
assaulted specific social practices and mores associated in Korea with
Confucianism, including ancestor-worship and filial piety, funeral
rites, forced and child marriages, non-remarriage of widows and the
merely functional view of women in general. They also accused Confucianism of agnosticism, materialism and obsession with office-
seeking.[35] In churches, the view that people were morally bound until
death to the social 'caste' they were born into was consciously com-
batted by gathering the whole range of society under one roof.
Although this attempt to ignore social distinctions in the conduct of
services met with indifferent success, active opposition was also
launched against legal discriminations based on class and sex.[36]

Confucian scholar–officials rapidly rose to defend themselves. In
1896, a high-ranking official and the then Minister of Education, Shin
Kisŏn, published his *Yuhak Kyŏngwi*, which was both an apology for
Confucianism and a counter-attack on 'Western' religion. It was a
misfortune for Confucianism that Shin's attack was apparently rather
crude, consisting essentially of the proposition that, because Christianity was a religion of 'barbarians', it was not worthy of consideration.[37] More thoughtful scholars possibly hoped Christianity
would soon go away; indeed, it had not yet shown signs of its imminent growth. When they did later take it seriously, it was often not
to refute but to accept it.

In any case, Christians immediately printed vindications of the missionaries and their faith. The *Tongnip Sinmun* praised the missionaries for their honesty and support of victims of injustice, their tireless
work in hospitals and schools and their service in printing works in
the vernacular *han'gŭl* script so that all Koreans might benefit. The
newspaper pointedly emphasised that all this was done for no official
or political reward and that such altruism could be found nowhere in

Korea except within the Church of Christ.[38] The Christmas Day editorial for 1897 put the record straight on the origin of the faith, by suggesting that the Western nations flourished because they were not above abiding by a religion that was not their own but had come from the East.

Shin Kisŏn represented a conservative backlash against the 1894–1895 Kabo Reforms, which had been introduced by reformers with Japanese support. Once appointed Minister of Education in June of 1896, Shin presumed to dismantle the educational reforms introduced by Education Minister Yi Wan'yong in 1895 and Acting Minister Yun Ch'iho early in 1896. Shin overstepped himself, however, for the reforms bore the status of imperially sanctioned law. In the furore that followed, incited by articles in the *Tongnip Sinmun* and protests by the Independence Club, Shin lost his portfolio and the laws stood.[39] After the fall of the club and Yun Ch'iho's internal exile in 1899, Shin once more became Minister of Education, but the conservative cause in education was all but lost as many leading officials and scholars began turning to Protestantism. By 1904 these included Kim Chŏngsik, former Chief of Seoul Police, Yi Sangjae, Hong Chaegi, Syngman Rhee, An Kuksŏn, Han Sŏkjun, Yu Kiljun and his brother Sŏngjun, and three scholars who became Korea's first ordained ministers: Ch'oe Pyŏnghŏn, Kil Sŏnju and Kim Pyŏngjo. Worst of all for Confucianism was the conversion of Yi Wŏn'gŭng, then considered to be Korea's greatest living Confucian scholar.[40]

Encouraged, Christian missions pressed ahead with education. In Seoul, the Methodists and Presbyterians expanded their outreach through the Pae Chae Boys' and Ehwa Women's Colleges, a girls' boarding school and the Intermediate School for Boys. The link between faith and learning posited in these schools is illustrated by the curriculum outline in a mission report on the Intermediate School, which in 1904 recorded a 100 per cent rise in enrolments over the previous year:

The subjects taught were, History—English, Korean and Ecclesiastical; Science—Astronomy, Natural History, Geography, Physics and Chemistry; Mathematics—Elementary and Advanced Arithmetic, and Algebra; Bible Courses on the Life of Christ, Gospel of St. John and Old Testament Theology, besides shorter courses in lecture on Romans and Ephesians, the Lord's Prayer, the Apostles' Creed and the Ten Commandments.[41]

In P'yŏngyang, the Presbyterians found the possibilities almost unlimited. By 1904 they operated 46 boys' and four girls' primary schools, an advanced school for girls and women, a teachers' training class and a theological academy which was training Korea's first Protestant ministers. In addition, the churches themselves held 'training classes' to educate their congregations, old and young, female and

male. In 1903–1904, over 5400 Koreans are claimed to have attended
these sessions, which emphasised Christian ethics and beliefs, mutual
acceptance among all members and leadership qualities. In the Sŏnch'ŏn circuit alone, in North P'yŏngan province, 21 primary schools
and 57 church groups operated in like fashion.[42] The appearance
by 1905 of at least 120 Protestant schools[43] is a measure of the degree
to which Protestants were wresting the initiative from neo-
Confucianism in education.

The Protectorate, the great revival and the alleged
anti-nationalism of the church, 1906–1910

Between 1906 and 1910, the odds in the Confucian/Christian rivalry
struggle swung decisively in favour of the latter. The Japanese
Residency-General noted in 1909 that, in all provinces save South
Hamgyŏng and North and South Ch'ungch'ŏng, the Christian
churches were replacing the traditional *yangban*-centred institutions as national foci, especially in conjunction with the *samin
p'yŏngdŭng* movement for social equality.[44] Shin Kisŏn's view of
Christianity was overthrown: the tables were turned and now it was
Confucianism that had to justify itself. The journals of some of the
newly formed educational and 'learned' societies joined newspapers
such as the *Hwangsŏng Sinmun* in echoing the earlier contention of
the *Tongnip Sinmun* that Confucianism was the villain behind
Korea's humiliations.[45] Koreans abroad added their condemnation of
the 'useless and empty' theories and ceremonies of the Confucian
scholars.[46] Henceforth Western education was to lead the long over-
due cultural and intellectual reformation.[47] By 1910, only about ten
religion-based schools were not under Christian management. The
Presbyterians and Methodists ran 805 schools, while Anglican and
Catholic schools numbered at least eighteen. 'The fact must not be
overlooked,' warned the worried Japanese officials, 'that schools in
Korea are being established under the missionaries. . . [These
schools] are the foundation of the present new education system.'[48]

The Japanese Residency-General, which had been installed in
November 1905, was under threat. 'In a day, that which centuries of
misrule on the part of her own rulers had failed to do, the Japanese
occupation accomplished: patriotism was born in Korea . . . All saw
in the Church the only hope for their country.'[49] This overstatement
by the Presbyterian William Blair in 1910, which stemmed less from
exultation than trepidation over the dangers for the church inherent
in this situation, reflected the spectacular growth of the time. The roll
of baptised Presbyterians reached 46 934 in 1911, whilst the Southern
Methodists, who were considered to be working in less responsive

areas, recorded an increase of 700 per cent between 1905 and 1911. At the close of 1910 the total number of Protestant adherents is estimated to have been more than 200000 in a population of about thirteen million,[50] or a little over 1.5 per cent. While this growth still centred on country rather than city and was greater among the lower classes, interest continued to increase among the scholars and some politicians, although the Japanese doubted that Christianity would ever capture the higher classes.[51]

The Russo-Japanese War was a factor in the early stages of this growth. According to mission reports, the missionaries 'gained tremendous prestige' from their seemingly unique ability to offer the Koreans protection in the war-torn countryside.[52] The leader of the Japanese nationalistic Kokuryūkai, Uchida Ryōhei, whom Prince Itō had invited to Korea to report on the situation, admitted this fact: 'At the time of the Russo-Japanese War, contrary to the [pro-Japanese] Ilchinhoe . . . the followers of the Western Religion were taken seriously by the Japanese Army,' so the church was felt to be a considerable force among the people. The church leaders profited by 'nursing their flocks, in contrast to the severities of army behaviour, like a Madonna her child'.[53] But if this held good during the war, it nevertheless lacks force as a full explanation of Christian growth after the war. For, as William Blair recalled, after Britain and America 'hastened to recognise Japan's control, a violent, anti-foreign, especially anti-American storm swept over the land'.[54] In 1907 another missionary, the Rev. C. E. Sharp, perceived a definite political motive behind the continuing growth. Upon hearing a Christian provincial governor state at a Sunday evening service: 'We are placed in a position where there is no alternative path to take other than believing in the Christian God,' Sharp concluded that God was using the political situation for a spiritual awakening.[55]

The Japanese were unappreciative of the divine strategy. Japan's victory over the pro-Ch'ing forces in Korea had expedited the rise of a new centre of resistance with considerable morale. Japanese police complained that 'wherever a dispute arises between Japanese and Koreans, missionaries take up the case of the Koreans . . .' Christian schools showed 'evil tendencies', mixing 'impurities', (i.e. politics) in their education.[56] As for the churches, the police asserted that Koreans joined them in order to resist the Japanese administration and that missionaries lured adherents by claiming that only through Christianity could Korea avoid annexation.[57] Uchida Ryōhei had already made the equation and his countrymen believed it: Christianity and anti-Japanese sentiment were one.[58]

If the turn to Christianity was in part politically motivated, the political context was largely the creation of Japan herself. Japanese political conduct had pushed reformers and Christians into opposition, and the fact that Christianity served as the 'spokesperson' of the national interest indicates the degree to which the new religion had penetrated national life. But this was not the whole story. The politically conscious Protestants were mainly higher class Koreans, and as such they were on the periphery of the rapid expansion among the rural and lower classes and of what was then the central religious experience and landmark of Korean Christianity, The Great Revival of 1907.

The Great Revival began in P'yŏngyang in January 1907 during an annual ten-day Bible-training conference and from there spread rapidly throughout the nation. At one of the evening sessions, attended by over a thousand people, a Korean church official publicly confessed to a grudge against a missionary and asked his forgiveness. This act precipitated what the missionaries called a 'terrifying' response. All assembled broke out in prayer in unison, confessing to sins and crimes and expressing a desperate desire for holiness and renewal. The same pattern was repeated for several days, and when the conference was over, the participants brought news of the events to their home towns with the same results. Before long, the revival spread among the Christian schools and colleges and among male and female, and lasted into 1908.[59]

The Great Revival was great not so much in its numerical effect—it occurred not prior to but in the midst of rapid growth—as in the profound effect it had on the nature and tone of Korean Christianity. 'The great awakening marks the spiritual rebirth of the Korean Church. The religious experience of the people gave to the Christian Church in Korea a character which is its own.'[60] Dr George L.-G. Paik, who penned these words in the mid-1920s, attributed the revival to a sense of failure and frustration at Japan's occupation, a desire for a higher level of spirituality whetted by reports from other lands and the 'definite attempt of the missionaries' to bring it about.[61] This opinion is corroborated by missionary writings and reports and by later church historians.[62] By all accounts, the revival was an intensely emotional movement, but it had practical results: indigenisation of Christianity; mutual understanding between missionaries and Koreans at a crucial moment; increased awareness of the ethical implications of faith and the need for Biblical study; and energetic evangelistic campaigns that ensured continued rapid growth through 1908.[63]

Since none of these results are overtly political or social, the revival was regarded by some of the more educated Christians, possibly including An Ch'angho, as irrelevant to Korea's burning problems. Debate still continues in Korea over whether the revival was not actually an anti-nationalist campaign directed by the missionaries. Given the political factors behind the growth before 1907, the revival appears, by contrast, to mark a turning away from national and political issues to personal spiritual concerns. There has been a tendency to regard this as a shift away from a 'social gospel' to an otherworldly pietism,[64] but before any judgment can be made there are some important aspects of the tension that need to be clarified.

The Great Revival took place during a period of national humiliation, and was pursued against a background of hopelessness concerning the future of Korean society. It was not at all unconnected with national issues, and it added considerable impetus to the Protestant educational endeavour. It also affected the nature of subsequent Protestant involvement in nationalism. Its legacy is apparent even in the reaction against it, and the attitudes of Christian nationalists to it highlight the tension inherent in the very term 'Christian nationalism.' This tension involved ideological, or rather theological, disputes which were not new to Christianity but were less familiar to Korea. At stake were the relationship of the church and believer with the world, eschatology, millennialism and the transcendent final cause of the faith. The tension also reflected the social composition of the church, which was mainly lower class and not as intellectually aware as some active high-class members desired.

It is important to note at this stage that the theological and social tensions did not follow the same demographic pattern. It was not a case of the educated believers adopting one doctrinal position and the commoners another. Much of the theological disputation took place among the intellectuals and between them and the missionaries, and although we have no direct evidence here, it appears that the less educated believers took their cue from their respective church leaders. The social tension underscored by the Great Revival was therefore somewhat independent of the theological: it concerned the manner in which the people expressed religious experience and the value they placed on it. This was a matter of difference between élite and commoner not only in culture but also in degree of national awareness. The intellectuals could not afford to ignore what, within the Protestant community, was a grass-roots movement, and so the tension was in the main a constructive one which led on both sides to a search for common ground. But the tensions cannot be appreciated sufficiently without further clarification of the issues.

The Protestant missionaries in Korea espoused the doctrine of the separation of the church and the state as a guideline to church–state relations. Far from implying submission of the churches to state authorities, this doctrine, which stems from the European Reformation, was designed originally to keep the churches free from government interference—free, in Korea's case, from the Confucian view that religion may exist only insofar as it serves state interests. The church was to reciprocate by not usurping genuine state functions, but it reserved to itself a 'prophetic' right to speak out on issues of national moral and spiritual welfare. This arrangement is not straightforward in practice and is especially problematic during a period of social and political upheaval such as that which Korea was undergoing in 1907.

Criticism that the revival withdrew the church from its national responsibilities, even under the church–state formula, had some basis. Though no mission body as such pontificated on the subject, certain individuals did seek to interpret St Paul's instructions on church–state relations as a condemnation of political resistance to the Residency-General.[65] This position was held in an extreme form by the 'Japanese agent,' Bishop M. C. Harris (a Methodist), who on occasion accused other missionaries of being anti-Japanese. But the view that, in opposing the Japanese, the Koreans were opposing authorities emplaced by God involved obvious absurdities, for it logically implied that whoever managed to force Korea into submission would have divine approval. If the Righteous Armies overcame the Japanese then they would have divine approval, but until then they were under God's condemnation.

The extremism of Bishop Harris was atypical of Korea's early missionaries. The church–state doctrine did recognise a distinction between the role of government (which was to restrain evil and promote good) and the people who filled government posts and who might act contrary to its purposes. The missionary Homer Hulbert, for example, toured the United States in November 1907 with the purpose of revealing that, under protestations of developing Korea for independence, Japan was pursuing terrorist politics.[66]

In the face of pressure to raise the banner of resistance over the church, most missionaries and Korean church leaders supported the separation of church and state in order to prevent the churches from becoming political institutions. It was in the context of suggestions that the church should officially join forces with the Righteous Armies that the Presbyterian Pastor Kil Sŏnju strove, with marked success, to convince Korean Christians that the church as such had no mandate in that direction. Missionaries in northern parts met to discuss the situation, and William Blair was convinced that if the Korean church officially declared itself to be against the Japanese, the people would adopt Christianity 'in a day', and so establish 'another Roman Church'.[67] Korean Christians could organise themselves politically if they felt they should, but not under cover of the church. This position was explicit in mission reports of the time:

The marked success of the Y.M.C.A. caused attempts to be made to use it politically, and, these failing, many young men of the churches began to band themselves together under a similar name within the churches, and under the sheltering folds of both church and society met nightly to discuss and denounce the actions of their government and of the Japanese. In time these were all suppressed, not because of any lack of sympathy on the part of the missionaries for all who were being wronged, but to prevent the Church becoming a political organ.[68]

Doubtless, the particularly inward nature of the revival was viewed with relief by the missionaries. There was unanimous agreement among the Presbyterians that its most salutary effect was the heightened consciousness of the need to repent of personal evil and a deeper appreciation of the concept of holiness.[69] It was easy enough to repent of one's ancestors' sins and far too easy to condemn the sins of a hated invader, but difficult to repent of one's own evil and to forgive others. It is only when this is accomplished that one reaches the heart of the matter, for in Christian terms it is the heart that *is* the matter. The missionaries' concern was not simply over a technical relationship between church and state, but also over the possibility of the essence of Christian spirituality (conceived as personal repentance and forgiveness) being submerged under a comparatively easier and certainly more popular political denunciation of Japan. Nevertheless, it is clear that the missionaries failed to understand sufficiently the Koreans' pain at Japan's predations. In that light, William Blair's counsel against church involvement in politics on the basis of his antagonism towards the Roman Catholic Church of some centuries earlier does seem to be a misuse of church history.

The missionaries were in a difficult position. The Japanese frequently accused them of encouraging anti-Japanese sentiment. When the Cabinet Minister Son Pyŏngjun accompanied Resident-General Itō Hirobumi to Japan in February 1909, he reportedly claimed that Christianity was the greatest problem in Korea. He even asserted that the mildly pro-Japanese Taehan Hyŏphoe's 'obstructionist' activities were the work of Christians and that the missionaries were inciting 'ignorant people' to commit acts of subversion. When Son publicly accused the missionaries of secret collusion with the former Korean Emperor and of political plots involving Prince Pak Yŏnghyo, they felt it necessary to meet to discuss ways of refuting him.[70]

In a sense very important to the survival and vitality of Christianity in Korea, the revival was not an anti-national movement. It had a particularly Korean flavour about it and, as their own unique experience, impressed upon the Koreans the fact that the faith belonged to their race and nation. No longer could Christianity be described as a Western religion. The Presbyterian missions in particular had encouraged this indigenisation through implementing what was called the 'Nevius Method' of self-support, self-propagation and self-government of the Korean church.[71] Around 1904, Dr H. H. Underwood had observed to the Korean Elder of Seoul's Chong Dong church that the idea that Christianity was foreign would continue:

just so long as you allow foreign money to be used in carrying it forward.
When you build and own your own churches, send out your own evangelists, and support your own schools, then both you and others will feel and
realise it is not a foreign affair, but your own.[72]

In 1907, the year of the Great Revival, the Presbyterian Church in
Korea became fully self-governing, and the structural and economic
strength of this and other denominations was of major importance
after the Japanese annexation in 1910.[73]

The revival also raised an issue quite other than theological for
some Christian nationalists. If, on observing the revival meetings, An
Ch'angho did exclaim, as hearsay has it, 'How shall we ever wake up
this foolish race!'[74] then he was referring not to any doctrine but to
the 'Korean' approach to religion. He was objecting to the very indigenisation the revival involved; to what appeared to be a reversion
to those traditional modes of behaviour and thought which An's writings clearly show he expected Christianity to abolish. This impression
is strengthened by later criticism by An's disciple, Yi Kwangsu, that
the Christianity of this period left a legacy of anti-intellectualism.[75]
This criticism reflects a class problem, but also anxiety lest this
'indigenisation' of Christianity should threaten its role in transforming society by losing its cutting edge as a distinct alternative. The
nationalists wanted a contextualised rather than an indigenised
Christianity; for them, Protestant rationality and concern for public
welfare appeared to succumb during the revival to traditional popular
emotionalism and self-concern.

There is, however, a theological aspect to this problem which involved divisions among the Korean intellectuals and missionaries.
This concerned the prevailing pre-millennialism of the Korean church
and the missionaries. Pre-millennialism is the belief that the
thousand-year period of peace and righteousness suggested in the Re-
velation of St John will be ushered in by Christ at his Second Coming
to end the course of human history as hitherto experienced. Opposed
to this is a post-millennial view which places Christ's return at the end
of a millennium of Christianisation of the world without any special
divine intervention. Distinct from both is amillennialism, which
denies that the millennium has literal meaning.

Pre-millennialists tend to hold a rather sombre view of history. The
millennium is to be imposed by a supernatural event cutting short the
evolution of demonic forces in history. Thus Christ's rhetorical question 'When the Son of Man returns, will he find faith on Earth?' is
interpreted negatively. Faith will only be found within an embattled
church standing in antithesis to the world. On this view, the 'Kingdom of God' is eschatological, not 'among you' in any concrete way,
but placed after the end of history. With their land ravished by two

wars, their emperor dethroned and their nation rapidly falling under foreign domination, the willing assent by many Korean Protestants to a pre-millennialist interpretation is not surprising. Amidst Earthly chaos, the believers could travel their Earthly pilgrimage in faithfulness to God, expecting either a resurrection to eternal life after death, or Christ's coming to destroy the evil age before their death.

Despite the foregoing construction, an historian is still faced with the seeming paradox of pre-millennialist missionaries and their Korean congregations establishing (as the Japanese complained) the framework of a whole new education system, founding hospitals and imparting political and social ideas which were considered nothing less than revolutionary. Part of this paradox can be dispelled by pointing out that it was the higher class converts, who were mostly not pre-millennialists,[76] who grasped the socio-political implications of the new faith and education. Further, the social concern nurtured in mission schools which were founded to facilitate outreach may be an instance of sociological laws working independently of original intentions. Yet the outworking of these 'laws' was certainly in line with the intentions of the activists, and this returns the discussion to the question of whether the other-worldly nature of the Great Revival weakened interest in nationalism among ordinary Koreans.

In theory, the church could be national without being nationalistic, and in practice the revival gave the church a 'national' face. But this misses the thrust of the charge that, in a time of national crisis affecting all Koreans, Christians were being discouraged from involvement. (The idea that the Great Revival gave the church greater cohesion as an anti-Japanese force in a recent study is a misleading simplification.)[77] Korean Christians abroad expressed anxiety at the revival's emphasis on life after death, and an evangelist then in San Francisco, Yang Jusam, printed a warning to Korean Christians in a nationalist newspaper not to forget that Christianity was expected to rescue Korea from Japan just as the Israelites were delivered from the Egyptians.[78] Judging from a Presbyterian mission report of 1904, it does not seem that even the conservative missionaries would have disagreed with this in principle.[79] But in 1907 there was a real question of *modus operandi*, and again, it is necessary to recall that the context of the debate was the 'temptation' for the church as a body to join the military resistance movement. This was thought to be suicidal, quite apart from doctrinal considerations, giving the Japanese every justification for the eradication of the faith from Korea. Such scruples were not limited to pre-millennialists or other-worldly believers. The influential Methodist intellectual and nationalist politician Yun Ch'iho had reflected on the issue as early as the 1890s. Then an exile and university student in America, Yun reasoned against official church participation in politics on the grounds that this amounted to a confusion of duties that would ultimately draw the church away from its primary spiritual charge towards the 'immediate, visible, tangible and temporal interest'.[80]

Yun saw a fundamental spiritual rationale for his church/state (or secular/sacred) division: 'The interest of the Kingdom of Christ can not, and must not, be identified with the interest of a party.'[81] Yun became convinced that Christianity was essentially inward, or as he put it, 'God in the heart; this is religion'.[82] It would be a misunderstanding to construe this position, which was widespread among the Korean Protestants, as a doctrine of the irrelevance or evil of the material world. It concerned the belief that inner renewal was essential to outward revival. Spiritual change was to work on the whole fabric of national life like leaven in the lump, while societal change without this inner transformation could never achieve genuine liberation. Christianity was not a political program, not because it was less than such, but because it was so much more.[83]

Viewed from this angle, adherence to any sort of millennialism appears less relevant. The Presbyterian Kil Sŏnju, ordained in 1907, was a fundamentalist who was accredited by the missionaries as being the major force persuading Korean Christians not to join the guerilla warfare. His personal history warns one off drawing easy conclusions on the basis of alleged beliefs. Converted to Christianity in 1897, Kil immediately teamed up with An Ch'angho in P'yŏngyang to establish the Manmin Kongdonghoe, or Assembly of All People, which was an offspring of the Independence Club. Did he change his mind by 1907? It would be truer to say he changed his occupation, from political activist to ordained minister. In any case, the Independence Club, Sŏ Chaep'il, Yun Ch'iho and An Ch'angho, had not seen any hope in armed resistance, and Kil in 1907 remained sceptical.

Thus the emphasis on personal salvation did not deprive the early Korean Christians of a social philosophy. The Great Revival clearly influenced the type of social philosophy that was adopted. It clarified and perhaps polarised two possible positions on the 'Kingdom of God', namely, either to identify it with an almost entirely immanent community that was thought to be emerging from the changes in Korean society, or to place it wholly after death or after Christ's return. The revival involved a position closer to the second pole, and this tended to discourage investment in systems or structures founded on human resources. At the least, it encouraged the view that national problems were analogous to, or a consequence of, individual spiritual weaknesses, and that therefore improving personal character would solve other, material, problems. This became a basic premise of Protestant self-reconstruction nationalism.

Hence, despite unhappiness among the nationalistic Protestants with the emotionalism and personalism of the revival, An Ch'angho represented many intellectuals in preaching that personal renewal was the foundation of national renewal. 'Christ told the Jews,' An wrote in the Kongnip Sinmun in 1907, 'that it was because they were full of evil deeds and devoid of all goodness that God took their rights from them and handed them over to others, and this surely applies to Korea today.'[84] National revival depended on personal improvement and thought reform. The principal difference between this and the revival doctrine was that An was at this time in the United States of America, where he based his individualist position on the marriage between utilitarianism and Protestant piety that was then in vogue in Western countries. Many Koreans in America appealed to J. S. Mill's doctrine that social laws could be reduced to laws of human nature: the Korean Youth Association in San Francisco held debates on the theme while their pastors implied that the purpose of personal Christian ethics was to produce a good national society.[85] So while the revivalists and nationalists held virtually the same premise, they differed in their conclusions. The former tended towards a mild political quietism, whereas the latter found in individual spiritual and ethical transformation the basis for a social and political program.

Where did the missionaries stand? One scholar has judged that 'indifference to the social application of Christian theology' was a 'feature of the Korean mission programme', and that this was due to the fundamentalism and pre-millennialism of the early missionaries.[86] But, regardless of their beliefs, had the missionaries gone to Korea with the purpose of encouraging a direct assault on the nation's social and political structure, their stay would have been very short. As it was, Kim Yunsik, then President of the Foreign Office, told Yun Ch'iho in 1896 that even Dr H. G. Underwood, whom Yun considered something of a 'royalist', had 'a great many charges against him for revolutionary schemes'.[87] Furthermore, as has already been noted, the missionaries were openly critical of time-honoured social institutions such as ancestor-worship, child marriage and aristocratic privilege.

Of considerable pertinence here is the missionary training program of the Australian (Victorian) Presbyterians, whose conservative and fundamentalist position is clear from a perusal of their mission archives. Australian candidates for the Korean mission field in the 1900s attended a series of lectures on the social effects of missions.[88] The lectures addressed the question of whether missions influence society as a whole beyond individual lives, on the premise that the 'social results are a later and more indirect product than the spiritual'. This did not mean retreating from the social sphere ('Christianity being sociological in scope, Christian Missions must be so considered.'), but it implied that the individual was the basic unit: 'Missions deal with the individual and through him reach society.' Social legislation 'may compel outward observance, but it cannot change the heart and disposition'. Hence social reform concerned first 'a change in the spirit of Asiatic Empires, rather than their material civilisation', for 'Christianity is not the bloom but the root', the 'pressure' behind reform. By implication the first and only task of the missionary was evangelism: without a significant number of committed Christians there could be no Christian reform and talk of a Christian society would be meaningless.

Social and political reforms were expected. The lectures continued:

> Christianity has a reconstructive function in the Mission Fields. Christian Missions have already produced social results which are manifest and society in the non-Christian world at the present time is conscious of a new and powerful factor which is working positive and revolutionary changes in the direction of a higher civilisation.

An anonymous Korean Christian leader's words are cited with approval:

> The only hope of the country is in the Churches . . . The Churches are raising up bands of men who know how to combine for a common object, who are quickened intellectually and who are full of character, courage and hope. To convert and educate the common people is the only hope of Korea.

This expectation of positive social change was also shared by Methodist missionaries, who, as early as 1898, had written on the 'part played by Christianity in the social progress of the world'.[89]

The argument that Korea's missionaries were uninterested in the social application of their faith and that this stemmed from theological conservatism and pre-millennialism is unsatisfactory. The real issues were the means of change, the priority of spiritual regeneration and the strict separation of church and state. They left direct action to the Koreans, discouraging such only when the means seemed un-Christian or where the separation principle was violated. There was some agreement among nationalists on these points. Yang Jusam warned that Christians must comport themselves in secular affairs 'in accordance with the Lord Jesus' command to follow righteousness and humanitarian principles', and judged that the guerilla approach fell short of this.[90] The similar position of Yun Ch'iho, an amillennialist and a non-fundamentalist has been mentioned above.

The church and the Righteous Armies

The principle of the separation of the church and state was most severely tested in 1907–08 after Japan forced the Korean Emperor Kojong to abdicate. From August 1907, guerilla forces intensified their attacks on the Japanese troops and police, but Japanese reinforcements were dispatched to suppress the resistance mercilessly. The atrocities perpetrated against innocent villagers turned 'hundreds of quiet families into rebels'.[91] Outrage filled the Korean Christians, and it has been claimed that, but for the influence of Kil Sŏnju, they might easily have risen in armed insurrection. The delicate position of the churches is illustrated by the case of the evangelist Ch'oe Sangnyun.

Ch'oe Sangnyun was one of 20 influential Christians selected by the Korean Minister of Justice early in 1908 to carry a royal proclamation to guerilla leaders ordering them to lay down their arms. Korean Christians had kept aloof from the Righteous Armies in the 1890s because they were at that stage anti-foreign and anti-Christian. But in 1907 Yun Ch'iho still faulted them. Although he confessed that the 'wanton and deliberate cruelty of the Japanese policy has alienated me—all true Koreans—from Japan',[92] Yun thought the Righteous Armies were pointlessly adding to the sufferings of the people. They were torn 'between the "patriotic" guerillas who levy supplies from villages and the "angelic" Japanese who burn up the villages turning thousands of harmless people into the mountains—there to starve and freeze and die, because they are compelled to give food to the guerillas'.[93] Reports in 1908 confirmed that in many areas 'people can neither sit down nor stand up', for if they were found with a 'self-defense corps' membership card they were executed by the guerillas, and if not, they were shot by Japanese soldiers as covert guerilla supporters.[94]

Most Christians agreed not to join armed resistance, but opinion was divided over the propriety of churchmen attempting to dissuade the guerillas on behalf of a government which was under the thumb of Itō Hirobumi. Did this not transgress the church/state principle? Criticism was sharpest from Koreans furthest removed from the struggle. In the United States, one Chang Kich'an attacked Christian ministers for becoming the tools of the enemy and suggested that, instead, they should encourage the guerillas not to rest until freedom was restored.[95] The evangelist Yang Jusam offered a more balanced view:

When first I heard that our Government had chosen a number of well-known members of the Christian Church and had sent them out . . . to deliver the Government order . . . I thought, here is an opportunity for the Christian religion to show itself to be the vehicle of peace, quieten the people and bring to pass a further flourishing of the Way in our land. But immediately upon thinking it over, I realised that should this mission really be undertaken it would bring harm and disrepute to Christianity, the religion which is prospering so and which is our nation's means of salvation, our people's sole hope—and finally bring terrible calamity upon our nation.[96]

Yang's fears that the people would misunderstand the Christians' motives and turn on them, as happened to the Chinese Boxers, were not unfounded. Dr Gale of the Methodist Yŏndong Church in Seoul received an anonymous letter from a guerilla early in 1908, which explained that the reason Christians had until now been treated with respect was that they were seen to be behaving honourably. But if the royal messengers were not recalled, their own and other Christians' lives would no longer be guaranteed. Some years earlier, Tonghak forces had regrouped and threatened to kill all Christians; only the Russo-Japanese War was thought to have prevented this.[97] Dr Gale took the warning seriously and consulted with the American Consul before negotiating with Itō for the recall of the Christian messengers.[98]

Ch'oe Sangnyun had, in fact, initially refused the government commission. Instead he wrote a lengthy letter to the cabinet urging each member to resign, go without escort to the guerilla strongholds and apologise in person, claiming that then the Righteous Armies would disperse.[99] It is a measure of the dilemma facing the Christians that within a month or so Ch'oe changed his mind, entering a guerilla base in Hwanghae province in February 1908. Ch'oe's meeting with the guerilla leader Min Kŭngho was a fiasco.[100] The whole project was abandoned and the resistance continued, but with enormous losses. Between August 1907 and June 1911 the Japanese recorded 2852 attacks involving 141815 insurgents, of whom 17697 were killed and 3706 wounded.[101] By 1913 the Righteous Armies were virtually eliminated.

The élite–commoner complexion of early Protestantism

Protestantism began in Korea in 1884 as a foreign religion whose existence depended on its not drawing attention to itself. By 1910 Korean Protestants numbered over 200000. They were predominantly rural and lower class, but also included politicians, accomplished scholars and many of the land's most influential nationalists. At first considered a potential political liability, by 1907 Christianity's possible withdrawal from nationalism was viewed with dismay.

The dramatic rise of Christianity, and with it Western influences, coincided with a traumatic political collapse. The phenomenal growth of Christianity between 1895 and 1910 can be—and often is—accounted for by the weakening of the traditional neo-Confucian, yangban-dominated social and political structure caused by the Sino- and Russo-Japanese wars and the imposition of the Japanese Protectorate in 1905. This enabled Christianity to become a contender in defining the nature and goals of society and nation. Thus an important cause of interest in Christianity was the relief it seemed to offer in the midst of political humiliation and social dislocation.

Not all who turned to Christianity were politically motivated. The Great Revival of 1907 revealed the essentially religious nature of the movement; from it there emerged an emphasis on personal repentance, on the vertical relationship with God and on the final cause of the faith: conformity to the nature of Christ through resurrection to immortality. Among Presbyterians, who comprised the majority, rote knowledge of the Westminster Confession's catechism was compulsory for all prospective members.[102] In response to the question on the meaning and destiny of human existence, the Shorter Catechism states: 'The chief end of man, is to glorify God and enjoy Him forever.'[103] A tension arose between an apolitical interpretation of this and the tendency to value the faith more for its perceived nationalist potential.

In 1907–08 especially, fears were expressed by educated Christian nationalists that the Great Revival was drawing the sting from the churches' socio-political challenge. Such fears may have had temporary validity. Yet once the theoretical and theological arguments over the implications of pre-millennialism and fundamentalism are examined, it appears as a matter of historical fact that the fears were a little alarmist. The revival also had positive effects on Christian involvement in Korean society. It created new interest in Christian education and helped give the religion a 'Korean' character, besides providing the numbers and structure without which the nationalists' talk of applying Christian notions to national life would have survived only as an idea.

The revival certainly manifested a division between the social élites and the commoners—the same sort of division that had long existed and been intensified under the Chosŏn dynasty. But here the important point is that this division was greatly relativised by certain factors. The evangelical Protestantism of the missionaries denied the relevance of class to spirituality, in the sense that no social position afforded spiritual advantage. But it also thus denied the validity of discrimination attached to class and so supported social reforms. The revival itself forced the élites to take the labourers, peasants and merchants into account. Conversely, the élites infused national consciousness and new ideas among the commoners through Christian institutions. Moreover, both groups recognised the primacy of personal renewal, even if their conclusions at times diverged. The tendency for élites, who are often the first to imbibe new ideas, to be cut off from the people by those very ideas, was greatly mitigated in Korea by the association of the new ideas with a new religion that had first gained acceptance among the commoners. Dr Allen's policy of reaching the nobility, the Methodist approach through education and the Presbyterian concentration on the countryside, together with a 'democratic' form of church administration, engendered mutual respect and solidarity among Protestants on the eve of invasion by a 'non-Christian', non-Western nation.

2 The ethical foundations of self-reconstruction nationalism

The greatest issue for the dying is how they should be living.

Yun Ch'iho.[1]

It was typical for members of the Korean Reform Party who travelled to Europe or America in the late nineteenth century to return impressed by 'Western' social values and conduct. Since they believed Western civilisation was formed by Christianity, the adoption of Christianity also became typical of the more radical reformers for whom the '[new] concept of God made impossible a recognition of ultimate value in the existing social structures.'[2] By 1910, reformers who had converted to Protestantism included Yi Sujŏng, Pak Yŏnghyo, Yu Kiljun, Syngman Rhee, An Ch'angho, Yi Sŭnghun, Yi Sangjae, Sŏ Chaep'il, Sŏ Kwangbŏm, Namgung Ŏk, Cho Mansik and Yun Ch'iho.

This turning to Christianity coincided with rethinking by the radical reformers on means and ends in the wake of their defeat during the Kapshin Coup of December 1884, which was an attempt to wrest control of Korean politics from Ch'ing domination.[3] The Kapshin Coup marks a watershed in the history of the Korean reform movement, for its failure underlined the need for future attempts to be broad-based national movements. The coup had been in the style of a traditional palace revolution. Thereafter a different strategy was called for, one of enlightening the people, informing them of Korea's condition and wooing their support for thorough reform. With this object in mind, Sŏ Chaep'il, now a Methodist, founded the Independence Club (Tongnip Hyŏphoe) in 1896, and with Yun Ch'iho and Namgung Ŏk began disseminating the 'new thought' through Korea's first vernacular newspaper, the *Tongnip Sinmun*.[4] High on the Protestant reformers' agenda stood the inculcation of a new civic ethic among the populace, and in this Yun Ch'iho played the leading role.

Yun Ch'iho is numbered among Korea's most eminent Christians and, at least up to 1918, was regarded as the foremost nationalist living in Korea. His political career commenced with his involvement in the Reform Party (Kaehwa Tang) in the early 1880s and in 1895–96 he served in the reform cabinet as Vice-Minister of Foreign Affairs and Acting Minister of Education. In 1897 he became an 'opposition' leader working for constitutional government through the Independence Club, of which he became president in 1898. He spent the years 1899–1903 in internal exile as the magistrate of the port cities of Wŏnsan and Chinnamp'o, but was recalled to Seoul during the Russo-Japanese War and appointed Acting Minister of Foreign Affairs. Upon the imposition of the Japanese Protectorate in November 1905, however, Yun refused all appointments and announced his retirement from government service.[5] The Japanese imprisoned Yun between 1911 and 1915 on charges of sedition, and on his release he devoted himself to education and the promotion of industry among Koreans through the Seoul Central YMCA and the Southern Methodist Mission. Of all the educated élite leaders to embrace Protestantism, Yun Ch'iho was the most unequivocal in breaking with Confucianism and the most deliberate and consistent in applying his new beliefs to national issues. His influence on other Protestants such as An Ch'angho was profound, and in his early career he laid the basis for much of the self-reconstruction movement up to 1937.

The apostle of ethical nationalism

The young reformer, 1881–1887

The eldest son of Yun Ung'yŏl of the old and prestigious Haep'yŏng Yun clan, and connected through his paternal grandmother to the powerful court clan of the Andong Kims, Yun Ch'iho was born in South Ch'ungch'ŏng province on 23 January 1865. A year earlier, Korea's King Ch'ŏlchong had died without an heir, leaving the court preoccupied with succession problems and clan strife. Yun's father, who in 1858 had begun an accomplished military career which brought the family to Seoul, was one of the first members of the Reform Party and advocated strengthening Korea's position through military reform. On his return from an official mission to Japan in May 1880, Yun Ung'yŏl had been appointed by King Kojong to train and command new troops according to the example of Meiji Japan.

This placed the Yun family in the centre of a bitter, often violent struggle over the optimum course for the nation, staged amidst the tripartite rivalry between Japan, China and Russia for pre-eminence in Korea.[6] Naturally enough, Yun Ch'iho followed in his father's footsteps and joined the initially pro-Japanese Reform Party.[7]

In April 1881 the Korean court sent Yun Ch'i to Japan as a member of a fact-finding group which included Yu Kiljun, the prominent reformer of later years and author of the influential *Sŏyu Kyŏnmun*, a treatise on Western civilisation. While Yu studied under the famed Japanese liberal, Fukuzawa Yukichi, Yun was placed under the supervision of one Nakamura Masatada, a specialist in Western studies. His observation of Asian politics from Japan hardened an earlier dislike of China which was confirmed by news of his father's exile to Wŏnsan on the north-east coast of Korea following the Military Riot (*Imo Kullan*) of June 1882, which he blamed on China. By 1883, Yun began referring to Korea's 'slavery' to China.[8]

Ironically, it was through the offices of the pro-Ch'ing forces that Yun gained influence in Korea's political affairs. On the death of Ch'ŏlchong in 1864, Princess Cho (the mother of Ch'ŏlchong's predecessor, Hŏnjong) chose as successor a child of the obscure Yi Haung, in the hope of bolstering her own Cho clan. As Regent, Yi Haung, known to posterity as the Taewŏn'gun, proved a competent and wily politician and surprised the Korean political world by skilfully rising to the top. But, following the 1882 Military Riot, the pro-Ch'ing Queen Min, wife of Kojong, co-operated with the Ch'ing to have the anti-Ch'ing Taewŏn'gun kidnapped and taken to China, following which the pro-Ch'ing forces in the court gained ascendancy.

In May 1883, at the age of 18, Yun was recalled after only five months' study of English (in Japan, under a Dutch diplomat!) to serve as interpreter to the first American Minister in Korea, Lucius Foote. In this capacity, he became involved in Foreign Office affairs and was frequently summoned to the throne to advise King Kojong and Queen Min. He found that the Chinese, represented by Li Hung-chang and Yüan Shih-k'ai, were confident of their pre-eminent influence over Korean foreign policy. 'I am the King of Corea whenever I think the interests of China require me to assert the prerogative',[9] Li informed the American Minister to Peking. Yun himself was irked by having to translate into English an 1883 document in which Li Hung-chang disapproved of independent trading agreements with foreign powers and warned Kojong not to allow 'any precipitate discussion with [foreign] plenipotentiaries, which shall nullify the purport of your former notice that Chosun is a dependency of China'.[10] In collusion with the powerful Yŏhŭng Min clan, which had been connected with the royal line since the reign of King T'aejong

(1400–1418), China had installed itself in the court as the foremost obstacle to the Reform Party's object of implementing Meiji-style reforms.

Although Yun decried this Chinese interference, it is clear that by 1884 he adhered to the self-strengthening position that the greater fault lay with Korea's internal weakness and disorganisation. 'If we but strengthen ourselves, there will be no real reason to fear anyone, he advised the king.[11] Yun at this time considered that tightening up the government machinery would solve the structural problems in both the central and the local administration which he felt impeded self-strengthening. His remedy was to keep civil and military affairs strictly apart and to regulate departmental business, so that, instead of interfering with other departments, officials would devote their whole careers to the business of their respective offices.[12]

When, towards the end of 1884, Yun learned of the radical Kim Okkyun's intention to take advantage of China's troubles in Indo-China to grasp power in Korea, he queried the wisdom of this type of solution. Yun's father especially disapproved of the plot on the grounds that reliance on Japanese troops without Korean support was bound to end in failure.[13] To Yun Ch'iho, the Kapshin Coup of 4–8 December was a tragedy. It placed all associated with the re-form movement under suspicion, strengthened China's hand and caused a reaction among the people and officials, who accused the reformers of intending to make Korea into a Japanese vassal.[14] While Kim Okkyun and others fled to Japan and Sŏ Chaep'il to America, Yun chose exile in Shanghai. There he entered Dr Young J. Allen's Anglo-Chinese Southern Methodist School on 27 January 1885. Two years later Yun converted to Christianity.

Experiments in nationalist theology and critique of Confucianism

From the beginning of 1886, Yun underwent a spiritual crisis which led to his baptism as a Southern Methodist in Shanghai on 3 April 1887. The decision came after intensive reading, discussion and thought, and Yun regarded it with utmost seriousness. The circumstances of his conversion are important for two main reasons. First, there is no indication that political considerations played any direct part. In fact, Yun later feared that his new faith would be a political liability.[15] Secondly, he regarded Christianity primarily as an inward, personal enlightenment which would, in time, produce a transformed life.[16] This inseparability of religion from ethics, the concept of re-newal commencing from within and working outwards, and his apolitical adoption of Christianity came to have a deep influence on Yun's nationalist thought; it also made him an enigma to the many Koreans who later embraced Christianity as a politically useful proposition.

Yet Yun was by no means blind to the implications of his new beliefs, which he began to relate to history and society after entering Vanderbilt University in America in November 1888. He keenly observed American social, political and religious beliefs and practice and, like An Ch'angho and Sŏ Chaep'il, attributed the nature of American civilisation to Christianity. This identification of civilisation with religion may be understood in relation to the standard dogma in Korea, where Confucianism and civilisation were virtually synonymous. Disenchanted with society and culture in Korea, Yun naturally concluded that Confucianism was at fault. Conversely, he concluded that if Christianity were the truth, then it would restore Korean strength and dignity:

> The rise and decline of a nation depends on the wisdom and nature of its people. Our people have for several hundred years been slaves of others, possessing no wisdom or manly character and, suffering for 500 years the oppression of an incomparably bad government, high and low, official and commoner, all seek miserably to preserve their lives through bondage to others. How then, given the present state of our country, can we hope for independence, and even were that attained, how will we be able to defend ourselves against subsequent evils and preserve our land? Thus the pressing need at present is to increase knowledge and experience, teach morality and cultivate patriotism. . . There is no other instrument able to educate and renew the people outside the Church of Christ.[17]

But would Christianity be able to save Korea? Here Yun hit a serious snag in the shape of social Darwinism. In fact, a great deal of his mental energy from mid-1889 on was expended on a struggle to reconcile his avowed belief in 'the inexorable law of the survival of the fittest'[18] with his Christian belief in a moral imperative and God's providential ordering of history.

Yun employed three key Christian concepts to analyse international behaviour and the Korean dilemma: the personal origin of evil; judgment in history (providence); and stewardship. On reading volume one of Macaulay's *History*, Yun was dismayed by the enormity of the crimes of one nation against another, but concluded: 'These international sins have their root and source in individual hearts. These sins look more grievous than individual sins simply because they are greater in bulk.'[19] Yet if history proceeds according to the law of might and 'international sins' are the prime mover in international affairs, what is the meaning of Providence? What is the point of talking of 'inalienable rights'? Yun took issue with Carlyle:

> In Carlyle's *Await the Issue*, he says, 'one strong thing I find here below: the just thing and the true thing'. There is as much truth in this statement as in the 'inalienable right of man' which men talk about now-a-day. That is, those who have *might* have inalienable right and justice and success,

but those who have no might have nothing but wrong, injustice, and failure. This is proved by the dealings of a stronger nation or race with a weaker nation or race. Therefore, one strong thing I find here below: might nothing more.[20]

One might speculate on the conclusions Yun would have drawn had he been exposed to the teachings on human institutions of other Protestant denominations on human institutions, or indeed to Pascal's thoughts on the relation of might to right in a fallen world, but in any case Yun did modify his judgment later:

We cannot say 'might is right' in the overthrow of one nation or race by another *unless* the conquered is better in morals, religion, and intelligence, therefore more *right* than the conqueror . . . But we find the stronger has been almost always better or less corrupted in morals, religion and politics than the weaker . . . Thus what seems to be a triumph of might over right is but a triumph of comparative—I do not say absolute—right over comparative wrong.[21]

From the notion of the survival of the fittest, Yun concluded that no right, even the right of a people to its nation, was inalienable. From the concepts of the personal origin of evil and of providence, he concluded that a people was morally accountable for its nation's survival. Invasion was as much the fault of the nation invaded as of the invader, for 'no sin is greater in a nation than weakness', and 'misgovernment has its own punishment as any other crime'.[22] Thus true fitness derived from spiritual health, while falling prey to social and national evolutionary processes was the logical outcome—or judgment—of spiritual stagnation. In Christian terminology, land, freedom and independence were gifts from God, and their retention depended on their proper stewardship.

Stewardship in Christianity may be traceable to the Creation accounts in *Genesis*, where God handed the earth and all its life and resources over to the care of humankind. However, the idea that government and citizens are jointly responsible for developing both the spiritual and material resources for the mutual benefit of all is contained in a number of religious systems besides Christianity, and certainly exists in Confucianism. But Yun believed Confucianism had been discredited precisely on this point. Korea had great potential— the people were endowed with good physique and intelligence, the climate was salubrious and natural resources abundant—yet her rulers and subjects neglected it.[23] Confucian precepts were powerless to rectify the Korean situation because they were flawed throughout by a ruinous preoccupation with filial piety. Moreover, in its detail, the Protestant version of stewardship possessed a social emphasis that was new to nineteenth-century Korea and which Yun considered crucial: namely, civic morality.

Civic morality is a term usually associated with English and American Protestantism and refers to those moral qualities which Protestants believe should accrue to the *individual* citizen.[24] Individual morality is seen to be the basis of social, and even national, health and vitality. Therefore one may understand the personalistic and religious social philosophy implied by this civic morality as being logically opposed to those philosophies which take social structure or class as their starting point. When expressing himself in English, Yun Ch'iho did not use the exact term 'civic morality', but he frequently referred to 'public virtue', 'public responsibility' and 'public spirit', and the content of these terms corresponds with the concept of civic morality outlined above. It was on the strength of this concept that Yun, shortly before leaving America in October 1893 to teach at his former school in Shanghai, stated his conviction that: 'Christianity is *the* salvation and hope of Korea.'[25]

What then of Confucianism? As a *yangban* educated in the Chinese Classics, it was natural that Yun Ch'iho should explain his new beliefs and advance a critique of Confucianism in ethical terms. But he also advanced a 'spiritual' critique, whereby he sought to demonstrate that Confucianism lacked the kind of transcendental power necessary both to explain and to implement its ethics. Yun's political exile, first in Shanghai and later in Wŏnsan and Chinnamp'o, evidently stimulated reflection on the role of Confucianism in the decline of Korean and Chinese cultures.

Yun Ch'iho firmly believed in the universality and objective existence of moral laws: 'Great and fundamental principles of morality are few and simple. The first great man who chanced to express them in neat and telling forms had, of course, as much right to give his name to them as Livingstone had to name his lakes and mountains.'[26] Therefore, although he shared the Reform Party's view that the Chosŏn era's neo-Confucian ethical system had become static and formalistic, Yun criticised Confucianism not for any alleged ethical poverty, but for the particular emphasis and construction it placed on filial piety. In Yun's view, although this duty was wholesome in itself, it had lost all proportion by being raised to an ethical absolute, as the touchstone of moral orthodoxy. The greatest casualty of this was public ethics: at the centre of Confucianism lay a distortion that subverted civic morality.

In Shanghai, Yun charged that filial piety, while 'covering a host of sins', freed one from concern for the millions without food, homes, education or spiritual understanding. It permitted idle speculation on questions of infinity and non-infinity in a 'perpetual war . . . in regard to the priority of 理 [*ri*] or 氣 [*ki*]', and encouraged 'the doctrine of the inferiority of women, of absolute submission to kings' and of 'everlasting go-backism'.[27] The ethical distortion went deep, not only justifying political and social oppression, but also supporting an ethical élitism (for only the privileged had the leisure and means to practise sufficiently the onerous demands of filial piety) which relieved one from mundane responsibilities. In contrast, Protestant morality signified to Yun a transition from outward legality to inward self-determination through a conscience informed transcendentally by God. Whereas Confucian ethics ended in moral élitism, Protestant ethics were a sort of 'everyman's' morality. In other words, it planted moral activity firmly in the ground of ordinary human existence.

Later, in 1902, as Magistrate of Wŏnsan in South Hamgyŏng province, Yun cited a contemporary case of political irresponsibility as an example of how filial piety, undergirding the ethic '不仁不義 [*purin puruĭ*] (one must not be uncharitable and unjust), may entirely subvert all public virtue'. On 25 March 1902, the Governor of Hamhŭng city, Kim Chonghan, had, through cruel extortions, caused a major insurrection. In his defence, according to Yun, Kim pleaded that his salary was too low, and that if he failed to support parents and relatives, 'he is necessarily a bad man, no matter if he is honest in the discharge of his duties'.[28] Yun also wrote scornfully of the *Government Gazette's* mention only of ceremonies and appointments of imperial gravekeepers as items of national importance at a time when eight of the thirteen provinces suffered severe famine and whole villages disappeared through death or migration. Given such official unconcern for the welfare of the people, Yun queried whether one could accuse God of injustice if Korea fell to others.[29]

Yun was equally disenchanted with the behaviour of the ruled. When in April 1902 a fire broke out in Wŏnsan, he experienced great difficulty in persuading even a few people to work the pump the Japanese fire-brigade had brought. Four houses burned down, and to his diary Yun confided: 'Altruism has always been condemned by Confucianists: hence public spirit is almost an unknown quality in Korea or China . . . where the gross materialism of Confucius has reduced the whole range of human duty within the four walls of one's house. . .'[30]

Bertrand Russell has pointed out that Confucianism laid down no ethical instructions that contradicted people's natural inclinations and saw this as a point in its favour. Yun Ch'iho believed this was its failing. Filial piety, interpreted as a concentration on the welfare only of one's kith and kin, was the greatest enemy in Korea of 'public spirit'. The whole business of morality was to turn attention away from natural inclinations to those needs of society and nation which transcended exclusively familial interests. Vipan Chandra correctly points out that Yun's criticisms of the materialism of filial piety do not easily apply to some of the more metaphysical schools of Confucianism or even to the writings attributed to Confucius himself.[31] But

Yun's standard here was the practice of filial piety rather than the Confucian canons.

There was more than an ethical problem for Yun in Confucianism; he perceived a vital lack in the system as a whole. Though he conceded the beauty of Mencian ethical maxims, he argued that they were *'powerless* and therefore *useless'* since they lacked any means of enabling people to practise them.[32] This was a lack, quite simply, of spiritual power—a religious rather than ethical disqualification. Yun required this spiritual power because, as a Protestant, he believed, *contra* Mencius, that humans tended naturally towards evil in action if not in sentiment, and that therefore fine ethical philosophy was inadequate by itself. Yun had already concluded in 1890 that Koreans, Japanese and Chinese did not need 'positive philosophy or altogether *knowable* religion', which they had in Confucianism. Rather, they wanted 'a living moral or rather spiritual power to enable us to do what we know to be true'.[33]

Thus Yun Ch'iho drew a different conclusion from that of Mo Tzu, the anti-Confucian philosopher of universal love, even though they shared similar premises. Both believed the ungoverned human will inclined towards evil and that some greater power was needed to bring about an ethical society. Even Yun's assertion that God's impartiality towards creation means humans should treat each other likewise employs the same kind of leap of logic as that used by the Mohists.[34] But whereas Mo Tzu appealed to a coercive outside force—the government—Yun appealed to a spiritual power that would take root within individuals. Nor was there any misanthropic pessimism here; Yun believed in the capacity of humans to change and then work voluntarily towards the highest common good. So against a background of centuries of sophisticated philosophical attention to the principles of Confucius, Mencius and Chu Hsi, Yun perceived that Christianity's strength in Korea would lie less in argument than in action, in a demonstration of its moral power to transform individual and national life.[35]

Yun's experience as Magistrate of the ports of Wŏnsan and Chinnamp'o (modern Namp'o) between March 1899 and July 1903 was a personal vindication of his contention that an application of Protestant social ethics would restore Korea's integrity. By all accounts he won unprecedented popularity for his honesty and justice in public affairs. In Wŏnsan, the people on one occasion fêted him with banquets, music and dancing, while in Chinnamp'o his popularity was such that when his transfer was announced, the people petitioned Seoul for its rescission, held demonstrations and for ten days prevented his departure.[36] It is ironic that the most successful period in his political life should have been these four years of internal exile. Yun Ch'iho gained a reputation during these years which soon became legendary and which even the later controversy surrounding his life could not wholly erase.

But for all his personal success in local administration, Yun was aware that Korea was steadily falling under Japanese and Russian control. If he had proved some points, his rule had nevertheless been paternalistic; and if the people had applauded his rule, their loyalty was to his person rather than to a concept of civic responsibility. In this Yun saw confirmation of a lesson he had drawn earlier from his experience in the Independence Club, to which we now turn: that democracy needed foundations. First Christianity had to replace Confucianism to generate public spirit at individual and national levels.

The Independence Club, 1896–1899

Towards the end of the 1894–95 Sino-Japanese War, a new, pro-reform cabinet headed by Kim Hongjip was formed under pressure from the victorious Japanese, and proceeded to enact what became known as the Kabo Reforms. Since Kim Hongjip had accompanied Yun's father to Japan in 1880, reformers who had fled after the abortive Kapshin Coup found it safe to return. Yun Ch'iho himself returned from Shanghai at the close of 1894 to seek a post in the Ministry of Education.

By any standards, 1895–96 was a tumultuous period politically, and Yun found little opportunity in government to apply his ideas. Vice-Minister of Education from 11 June 1895, he was reappointed as Vice-Minister of Foreign Affairs in July, after the re-exile of the then Home Minister, Prince Pak Yŏnghyo, on false charges of treason levelled by supporters of the still pro-Chinese Queen Min. Yun himself became very suspicious of the Japanese Minister Inoue's intentions, which he believed were 'to manage Corean affairs. . . until Japan may feel strong enough to defy [Russia].'[37] However, Inoue's replacement in August by Count Miura Gorō proved far more sinister. Before dawn on 8 October, Queen Min was murdered in the palace with the complicity of Japanese troops under Miura and a Captain Sugimura, whereupon the king became Japan's virtual prisoner. On 28 November Yun Ung'yŏl organised an attempt to smuggle King Kojong out of the palace with his son's knowledge and support, but failed. Thereupon Yun Ung'yŏl fled to Chefoo in China, while Yun Ch'iho was dismissed from the Foreign Office under Japanese pressure.[38] On 11 February 1896, the king was safely escorted to a haven inside the Russian Legation, whereupon Kim Hongjip and others in the pro-Japanese cabinet were assassinated.

Yun emerged from hiding, received a royal pardon and was appointed Acting Minister of Education the next day. However on 1 April he departed from Seoul with Prince Min Yŏnghwan on the first Korean mission to Russia.[39]

Despite the circumstances of his brief stay in office, Yun succeeded in having two primary schools established and initiated a move to recall two-thirds of the Korean students in Tokyo to help set up a modern education system in Korea.[40] Among the three education laws Yun framed while Acting Minister of Education from 12 February to 31 March 1896, the most important provided in principle for the implementation of universal primary education.[41] As Vice-Minister of Foreign Affairs, he also initiated the practice of publishing reports on foreign events in the *Government Gazette*, in particular on the situation in India under British rule.[42] But the implementation of educational reforms and the Kabo Reforms in general was frustrated by government instability and conservative opposition.

Just as problematic as conservatism, in Yun's view, was the disastrous philosophy of change that lay behind the vicissitudes of 1895–96. Despite the lesson of the Kapshin Coup, the philosophy prevailed that 'by one blow, they could rid Korea of all known and unknown evils', despite the fact that they had thereby progressively endangered the existence of the nation.[43] On his return from Russia in January 1897, Yun sought no political post but instead joined the Independence Club (Tongnip Hyŏphoe), the reform lobby which Sŏ Chaep'il had revitalised on his return from exile in America in April 1896.

Yun Ch'iho at first called the Independence Club a 'farce', a 'conglomeration of indigestible elements',[44] but soon became an enthusiast, speaking with Sŏ at Christian meetings to solicit support. Under club auspices, he organised a debating society which evolved into the famed Assembly of All Peoples (Manmin Kongdonghoe), and introduced what became a club tradition of memorialising the throne on national affairs.[45] Elected vice-president of the club in February 1898, Yun became its president in May.

The Independence Club published a newspaper, the *Tongnip Sinmun*. As the first Korean newspaper to be published entirely in the native Korean phonetic script (*han'gŭl*), it was designed to reach the widest possible readership, inform the public of domestic and foreign events and problems, introduce the new learning of the West, and instil the concepts of civil rights, self-reliance and democracy. The tone was Christian, and several leading articles dealt with allegedly harmful socio-economic effects of Shamanism.[46] Upon Sŏ Chaep'il's return to the United States early in 1898, Yun Ch'iho took over management of the paper, at which point circulation had risen from an initial 300 to 1500 copies. Under Yun's management, issues were increased from three to six per week, while circulation doubled to 3000 by the end of 1898.[47]

On accepting management of the paper, Yun emphasised the role of the *Tongnip Sinmun* in making people aware of their civil rights and of the need for their action and perseverance to attain these. Koreans, he said:

> . . . were not horses and oxen set to work like beasts of burden to carry baggage for monarch or yangban, nor could they simply gather up inalienable rights and prosperity by chance from off the streets. Rather, these things were acquired only after a long period of effort, study and struggle . . . . If they desired to enjoy such rights and prosperity, they must work, strive, indeed fight for them.[48]

From April 1896 to its final issue at the end of 1899, the *Tongnip Sinmun* addressed this theme with religious fervour. Its editorials preached that religion, education and democracy, and hard work, co-operation and honesty, were the only path to self-reliance. A link was posited between God, patriotism and industry on the one hand, and unity, prosperity and strength on the other,[49] while the West was held up as verification.[50] The *Tongnip Sinmun* served as the vehicle of an intense campaign for the modernisation of the total life of Korea along Western lines. Western education was therefore advocated as an alternative to armed revolt and continual government reshuffling.

In the editorials of the *Tongnip Sinmun*, the ethico-spiritual analysis of Korea's position was for the first time openly publicised among the Korean people. Korea's troubles were characterised as 'the accumulated result of the ways of thinking and studying in Korea over the last several hundred years'.[51] Her weakness was the result of 'worshipping empty theories', while Eastern learning in general was caricatured as 'a high fence, within which one may look about, but outside of which one is not permitted to see a single thing', thus stifling all innovation.[52] The strength of the West, on the other hand, was attributed to its dynamic tradition of studying factual reality over a long period and of applying the conclusions to the promotion of the people's welfare.[53] The Western values behind this were said to be Christian: Western civilisation was wont to 'make use of the Creator's beautiful soil for the good of His people the world over'. Insofar as this civilisation was 'the outcome of sound education', editorials proposed that it be pursued through three channels: Church, school and press.[54]

The *Tongnip Sinmun* discussed such major themes as the nature and necessity of unity,[55] modern economic and political theory[56] and the meaning and value of normative law.[57] The *Chosŏn K'ŭrisŭtoin*

Hoebo, a Christian periodical, added its support to the campaign for civic morality, especially in its call for a new style of education. Warning that bringing up one's children only in the knowledge of their own interests invites egotism, arrogance and laziness, it argued that since children, too, are gifts from God, parents are stewards charged with educating the young in a responsible manner.[58]

The Independence Club debates were much more overtly political. As speeches became pointed in their reference to the king's 'slavery' to Russia, Yun Ch'iho proposed in February 1898 that the club memorialise the throne to the effect that 'it is the misadministration of internal affairs and not the presence of foreign gunboats that threatens the safety of the kingdom'. Passed by a vote of 50 to four against, the memorial caused a sensation.[59] As memorial followed memorial, Yun remarked that 'the waves of democracy are faintly beating on the rocky shores of Korean politics'.[60] By the end of the year, however, the club became politically isolated, and as Yun's formerly cordial relationship with Emperor Kojong suffered mounting strain, he began daily to expect assassination or arrest.

During his absence on the Korean mission to Russia, Yun had been appointed a Privy Councillor, a position he retained after joining the Independence Club. In July 1898 he tendered his resignation in connection with certain memorials criticising the throne, but at that time the Emperor rejected it. In October, after repeated memorials, Yun was censured by Kojong but his integrity was so prized that he was appointed vice-president of the Privy Council shortly afterwards.[61] Then, on 30 October, an extraordinary event took place. Several cabinet members and important officials joined the Independence Club and Assembly of All Peoples in a gathering before the palace, to demand rectification of government shortcomings and reform. This gathering, known as the Kwanmin Kongdonghoe (Assembly of Officials and People), presented the famous Six Articles, a demand for constitutional politics.[62]

Appearances belied reality. Yun Ch'iho later recalled the action of the politicians and officials as a most cynical act motivated by fear of 'public opinion,' a ploy to put the people off guard and await the chance 'to send down a thunderbolt of oppression'.[63] The Independence Club had already lost favour with the foreign legations by opposing the moves of Russia, Japan and America to gain special influence in the court;[64] now it was exposed fully to the hostility of the court itself. During the night of 4 November, the eve of the day on which it was promised to introduce political reform, the arrest of Independence Club members began. Syngman Rhee, Yi Sangjae, Namgung Ŏk and fourteen others were taken, but Yun escaped via an exit in his back fence specially prepared against this contingency. From hiding, Yun again submitted his resignation from the Privy

Council. But after popular pressure persuaded the authorities of the wisdom of releasing the prisoners, Yun was granted a special imperial pardon and during the period 22–23 November he was reappointed vice-president of the Privy Council and appointed Mayor of Seoul.[65] Nevertheless, Yun refused the appointments (since his father warned him against remaining in Seoul) and the political experiment was over.

On 21 November a fracas broke out between supporters of the Independence Club and the strong, conservative Pedlars' Guild led by Hong Chŏngu, the assassin of Kim Okkyun, which left several people dead or injured. At the same time, forged posters appeared on public buildings bearing the message that the time had come to depose the monarch, establish a republic and elect a president.[66] Kojong fell for this deception and finally withdrew his protection from Yun. In January 1899 the club was forcibly dissolved and prominent leaders again imprisoned. Yun was exiled to Wŏnsan in March, and nine months later the *Tongnip Sinmun* was discontinued.

The suppression of the Independence Club came as no surprise to Yun Ch'iho, who since May 1898 had suspected that the experiment would fail. The primary cause in his view was not conservative opposition so much as the continuing 'lack of public spirit among the people', without which democracy had no basis. Even the euphoric meetings of the Assembly of All Peoples later that year did not impress: Yun was surprised rather by the 'abominable indifference of the general public'. Among club members themselves, he lamented, perhaps as many as nine-tenths were corrupt. He had therefore opposed the demands of the 'radicals' like Syngman Rhee for direct political confrontation, since without popular support the only winners would be Japan or Russia. Before democracy must appear a public conscience; and before that, the 'blood of the race has to be changed by a new education, a new government and a new religion'.[67] Sŏ Chaep'il was of the same opinion.

That this account of the failure of the movement was more than a little self-serving has been cogently argued by Vipan Chandra.[68] Sŏ was unwilling to risk his skin by fomenting a revolution against a monarchy he was comfortably employed to advise, and opted to return to the United States, where he was a citizen. Although he was clearly bolder than most in his memorials and speeches, Yun was careful to maintain relations with the monarchy which were as amicable as possible, thereby saving himself from certain imprisonment. (In 1898, however, at the height of the Independence Club's strength, Kojong had ordered the assassination of Yun, who was saved only because the order was disobeyed.)[69] Both men failed to throw themselves unequivocally behind a political revolution, and Yun's break with younger members such as Syngman Rhee seriously weakened the movement. This is perhaps not so inconsistent with the brand of liberalism Sŏ and Yun held. Yun, at any rate, favoured an evolutionary course of national transformation, and was more attracted to a constitutional monarchy grounded on liberal values than an outright republic. Yun always eschewed violent means of change—in fact, he seemed to believe that no positive change could result from violence—and this may have been linked to his belief in the inner, spiritual source of change.

It is difficult to assess the importance of the Independence Club during its hectic three years of activity. It was the first organised front pressing the court to adopt a course of modernisation to strengthen and secure national independence. It created not only the first vernacular script newspaper, but the first real 'opposition' newspaper in Korean history. Although the club prompted only limited reform, such as the enactment of regulations governing concessions to foreign firms and provision for the election of some members of the Privy Council, its legacy became clearer in the twentieth century when former club members became stars of the nationalist movement. Moreover, its most active members—Yun, Sŏ Chaep'il and Namgung Ŏk in Seoul and An Ch'angho and Kil Sŏnju in P'yŏngyang—were Protestants, while others such as Yi Sangjae and Syngman Rhee embraced Christianity during their imprisonment from 1899 to 1904. The Independence Club enjoyed greater influence as a legacy than as an institution.

Civic ethics and capitalism

There was, however, one important area in which the ethical and individualist approach represented by Yun and Sŏ was influential among reformers as a whole in the 1890s, and this was the area of change. Yun, somewhat mischievously, ascribed his own belief that lasting change would issue only from change in the will of individuals to the Imperial Decree of November 1897, which proclaimed that Korea was thenceforth an empire ruled by an emperor. In a speech in honour of the Decree, Yun interpreted it thus:

> The point of the Imperial Decree in urging us to amend our ways and pursue new ones, is not that we must willy-nilly change our occupations—scholar, farmer, artisan or merchant—in order to become true citizens. Rather, it means that if we once cast from us all those customs and habits of old that have inured us to indolence and duplicity, and instead work conscientiously to fulfil our respective duties in whatever office or business we may be engaged, then not only will our nation *naturally become*

prosperous and strong, but we will also indeed become Taehan citizens worthy of the name.[70] [Emphasis added.]

This appeal to the conscience and will of each citizen appeared frequently in the *Tongnip Sinmun*, especially in discussions of economic issues, where it was maintained that a change in moral outlook would bring about changes in the structure of economy and society. Further, it was claimed that the essence of Western capitalism was 'public spirit'. Whereas no-one with money in Korea ever thought to put it to public use, in the West it was considered that 'money is not just for the use of one person, but is rather a convenient means of exchanging goods among the peoples of the world'.[71] Money put into industries producing useful goods was money serving the people. England exported goods throughout the world; America supplied the world with food; but Korea, despite its fertile soil and ideal climate, had not even developed its agriculture let alone deep-sea fishing. Westerners used their surplus to establish schools, hospitals, libraries and the like; that they did so even in foreign lands demonstrated the universal reach of Western ethics.[72] It is important to grasp this highly optimistic view of 'Christian' economics and the non-violent approach to change held by the management of the *Tongnip Sinmun* when examining the reform proposals of the 1890s.

The two principal reformers involved in economic reform during the Kabo Reforms of 1895–96 were the 'moderate' reformer Kim Yunsik and Yun's erstwhile colleague, Yu Kiljun. Both were influenced by earlier Silhak scholars' idealistic schemes for equal land distribution. Yet both rejected this idealism in favour of infusing the existing landlord–tenant structure with capitalist functions, modern agricultural techniques and a secure landownership system which would protect the right of individuals to own land. As a Confucian, Kim Yunsik was unimpressed by the Western rationale for such a system. He was a pragmatist who was guided by Japan's experiences and his perception that justice and domestic peace were best secured by tax-reform and the protection of private property.

In practical terms, Yu Kiljun's position was similar to Kim Yunsik's. In 1891 he had argued in his *Chije Ŭi* that the traditional ownership system, improved and secured by issuance of land deeds after a fair survey, could best serve the modernisation of agriculture.[73] But Yu's admiration for the West and its values aligned him much more closely with the tone of the *Tongnip Sinmun's* pronouncements on the subject. Yu argued that development of commercial companies, which were basic to the West's economic strength, could only occur through voluntary investment by those already possessing capital. A sudden equal distribution of land would not only remove the only rural component—the landlord class—that could provide the wanted capital, it also missed the point. A redistribution would hinder rather than enhance the emergence of a sector willing to put money into public development. In Korea, the local Gentry Associations which were able to mobilise the rural population through the Village Codes they composed were the obvious vehicles of reform.[74]

Yu Kiljun and the *Tongnip Sinmun* clearly put a great deal of faith in the willingness of the landlords and monied classes to free their capital for investment in agricultural enterprises and, having done so, to increase wages as returns increased. The Korean economic historian Kim Yongsŏp comments that, with Kim and Yu, 'the traditional landlord system was rationalised according to Western European economic and political thought'.[75] Of Yu Kiljun and the *Tongnip Sinmun* editors it would perhaps be truer to say that it was rationalised according to their *romantic conception* of Western economic practice. Yu Kiljun, who had edged towards Protestantism by this time, believed that competition was the source of prosperity and happiness and that competition was a natural, and proper', outcome of the 'pursuit of knowledge and the cultivation of virtue', which Confucianists had talked of but not understood.[76]

The contrast between the alleged Korean practice of confining the use of money to one's home and the capitalist practice of putting one's money to use in the wider society led Yun Ch'iho, Sŏ Chaep'il, An Ch'angho and other reformers besides Yu Kiljun to regard capitalism as unselfish in spirit. Just as responsible engagement in local and national affairs was civic morality in the political arena, so capitalism was civic ethics applied to the economic sphere. This rosy view of capitalism undergirded the economic self-reconstruction thought and activities of Protestant nationalists such as Yi Sŭnghun, Kim Sŏngsu and Cho Mansik right through to the 1930s.

Further, in concert with political liberalism, such a process of economic change would obviate the need for sudden upheaval and assure the stable development of civil rights, democracy and national strength. The only alternative seen in those troubled times was a violent revolution such as the 1894 Tonghak Rebellion which, as Yun had foreseen five years earlier, served as an excuse for foreign powers to 'Polandise' the Korean peninsula.[77] In this connection it may be justifiable to claim that 'imperialism was the catalyst of [economic] change.'[78] But this ought not to suggest that the Protestant reformers or their collaborators were passive agents. It may be true that by the beginning of the twentieth century the traditional merchant class had to adopt capitalist models, establish trading banks and so forth simply in order to survive,[79] but Protestant reformers saw intrinsic value in capitalist formation.

Education and the model settlement, 1905–1910

When Yun Ch'iho returned from internal exile to Seoul in February 1904, a showdown was occurring between Russia and Japan which was to have a fateful impact on Korea. A final attempt to reform the peninsular empire along traditional lines—the Kwangmu Reforms[80]—had already been frustrated by intensified Russo-Japanese rivalry. The Russo-Japanese War had commenced, and the deployment of a large Japanese force in Seoul warned Yun that 'the life of Korea as an independent country is suspended by a thread'.[81] In March he was appointed Vice-Minister of Foreign Affairs, a post which over the next twenty months entailed humiliating negotiations with the Japanese. Foreign Office affairs became distasteful to everyone. The Minister of Foreign Affairs, Yi Hayŏng, fell conveniently ill at strategic moments, and so Yun, as Acting Minister, was left to sign 'agreements' with Japan which gave her progressive control over Korean affairs.[82]

Yun was in no doubt over his own position. It was 'morally wrong' to 'hand over the whole country with eyes open, for dirty bribes, to Japan', and he refused to accede to the 'Nagamori Concession', a scheme of the Japanese Minister Hayashi to have Korea's 'wastelands' transferred to Japanese management. It was, he perceived, 'annexation minus the name'.[83] Hayashi himself confided to Yun, whose grasp of the Japanese language and customs was excellent: 'We expect much of you and ask you and your friends to co-operate with us.'[84] He became disgruntled over Yun's obstinacy. Tragically unable, in the flush of victory, to understand why Korea's 'progressives' should oppose them, Japanese officials grew incensed at their coolness. Following Russia's final defeat in October 1905, Prince Itō Hirobumi entered the palace with a force of gendarmes and on 17 November compelled the cabinet to sign a Protectorate Treaty which made him Resident-General. Thereupon Yun resigned from the government and, to the displeasure of Japan, flatly refused the Foreign Affairs portfolio which was pressed upon him repeatedly in following weeks.[85]

The instalment of the Residency-General in Seoul added urgency to Yun's conviction that new learning based on Protestant spirituality was Korea's only hope. Earlier, in July and August 1904, former Independence Club leaders had been released from prison. In the reunion that followed, Yun discovered that a good number had become Protestants. As news of the activities of the Presbyterian An Ch'angho and Yi Sŭnghun reached him, Yun realised he was now one among many influential people who believed that spiritual training to foster civic virtues was the proper means of gaining and maintaining independence. In a letter to Mr Durham Stevens, an American employed by the Japanese in the Finance Department, Yun explained that, while he had no sympathy with the puppet government, he had no intention of joining the Righteous Armies either. 'I believe that Koreans must take the situation that is imposed on them and make the most of it. I can help my country better in a private capacity than I may in the Cabinet as now planned.'[86]

By 'private capacity', Yun meant educational, and specifically Christian-based educational, work. As early as 1893 he had conceived a plan of establishing an industrial school in Korea, for which he had entrusted $200 to Dr Candler, then President of the Methodist Emory College.[87] Back in Korea, Yun wrote to Dr Candler: '[If] we desire to have a school of any sort at all, it must be an industrial school where the Corean youth may learn through saving truth that work is no disgrace; that Corea's future depends on work; that Christianity is a working religion.'[88] It was 'one of the obligations of Christianity' to teach the virtue of hard work, and a Christian industrial college would 'not only encourage self-reliance but also give the means of self-reliance'.[89] This self-reliance, of course, would be the foundation of national independence.

From early 1906 Yun began preparations for the school with financial support from his father. In October he opened the Han–Yŏng Sŏwŏn (Anglo-Korean College) at Songdo (now Kaesŏng) to the north of Seoul, in conjunction with the Southern Methodist Mission. As principal, his fame attracted students from all over Korea. Commencing with just fourteen students, the roll increased to 225 within two years and by 1910 reached 329 students, 54 of whom were high-school pupils.[90] The industrial side of the curriculum at first concentrated on the fruit and vegetable industries, later expanding to include carpentry, pastoral farming and the textile industry. In time the college provided Songdo with a modern carpentry business, a textile plant which began exporting in the 1920s, a dairy farm operated by Yun's eldest son, Yŏngsŏn, and an apple orchard and vineyard.[91]

A number of other institutions which shared Yun's convictions were founded concurrently. The return of the youthful An Ch'angho from America in February 1907 heralded a flurry of activity within the new Protestant community. In the north, Yi Sŭnghun founded the famous Christian Osan College, while An himself founded Taesŏng College. Uchida Ryōhei termed P'yŏngyang the 'hotbed' of Christianity and estimated that at least half of its population were Christians (which could not have been so). 'In P'yŏngyang,' he reported, 'there are the Minkai [Minhoe: Citizens' Councils, or Sinminhoe?], the Self-Strengthening Society and youth associations [Ch'ŏngnyŏn Hakuhoe?] . . . Everything is run by Christians. . .' An Ch'angho especially inspired Christian activism. He embarked on lecture tours to persuade Koreans that independence depended on themselves, not foreign nations. Uchida's spies quoted An as teaching: 'If we believe in Christianity then we have no real enemy under Heaven . . . The nation's independence is up to you citizens, not the protection of foreign peoples. God alone can be called our Protector.'[92]

The years 1907 to 1908 saw a mushrooming of educational and industrial institutions under Christian leadership in several parts of the nation. Yi Tonghwi, though harassed by police, founded and headed the Poch'ang School in the Kanghwa district on the mid-west coast; Yi Sangjae became principal of the Kosŏng School in Seoul; Namgung Ŏk edited a monthly educational journal, *Kyoyuk Wŏlbo*, for Koreans who were unable to attend schools; and Yi Tonghwi and Kim Tongwan helped establish industrial centres in Seoul and Song-do. The return of Yu Kiljun from exile in September 1907 further stimulated interest in industry, education and local self-government ideas in the mid-western provinces around Seoul. Just before his forced abdication in 1907, Emperor Kojong granted Yu an official pardon and offered him a government post. Like Yun Ch'iho, Yu declined and reportedly stated his intention of 'working in the capacity of an ordinary citizen, serving the needs of education'.[93] From November, Yu devoted himself and his money to primary education, workers' education and industrial development. Enlightenment through learning and cultivation of morality, Yu proposed, were the twin pillars of true civilisation.[94] Like Yun Ch'iho he impressed on Korean workers the moral that their hard work would save the nation.[95] He also joined Namgung Ŏk in organising a number of self-governing, elected citizens' councils. Still an idealist and now a firmly Christian idealist, Yu Kiljun was by 1908 espousing 'pure' socialism.[96] Upon annexation in 1910, the Japanese attempted to gain the support of this extremely talented individual by including him on their list of high decorations, but Yu refused the gesture. (Yu died as something of a mystic in 1914. His brother Sŏngjun and son Ŏkkyŏm both became Protestants and leaders in later self-reconstruction nationalism, the latter as a protégé of Yun Ch'iho.)

A negative byproduct of this activity was the development within the Protestant community of the traditional regional rivalry between the northwest and mid-west provinces. To the former belonged An Ch'angho, Yi Sŭnghun and Cho Mansik; to the latter Syngman Rhee, Yi Sangjae, Yu Kiljun and Yun Ch'iho. Cognizant of this development, An and Yun worked to minimise its effects. Yun became principal of An's Taesŏng College and An encouraged 'southern' participation in the leadership of organisations he inspired, particularly the Sinminhoe (New Citizens' Society) and the Ch'ŏngnyŏn Hakuhoe (Youth Student Fraternity). The Sinminhoe was designed to promote national unity, spiritual and moral growth through education, and commerce and industry through Korean capital and expertise. While president of the Self-Strengthening Society, Yun was also involved in the Sinminhoe and Ch'ŏngnyŏn Hakuhoe.

The manifesto of the Ch'ŏngnyŏn Hakuhoe, which was almost certainly composed by Yun Ch'iho and not, as has been claimed, by Shin Ch'aeho,[97] described the type of new citizen Yun envisaged:

> To all who desire reform of corrupt old customs and are willing to cultivate true public virtues we declare that this cannot be achieved by academic ability or by fine writing and rhetoric alone. It will be attained by forming a grand spiritual organisation of young men of one mind; by the mutual exchange and application of knowledge; by formulating forward-looking policies, despising backwardness and danger; by stemming the angry tide of convention regardless of the cost; and by making your youthful renewal in pursuit of the way of happiness the pivotal point of our [national] revival.

It was a measure of the social changes occurring in the early twentieth century that Yun and his colleagues perceived that Korea's main hope lay in its youth (i.e. the 20–35 year range). In a sense, the YMCA (led by Yun, Syngman Rhee, Yu Sŏngjun and Yi Sangjae) and the Ch'ŏngnyŏn Hakuhoe were the new Independence Club, while the latter's mouthpiece, Ch'oe Namsŏn's *Sonyŏn*, was heir to the *Tongnip Sinmun*. In the issues of *Sonyŏn* published between 1907 and 1910, civic courage was opposed to materialistic bravado, the citizen's responsibility for the nation and the need to reject toadyism were proclaimed, and pointed biographies on great leaders such as Garibaldi and Abraham Lincoln abounded.[98] In December 1908, *Sonyŏn* carried an article explaining how America gained independence, in which the anatomy of civic morality was described in detail. Perseverance and a self-reliant spirit were heavily emphasised, and the description concluded with the old theme of the unselfish spirit behind Western civilisation.[99]

Encouraging though the proliferation of such organisations was, Yun Ch'iho was also conscious of the diffused nature of the campaign. A concrete embodiment of the new principles was necessary. By April 1907, in view of the support accorded his convictions and the generous donations of funds for his school even by non-Christians, Yun judged that the time was right to establish his dream—a 'model Christian settlement'. This he described in a letter to Dr Candler: 'To do this one must have (1) a missionary centre, (2) a good educational plant, (3) a reasonably large tract of land for the accommodation of at least a hundred or more cottages with good streets, etc., (4) money to initiate these elements of a settlement.'[100] The project was important to Yun as a visible alternative to the methods of the patriotic guerillas. He wrote: 'We shall present to our non-Christian population of the whole country a model settlement' with 'a hospital, a school, a missionary settlement, and cheap and beautifully located sites and farms to begin with'. He even appealed to Dr Candler to seek people willing to invest up to $20 000 in the scheme, adding: 'All the members of the Mission approve the plan.'[100]

However, time was against Yun and like-minded Koreans. In October 1909, a Catholic, An Chunggŭn, assassinated Prince Itō in Harbin. The Residency-General began trailing An Ch'angho and attempted to entrap him with 'plants' in order to link him with the assassination, and Christian activists began fearing for their safety. When annexation appeared imminent, a number of leading Protestants fled the wrath to come. On his return from YMCA deputation work in England and America early in 1910, Yun was unsettled to find that An Ch'angho had departed. But he himself resolved to stay and expand the school and mission settlement in accordance with his ideals. On 29 August 1910, Korea was formally annexed to the Japanese Empire. The following year Yun was arrested, and work on a pilot community to implement the new civic ethic was cut short.

Conclusion

The American diplomat William Sands believed that the Independence Club members would have carried off a real revolution but for the Russo-Japanese rivalry that precipitated war in 1904. Even after the war, he considered them still capable of engineering a revolution.[102] A revolution something like the Chinese 1911 incident was certainly in the offing; only outside intervention and internal division and uncertainty forestalled it. Should the reformers have allied with Japan? Apart from the fact that opposition to foreign reliance was a major item on the radicals' platform, there is no evidence that Japan would have been a trustworthy ally. An Ch'angho himself pleaded with Prince Itō in 1907 to allow the Koreans the same opportunity to reform that Japan enjoyed in the 1860s.[103] But the very fact that a statesman of Prince Itō Hirobumi's stature should have forced the Korean cabinet to sign the Protectorate Treaty at bayonet point indicates the importance over and above their avowed idealistic purposes which the Japanese attached to control over the peninsula. Especially after 1905, there is a strong basis for Marius Jansen's assessment that the 'likelihood of substantial Japanese support for liberal and republican forces in Asia was very slight'.[104]

In view of the external threat, a compromise with the conservatives might have been expected. Was not Korea's danger such that the immediate necessity of defending it had a right to override the question of just what it was that was being defended? On several occasions between 1884 and 1905 Yun Ch'iho was looked to as the only politician capable of forging such an alliance: he once confided to his friend Yu Kiljun, 'I cannot be a partisan; I look at both sides of a question too much.'[105] But this is an admission of ambivalence, which seriously compromised his leadership at crucial moments. After 1905, he cut his links with officialdom, convinced that it was pointless trying to maintain the superficial independence of a corrupt and anachronistic system. In his thought, means and ends became inseparable: the end he desired for the nation was simply the continued practice of the religious and ethical means he prescribed for attaining the new Korea. Yun refused to distinguish independent statehood from the *quality of life* of the people. As the journal *Sonyŏn* argued, the American people had become independent before England bowed out.[106] In Yun's thought it always had to be that way round: foreigners would always interfere in Korea unless the people first developed the spirit of independence.

The essence of Yun Ch'iho's ethical nationalism is thus seen in his response to the final loss of independence in November 1905. With the situation beyond his control, Yun decided to pursue his ideals through the open avenues of education and religious societies, rather than beating against closed doors. If perfection were pursued in society, sooner or later that society would be renewed. This is not, as George Bernard Shaw wittily characterised it, an instance of viewing the world as a 'moral gymnasium'. It is comparable, rather, to a Chinese tradition which Lin Yü-sheng describes as the need to establish an intellectual and cultural foundation for change.[107] Ironically, Yun and An Ch'angho, together with other Protestants who played active roles in the Independence Club and enlightenment movements, fell back on a revered ingredient of their élite tradition in order to pursue cultural iconoclasm.

There is some uncertainty about how deeply the new tradition could have penetrated Korean society. Certainly the ideology of the *Tongnip Sinmun* was an import of high-level Western liberalism expressed through high-level journalism by high-class intellectuals. It informs the historian about ideas circulated among élites—that is, educated rather than economic élites. But the medium was part of the message. The *Tongnip Sinmun* was printed in pure vernacular script: it was meant for wide readership, to instil democratic ideas and to plant the seeds of a new order. It has been judged that the *Tongnip Sinmun* played a crucial and unambiguous role in forging a new national cultural identity.[108] The *Sonyŏn* journal took the next step and aimed its message at the new generation of anxious and restless minds. Here, in the midst of the Great Revival, the identification of the new values with Protestant principles was vital, as it established a sense of comity between upper and lower social levels which opened a crucial channel of communication between the two.

It was the Ch'ŏngnyŏn Hakuhoe which most influenced self-reconstruction nationalism after the annexation. The organisation was founded as a result of much reflection by An Ch'angho on the limitations of the Independence Club and the Self-Strengthening Society, which had been hampered by their political involvement. The Ch'ŏngnyŏn Hakuhoe was therefore strictly nonpolitical in an overt sense and dedicated to the reformation of individual and social behaviour.[109] Through it, An's 'Four Principles' of living—truth, ability, loyalty and courage—and the 'Three Categories' of education—moral, mental and physical—were expounded for the first time. The Protestant activity from 1896 to 1910 would seem to support Lévi-Strauss's discovery that humankind builds big at the beginning. The groundwork for the whole self-reconstruction ideology up to 1937 and later had been laid during this period. There was hardly a development within the movement thereafter that was not an extension of some principle in ethical nationalism. The eureka had been sounded and attention focused subsequently on its possibilities—and on its problems.

3 The Dark Ages, 1910–1919

The period 1910–19 in Korean history may be described as a 'dark ages' with regard not only to the fate of Christian and nationalist activities, but also to the paucity of materials available for research. The annexation terminated both the Chosŏn dynasty and the energetic enlightenment campaign of the previous five years, and few Korean documents have survived from the decade of military rule that followed. The religious policies adopted by Governors-General Terauchi Masatake (1910–16) and Hasegawa Yoshimichi (1916–19) were essentially hostile to any independent religion.[1] Despite unofficial contact with the West through the mission boards, Korean Christians probably suffered more than any other group (with the exception of the guerillas) during this first decade of direct Japanese rule. Though the Protestants organised no political movement and threw out no overt challenge to the authorities, they found themselves locked in a struggle with the Japanese for the 'soul' of the nation and their own survival. Education, a major emphasis of the Sinminhoe and Ch'ŏngnyŏn Hakuhoe, was the principal avenue open to Protestants. Together with the churches, schools became the means of forging Protestants' identity as a reconstructive community on which, its members believed, the fate of the nation rested. But the scope of Protestant activity, and indeed that of every other Korean group, was severely constricted by the colonial policies of the military Government-General of Chōsen.

The policy and practice of assimilation

Japan's colonial theory in Korea cannot be treated here in detail,[2] but its central motif of assimilation requires some description. Conceiving of Korea as a dagger pointed towards her heart, a natural highway leading China and Russia to her, Japan had pleaded defensive and strategic justification for the annexation. Especially after An Chunggŭn's assassination of Itō Hirobumi in October 1909, both the public and the political parties had pressured the Saionji cabinet for a 'decisive policy,' and the 'Treaty of Annexation . . . was universally proclaimed as a great achievement'.[3] Behind this acclamation lay Japan's belief that she was the 'Light of Asia', destined to lead the East into strength and prosperity. From this idealistic motive, as well as to secure more mundane purposes, the assimilative policy appeared most suitable.

The main assumptions of the assimilative policy appeared in the summary prepared by Governor-General Terauchi for the 1910–11 Annual Report of the Administration of Chōsen. Citing the close geographical and cultural affinities of Korea and Japan, he asserted: 'It is a natural and inevitable course of things that two peoples whose . . . interests are identical, and who are bound together with brotherly feelings, should amalgamate and form one body.'[4] Not all Japanese favoured assimilation on these or any other grounds, and later Dr Suehiro Shigeru of Kyōtō Imperial University identified the policy as the root of all Japan's failures in Korea.[5] Few Koreans desired to acknowledge any ethnic bond, and since Korea had been the means of Chinese culture reaching Japan, particularly T'ang Buddhism and fourteenth-century neo-Confucianism, the Korean people were embittered by Japanese condescension. For, protestations of brotherly love notwithstanding, the racial contempt of the Japanese for Koreans, already evident in the 1890s, became firmly institutionalised after 1910 in the political apparatus, in education and in legal and economic systems.

The immediate problem of applying political rights to Koreans had been circumvented quite simply: annexation of Korea had not been anticipated in the Japanese Meiji Constitution of 1868.[6] While adopting this recourse, Premier Katsura nevertheless announced in December 1910 that Korea was not a *shokuminji* (colony) but a *gaiji* (outer territory), of which Japan was the *naiji* (inner or home territory). Under this arrangement, the Government-General was separated from the Japanese Diet in such a way as to give the Governor-General almost unlimited authority over the peninsula. He exercised direct control over the Secretariat, the five bureaus and seventeen affiliated offices of the Government-General and literally ruled the land by decree.[7]

Since the administration at the local level was also highly centralised, the political apparatus, to be effective as a means of control, was
inimical to meaningful Korean participation and therefore to Korean
political assimilation as well. There being no representative body for
Koreans, bureaucratic recruitment was the only door to political involvement; however, since the function of the bureaucracy was to
implement Japanese rule, such employment bore the stigma of collaboration, and most 'patriotic' Koreans such as former Governor of
South P'yŏngan, Yi Siyŏng, had been removed by 1910. Between
1910 and 1913, 43.9 per cent of Korean senior officials, including 90
per cent of the highest, chokunin, rank and 24.7 per cent of Korean
junior officials were dismissed.[8]

The aims, practice and results of Japan's economic management of
Korea have occasioned some polemical disputation. But Koreans
felt, and no doubt were, exploited, for in terms of Japan's avowed
strategic interest in Korea, commercial factors ranked high.[9] The
Government-General centralised the economy, maintaining monop-
olies in forestry, mining, tobacco and railways. In the early years,
however, the most visible economic measure of the Koreans' loss of
nationhood was the Japanese acquisition of land.

Japan had begun acquiring real estate well before the annexation.
Even prior to the Protectorate, an observer noticed 'certain extraordinary and incredibly usurious real estate mortgage operations [by
the Japanese], which seemed to have the definite purpose of acquiring all the land possible by foreclosure'.[10] After 1910, the land sur-
veys, unfamiliar in form to the illiterate Korean farmers, facilitated
legal confiscation of land on technical grounds. The Japanese Christian and liberal Professor Yoshino Sakuzō reported in the Tokyo
Chūō Kōron after a tour in Korea in 1916: 'Without consideration
and mercilessly [the Japanese] have resorted to laws for the expro-
riation of land, the Koreans concerned being compelled to part with
their family property for nothing'.[11]

Only in education did the Koreans retain some measure of control.
This is significant, for political means of assimilation having been
rejected, education was elected the most suitable alternative. Dr
Mizuno Rentarō, later Director-General of Political Affairs in the
Government-General, urged that education be introduced benev-
olently as a tool of assimilation, with sufficiently encouraging in-
centives.[12] While his principle was adopted, his recommendations
on its implementation were not. Instead, Terauchi erected a separate, unequal school system to that provided for the Japanese in
Korea, on the basis of the alleged racial and intellectual inferiority of
the Koreans. 'Assimilation', rather than advancing the Koreans'
knowledge and expertise to a level on par with that of the Japanese,
was intended 'to cultivate such character as befitting the imperial

subject through moral development and dissemination of the national [i.e. Japanese] language'.[13] The Japanese were conciliatory, even supportive, towards Confucian schooling. By contrast, relations with Christian-based schools were plagued by prolonged conflicts; the Japanese perceived in these schools a major threat to their assimilative designs. Governor-General Terauchi responded with a two-pronged attack directed first against the Christian leadership and secondly against the Christian schools.

The Japan Congregational Church

It was Terauchi's hope to have Korean churches reorganise as branches of the Japan Congregational Church and to enlist the support of the missionaries in drawing the sting from the Korean Christian community. However, neither ploy enjoyed much success.

The Japan Congregational Church (Kyōdan kyōkai) had established a church in Seoul in 1904 and another in P'yŏngyang in 1907. In 1910 the church publicly endorsed the assimilation policy and, blaming foreign missionaries for the Korean Christians' anti-Japanese stance, advocated evangelism by Japanese Christians only as the path to harmony between Korea and Japan.'[14] Not all Christian denominations in Japan supported assimilation, but all approved the annexation. The famous Japanese public figure Uchimura Kanzō, who was much admired by Yun Ch'iho, stood alone as the only influential Japanese Christian to oppose annexation in 1910.[15]

Terauchi was quick to grasp his opportunity. Letters and other documents of the Japanese Christians concerned mention the Governor-General's political and financial support of the Japan Congregational Church. He also personally encouraged wealthy Japanese to add their assistance in order to counteract the evils of 'Western Christianity'. Ōkuma Shigenobu, Shibusawa Eiichi and several *zaibatsu* firms—Mitsubishi, Mitsui and Furukawa—donated funds, and the Congregational Church was able to entice already-established Korean congregations to affiliate with its superbly financed denomination. In this way, together with relatively minor success in evangelism, the denomination grew to have 150 churches for Koreans by 1919, with a membership of 14 387.[16]

Terauchi's successor, Hasegawa Yoshimichi, continued the policy more openly. In his review of the first decade of Japanese rule, he mentioned the administration's constant concern over the Korean Christians' dependence on foreign missionaries, whom he accused of pursuing the politically harmful evangelistic tactic of advocating 'freedom and pro-Americanism'. He then revealed that the Japan Congregational Church had been given Government-General aid over the decade, but lamented its meagre returns.[17]

In terms of the aim of assimilating Korean Christianity, the Congregational Church's attraction of only just over 14000 of the at least 300000 existing Korean Christians over a period of ten years was perhaps disappointing. Yet among those who transferred to the Congregational Church were some important leaders. After an altercation with an American missionary, Yi Wŏn'gŭng's Seoul Myodong Church became independent and then in late 1916 affiliated itself with the Japanese denomination.[18] The former Chief of Seoul Police, Kim Chŏngsik, who had been serving as president of the Korean YMCA in Tokyo, also joined the Congregational church on his return to Korea at the end of 1916. At this point the denomination experienced rapid growth from roughly 6000 to 11000 members.[19]

Government-General sponsorship of the Japan Congregational Church was only one side of the coin of its strategy to contain Christianity. On the reverse side were legal and other disincentives placed on the practice and propagation of the faith among Koreans. In August 1915 a new religious ordinance distressed missionaries by the powers it gave the authorities to control church personnel.[20] From Japan, Dr Speer advised missionaries not to be alarmed 'in the slightest degree', since such regulations also pertained in Japan.[20] But the missionaries' fears were grounded in the experience of the church over the preceding five years under less troublesome laws. From 1911 reports emerged from Christian strongholds such as Sŏnch'ŏn that 'services, Sundays and week days, were regularly attended by police . . . and our schools were under very close scrutiny almost daily'.[22] Even more pertinent was the fact that, shortly before the new laws were devised, the Korean Christian community had been rocked by a serious assault on its leadership, known as the '105 Incident', or 'Conspiracy Case'.

The Conspiracy Case, 1911–1913

An Ch'angho fled to America; Yun Ch'iho elected to stay. In their own way, both choices were fateful: the former suffered the frustrations of diaspora life, while the latter endured the psychological and physical assault of the Government-General. Yet as far as Korean Christianity and nationalism were concerned, An Ch'angho lurked in the wings while Yun Ch'iho stood, willy-nilly, on centre stage.

The dress-rehearsal of the drama about to enfold around Yun took place in Anak, Hwanghae province in November 1910, when Kim Ku and a number of others, mostly Christians, were sentenced to imprisonment for alleged involvement in a subversive plan attributed by police to An Myŏnggŭn, the brother of Itō's assassin, An Chunggŭn. Since their guilt was unproven, the Anak Incident was regarded by many as the beginning of a plan to crush Christianity. Less than a year later, these fears were realised.

The Government-General struck first in Sŏnch'ŏn, a provincial centre in North P'yŏngan where over half the 8000 inhabitants were Christians. Arrests began in late September. Before long, over 80 people, including five pastors and the pupils and faculty of the Christian Boy's Academy, were arraigned on a charge not yet revealed. When accusations of an aborted plot to assassinate Governor-General Terauchi at Sŏnch'ŏn railway station on 28 December 1910 finally emerged, they were met with universal disbelief among Koreans and foreigners alike.[23]

Identical attempts on Count Terauchi's life at other stations were alleged, accounting for the arrest of Christians in P'yŏngyang, Seoul and other centres where Christians were influential. Of approximately 700 persons detained during the operation, up to 157 were remanded for trial, of whom only 22 were not Christians.[24] On 9 February 1912, Yun Ch'iho was charged with having masterminded the whole conspiracy. The first trial commenced on 18 June 1912 at the Seoul District Court. During it, 123 persons were arraigned and 105 convicted on the strength of stereotyped confessions. Three men died from torture employed to exact the confessions.[25] Although careful not to openly accuse the Government-General of persecution of Christians, missionaries' reports and letters show that they solidly supported the view of the Korean population that the conspiracy was a Japanese one against the life of the church. It was claimed that even Japanese residents and police said as much.[26]

Two factors robbed the Government-General of full satisfaction. First, the trial itself exposed the improbability of the charges, and it became evident that in their zeal the police and prosecution had lost all sense of proportion. In July 1912 a Presbyterian missionary in Taegu wrote that it was 'so evident that the authorities have overreached themselves and made a travesty . . . of the whole affair, that we are much comforted.'[27] Secondly, the accused themselves made a fool of the interrogation methods by implicating foreigners. On 11 July 1912, confessions read in open court implicated nineteen missionaries, including Drs Underwood and McCune, the premillennialist and fundamentalist Dr Moffett and Mr Blair and, absurdly, the pro-Japanese Bishop Harris.[28]

Astonishment and glee at the folly of the prosecution has obscured the question of whether this was not actually a brilliant move by the tortured defendants. The door was thrown wide open to justified foreign protest, so that, buffeted by international outrage, the

Government-General was obliged to reopen the trial. The initial judgment of 28 September 1912 had declared 105 persons guilty of treason. Six, including Yun and Yi Sŭnghun, were sentenced to ten years in gaol, eighteen were sentenced for seven years, 39 were sentenced for six years and 42 were sentenced for five years.[29] The incongruity between the charge and the sentences suggested that even the judges viewed the case simply as an expedient for removing influential Christians from public life. Two eminent lawyers from Tokyo, Messers Ogawa and Ozawa, unequivocally denounced the trial as itself criminal proceedings and charged that there was 'evidence from the records in this case that the Administration was oppressing men on account of their beliefs. . .'[30]

During the two retrials which followed, Yun Ch'iho and An T'aeguk especially produced solid alibis and successfully refuted the testimony against them. All this the magistrate accepted. But in his fiinal verdict he concluded, in effect, that there was insufficient reason to abandon the overall charge that the six 'ringleaders' had plotted mischief against the Governor-General.[31] The sentences of Yun, An, Yi Sŭnghun, Yang Kit'ak and Im Ch'ijŏng were reduced to six years and that of Ok Kwanbin to five years, while the remaining 99 defendants were acquitted.

In October 1914 Bishop Harris learned that the Japanese Premier, Ōkuma Shigenobu, had advised Terauchi to adopt a friendlier attitude towards the Christian missions in Korea.[32] Accordingly, the six Christians were released under a special amnesty on 13 February 1915. However, Terauchi continued to insist on the conspiracy's reality, attributing it to 'misunderstandings concerning the purport of the annexation'.[33] The Japanese press in Seoul went out of its way to suggest that the prisoners were tremendously grateful for the amnesty and now fully understood the grandeur of Japan's history and its beneficence towards Korea.[34]

If the conspiracy case was irrational in its prosecution, the Government-General's objective, on its own terms, was not illogical. The Christian community, though not a strongly organised force politically, was still the most troublesome single focus of national identity. Its potential to seriously challenge the authorities should its growth continue unchecked was lost neither on the Japanese nor on the Koreans. Count Terauchi reportedly explained, in a speech he gave in Tokyo on 17 December 1913, that: 'The Christian Church is the most powerful force in Chosen. Therefore [we] must keep especial watch on the Christians there.'[35] Among Koreans, the common perception was summed up thus: 'To the Japanese, the most worrisome element is the Christians. To the Koreans, the most hopeful thing is the expansion of the Christian Church.'[36] The Christian community, it was thought, was inassimilable.

But why should Yun Ch'iho, a cautious man who had counselled against open political resistance to the annexation, have been singled out? Many Koreans did not find this at all puzzling. 'Needless to say, Mr Yun's withdrawal from officialdom was the primary reason he was seized in the Governor-General assassination conspiracy case,' Yi Kwangsu commented later.[37] In his own detailed report of the case in 1912, the missionary J. Jardine also opined that Yun's repeated refusal to join the government during the period of the protectorate was taken very badly by the Japanese, who had hoped thus to legitimise their presence.[38]

It was the reason for Yun's withdrawal that was considered subversive. Yun had written to Durham Stevens that it was a protest against the shameful act of signing the Protectorate Treaty.[39] The full import of his 'retirement' had been impressed on the Japanese by his involvement with An Ch'angho in the Sinminhoe, Ch'ŏngnyŏn Haku-hoe and other nationalist movements. At the retrial in Taegu in July 1913, the prosecution began with Yun's presidency of the Sinminhoe, a body organised, it was claimed, to instil patriotism and anti-Japanese thought in the people's minds in preparation for the overthrow of the 'empire'. The 'conspiracy' was directly linked to this background.[40]

That the Sinminhoe—like the Myŏnhakhoe which was linked to the Anak Incident—was founded and led by Protestants was food enough for thought, but Christian leadership of the major schools was no less irritating to the authorities. As Yun Ch'iho's Methodist Han-Yŏng College in Songdo and Yi Sŭnghun's Osan College in Chŏngju attracted large numbers of spirited students, the Japanese were alerted to the fact that in education, where they hoped to create 'loyal subjects', a quite contrary movement was being nurtured. It mattered little that Yun and the missionaries cautioned against political resistance when they presided over a whole religious and educational enterprise that, of its nature, inspired 'evil' tendencies. The Conspiracy Case was more than simply vengeance for Itō's assassination or spite against influential Koreans snubbing officialdom: it was a clear signal of Japan's determination to eliminate any independent element that might endanger its strategic stake in the peninsula.

The education controversy

Residency-General documénts suggest that the Japanese had the closure of all religious and possibly private schooling in view from at least 1909. As the first step, the Residency-General had instituted measures to remove any publication considered harmful to its interests. Among the first to be banned was Yun Ch'iho's *Usun Sori* (otherwise known as *Sohwa*), a collection of stories with patriotic overtones and civic morals.[41] According to one Korean report, the police burned 3700 volumes in May and June 1909.[42] In August 1909, guidelines for textbook censorship were devised and finally, on annexation, all Korean newspapers, magazines and journals were banned and replaced by official, pro-Japanese publications.

The corollary of this onslaught was an active campaign to suppress the Korean language, discredit Korea's cultural heritage and assert Japan's historical and moral rights over Korea. Japanese teachers taught their Korean pupils that their rightful emperor resided in Tokyo and that there was no such entity as 'Korea'. The campaign was crude: Japanese histories of Korea were little more than 'a collection of nursery tales'.[43] In retaliation, some Koreans, especially those abroad, began producing their own platonic 'noble lies', extolling the glories of Korea's past and charging Japan with having interrupted the natural unfolding of the country as one of the lights of the modern world.

Korean Protestants who subscribed to the ethical theory of the Chosŏn dynasty's collapse favoured a different kind of response. An Ch'angho had not bothered to dispute with Itō over the diagnosis of Korea's ills, but he insisted on Koreans being left to administer their own cure. After all, was it not the Christians' aim to reconstruct national life? The Government-General readily agreed it was, but there lay the nub of the problem. The Protestant version of reconstruction pointed away from assimilation to the Japanese empire towards a self-reliant, independent nation-state. The Christian educational enterprise had to go.

As the effects of the Conspiracy Case began to wane, the Government-General passed new educational laws in March 1915 which explicitly prohibited religious instruction in schools and aimed at phasing out any language but Japanese in the classroom.[44] Count Terauchi stated that, throughout the empire, the principle was 'to keep education independent of religion'. He expressed concern lest the private schools, which admittedly were very influential, should 'go contrary to the general principle of the State' with consequences 'most grievous from the point of view of national welfare'.[45] For the transition to teaching in Japanese and the full adjustment of courses, Count Terauchi announced a 'period of grace' of five and ten years respectively for schools already established. Undoubtedly this was a period of grace also for the Japanese, since, as Terauchi had observed in 1914, closing down mission schools immediately would 'leave a great gap in the educational work of Chosen'.[46]

The missionaries were quick to dispute the claim that Japan was following accepted Western custom in separating religion completely from education. It was pointed out to Mr M. Komatsu, Director of the Foreign Affairs Bureau in Korea, that the Japanese version amounted to state interference in religion; that it removed all justification for soliciting and receiving funds in support of private schools; and that, therefore, the private schools would be unable to continue.[47] This of course was what the authorities had in mind, but not instantly, and in any case the Rev. J. Adams of Taegu, chairman of the Senate of the Educational Federation of Christian Missions in Korea, reminded them of earlier assurances that there would be 'no interference with the full freedom of religious instruction in the Christian schools'.[48] Not all missionaries were so anxious, and Dr Speer in Tokyo predictably advised Korea's missions to think nothing of it.[49] But when Mr Komatsu finally responded in November 1915, it was clarified that the source of the new laws had been irritation at the obstacles Christian schools placed before assimilation.[50]

The Presbyterians and the Methodists differed in their responses. For the most part, the former, who valued education more for the opening it gave to religious instruction, resolved not to register under the new regulations, whereas Bishop Harris influenced the latter to comply. In February 1916, Shin Hŭngu's Northern Methodist Pae Chae College in Seoul became the first mission school to register under the new laws, as Pae Chae Higher Normal School. When the Southern Methodist Han–Yŏng College at Songdo followed suit, the Japanese press eagerly rushed to the conclusion that Yun Ch'iho, who had resumed headship of the college after his release, was therefore 'decidedly in favour of the proposal'.[51] In fact, Yun does not appear to have greatly feared that educating Koreans under Japanese laws would be unendurable. (By this stage his Christian activities were focused around his leadership of the Seoul Central YMCA.)[52] But the registration of his college had occurred under duress, and appeared to vindicate the pessimists.

In mid-November 1916, three Han–Yŏng College teachers were among a group arrested on charges of having unlawfully printed and distributed two volumes of seditious songs. Among the songs was one paying tribute to Itō's assassin, An Chunggŭn, another calling for 'heroes of an independent nation' and Yun Ch'iho's *Aegukka* (National Anthem). Both volumes were prefaced with an explanation of the power of songs to inspire true spirit in citizens, on which the rise of the nation depended.[53] The secret publication of the volumes confirmed the police's suspicions that the college was still 'brimful with seditious thought',[54] although Yun himself saw nothing seditious in the materials.[55] Nevertheless, a thorough search of the school exposed further publications 'injurious to public peace'. Finally, after it was revealed that the song books had also been distributed among pupils of the nearby Southern Methodist Holston Girls' School, police indicted 22 staff and pupils of the two institutions.[56]

The Governor of Kyŏnggi province summoned the head of the Southern Methodist Mission in Songdo, Mr Wasson, demanding that he explain why he had not registered the school, and warning that if Mr Wasson was indisposed to conform after assurance that the teachers would be licensed it would be interpreted as reluctance to work in harmony with the Government-General.[57] After his compliance, however, Mr Wasson was informed that he had only one year's grace to build separate premises for purely religious instruction, while the school's curriculum had to change 'instantly'.[58] Similar cases followed, and many schools' applications for the license of teachers were refused, so that in the end even the formerly sanguine Dr H. H. Underwood wrote:

> An administration which looked with grave suspicion on all private education and frankly looked forward to its rapid elimination was not inclined to make it easier for these schools to readjust themselves to the new conditions. . . . Many elementary schools were forced to close and all schools felt that their existence was precarious.[59]

But for the 'conciliatory' policy introduced by Baron Saitō Makoto after the March 1919 uprising, Protestant schools may well have closed before the ten years' grace expired.

To the missionaries, the confrontation was essentially over the issues of religious freedom and the role of the state in national life. The separation of the church and the state did not mean to them the removal of the church from education. Theologically, it was the old question of whether an imperial system was not actually demanding that its subjects render to itself what belonged to God. From 1 April 1915, the Government-General instructed Christian schools to observe strictly and with prescribed ceremonies the days on which the Japanese Emperor offered imperial sacrifices. A compulsory textbook on ethics and morals, with injunctions on ancestor worship, was issued to Christian schools. When Christian pupils and teachers were ordered to bow to the portrait of the emperor they objected that it was idolatrous, 'since, to a good Japanese, he is a divine being'. The missionaries naturally accused the authorities of 'a remarkable inconsistency'.[60]

On their own terms, the Japanese were not so inconsistent, for they accepted a different definition of the issue. Like the former Korean neo-Confucian monarchy, the authorities wished to link filial piety, albeit of a Shintō variety, with loyalty to the state. The Japanese in Korea regarded religion as subordinate to politics; the missionaries insisted the two were distinct and that ethics were a function of religion. Though Korean Protestants generally went along with the latter, to them the confrontation obviously had another dimension: national survival.

4 The reconstructive community, 1910–1919

As shown in the preceding chapter, the loss of statehood in 1910 and subsequent Japanese policy forced the Protestant community to reflect upon its survival. The exodus of Christians that had begun before 1910 increased, and such large numbers emigrated north to Manchuria and Siberia that, even as far south as Pusan, missionaries reported cases of almost entire congregations emigrating. Dispossession of land provided a major inducement to leave, but in some cases emigration was blamed directly on the wave of persecution against Christians.[1]

Though their ranks were depleted, the Protestants were still the most 'progressive' force in Korea in terms of education, political philosophy and self-reliance. Unable to express their ideals explicitly, Protestant nationalists articulated their values and vision of a free Korea through the language and symbols of their faith. The Korean church thus communicated an image of the future which inspired and maintained hope during the dark decade of 1910–19. The Presbyterian and Methodist denominations not only survived, but even increased their core membership from 62 000 baptised members in 1911 to 87 000 in 1919.[2] But persecution drew differing responses among them, and from 1910 the original vision of a reconstructed civilisation had to be defended against mounting pressure to define nationalism negatively as 'anti-Japanism.'

The question of means

The Protestant community in Korea was by no means monochrome in its attitudes. Quite apart from the views held by those in the exile centres in China, Manchuria, Siberia, Hawaii and on the American continent, there were many shades of emphasis between the positions adopted inside Korea, for instance, by Kim Ku on the one hand and Yun Ch'iho on the other. The pre-annexation groupings— Sinminhoe, the YMCA and so on—still maintained some cohesion and tended to identify with an organisation in exile. Variation also arose out of the identification of movements and emphases with the different 'nationalistic' schools: Yangsan School in Anak (Kim Ku), Taesŏng College in P'yŏngyang (An Ch'angho), Osan College in Chŏngju (Yi Sŭnghun and Cho Mansik), Han-Yŏng College in Song-do (Yun Ch'iho), Pae Chae College in Seoul (Shin Hŭngu and Nam-gung Ŏk) and the mission schools in P'yŏngyang, Sŏnch'ŏn, Seoul, Taegu, Pusan and Masan. Parochial loyalties to the regional *kiho p'a* and *sŏbuk p'a* also remained.[3]

Initially, the Protestant nationalists were more united by what they held in common than divided by their differing emphases. The generation of civic ethics and the reconstruction of a strong nation were major aims common to all. Up to 1910, Kim Ku had striven to instil 'national spirit', complaining that most adults 'did not even know what a nation was'.[4] But after 1910, when action inside Korea became further restricted, his attention was drawn to overseas military science training. Shortly after annexation, Kim Ku, Yi Sŭnghun, An T'aeguk, Chu Chinsu and Yang Kit'ak were 'elected' representatives of Hwanghae, North P'yŏngan, South P'yŏngan, Kangwŏn and Kyŏnggi provinces respectively, and charged with the initial task of arranging emigration of youth to Manchuria to train as nationalist troops.[5] All these 'representatives' were arrested in the Anak and Conspiracy Case incidents, although Kim Ku and Yi Tonghwi subsequently escaped across the Yalu river.

The arrests did not extinguish interest in military preparations, however. In 1915 the Japanese police discovered links between several Christian schools, particularly in P'yŏngyang and Anak, and Korean military camps in Manchuria and America.[6] Early in 1917, a branch of the Korean National Association (Taehan Kungminhoe), formed by An Ch'angho, Syngman Rhee and other overseas dissidents, had been established inside Korea. Members were recruited from among students from all provinces who attended the P'yŏngyang Presbyterian Seminary and Sungsil College. The Korean branch formed two bodies in June 1917, called the Korea Independence Corps and the *Kyŏlsadan* (often translated 'suicide squad', though it was a fairly typical underground resistance organisation), and emphasising military strength as a means for realising a 'Korea for Koreans'. More than half of the 25 members arrested in February 1918 were connected with the P'yŏngyang Seminary, Sungsil College and the Presbyterian Yŏnhŭi Special School in Seoul.[7]

However, the number of Protestants inside Korea directly or indirectly involved in military preparations accounts for only a small percentage of the many hundreds who passed through Christian schools as pupils or staff during this period. Nor do the Japanese documents mention any participation among church congregations. Indeed, Kim Ku's thought reflects no specific Christian inspiration and his position was 'Christian' mainly by association. His writings betray an interest in Christianity that derived solely from political expectations: God was nothing if he was not a champion of Korean nationalism.[8] Some divergence between his and An Ch'angho's approaches was inevitable, since An deliberately related his reconstruction program to Christian doctrines, and in later years they were hardly in the same stream. If Yun Ch'iho's views are placed against Kim's, the divergence becomes a chasm. Among the Protestant churches and many of their nationalist leaders inside Korea—Cho Mansik, Yi Sangjae, Shin Hŭngu and Namgung Ŏk—the approach of Yun, and to some extent of An, was still regarded as the authentic one.

The reconstructive community in Korea

In contrast to the centralising activities of the Residency-General and later the Government-General, the missions had encouraged, through the Nevius Method and their implicit political views, administrative autonomy and local self-support among the churches. The emphasis on personal liberty, respect for impartiality in legal cases, resistance to unlawful seizure of property and illegal taxation, especially in the northwestern provinces, had contributed to what Yi Man'yŏl terms 'autonomy-consciousness'.[9] The 1907–08 Great Revival, far from being over in 1910, was only beginning to bear its more long-term fruits, and the evangelistic 'Million Movement' of 1910 was pursued in the expectation that a time of severe trial for the nation was imminent. Under the circumstances, evangelism really amounted to recruiting members for an organisation implicitly at variance with the Japanese colonial policy of assimilation. It is in this light that Yi Man'yŏl suggests that the extent to which the missionaries 'directly and indirectly inspired in the Koreans the spirit of independence . . . is incalculable'.[10]

By intensifying the sense of national loss, the annexation influenced many Koreans to regard the Christian church in a special way. According to George L. G. Paik, at that time a member of the rising generation of Christian youth, loss of statehood encouraged Christians to depend on the church and look to it as a substitute for the state.[11] This involved an important transfer of loyalties. Among the higher classes, the highest political and social value in Korean life had been filial piety, the apogée of which was loyalty to the monarch. This orientation had already been relativised by the late nineteenth century reformers, and with the loss of both emperor and statehood the people were compelled to seek a new focus among themselves. A transfer of loyalties to the people took place whereby the idea of a nation-state replaced the old monarchical order and serving the state meant serving 'the people'. The monarch had not been a nationalistic symbol (although he became a very effective one in 1919), but Koreans of all classes were well aware of his, and their own, place in the political order. An Ch'angho, in 1920, summed it up thus: 'Is there no emperor in our country today? There is. In the past the emperor was just one person, but today all twenty million citizens are the emperor. . . . What is "emperor"? It is the name of the supreme ruler. Hitherto the sovereign was a single person, but now you are all sovereigns. . .'[12] Most of the reformers who converted to Protestantism regarded Christianity as 'for the people', and the Christians who had fled abroad were expected in due course to return and take up leadership of a new Korea.[13]

If, because of the discontinuity of Korean political life, the Protestant church had become a repository of national ideals and aspirations, it does not necessarily follow that these were themselves 'Christian' in nature. But Korean intellectuals were convinced that there was an integral connection between their beliefs and democratic values. Referring to the self-government of the Korean churches, Henry Chung (Chŏng Han'gyŏng) declared without qualification that 'Christianity from time immemorial has sown the seed of democracy.'[14] Hugh Cynn (Shin Hŭngu) believed that Christianity implicitly inspired democratic sentiment in Korea. He noted a distinct relationship between the rise in the number of Christians and growing interest in democracy, citing the influence of hospitals and churches in breaking down class and sex segregation and in promoting the egalitarian ideas disseminated through schools. He observed further that the schools served as important links between the Christian and non-Christian communities as the organs through which Protestantism introduced a universalistic ethic and thereby turned the eyes of the Hermit People toward new social and political values.[15]

What were these 'new' values? Some have been raised already: civic ethics, stewardship and service of one's fellow-citizen in lieu of absolute obedience to the monarch (or equivalent). But since it was no longer possible to voice 'dangerous thoughts' openly after 1910, the values had to become implicit in the teaching and theological principles of the Protestant schools and churches. Here, two broad areas emerge: the structure of the church as a community and the emphasis on individual conscience.

The pattern of social relationships within the church communities served as the 'plausibility structures' of their values and beliefs.[16] Unfortunately, records of sermon content during this period are scant, but by piecing together information from scattered sources we learn that it was taught that all believers, regardless of social background, education or possessions, held the same system of values, among which was the principle that all members were equally responsible for decisions affecting their lives.[17] This principle had particular poignancy in a Confucian society. Yim Louise (Im Yŏngsin), a pioneer in women's rights and education, and later founder of Chungang University in Seoul, recalled that experience of this principle marked a turning point in her life. As a high school pupil in 1915, Yim was introduced to the Rev. Kim Inju of Chŏnju: 'He spoke to me as an equal. It was the first time I had been addressed like this by any Korean man.' Inspired, Yim started prayer meetings among Korean women and founded 'cell groups' in which women began deliberating on their role in national social affairs.[18]

The inviolability of the individual conscience is expressed in the distinctive Protestant doctrine of the 'Priesthood of all believers' and is implicit in the main Presbyterian textbook for members at the time, the *Westminster Confession of Faith*. This doctrine was basic to the voluntary composition of the community and permitted freedom even in major decisions such as choice of marriage partner, vocation and possibly (this is far from clear) even subordinate articles of faith. It encouraged acceptance of limited social pluralism and was regarded as the basis of democratic sentiment. Equally importantly, the doctrine implied responsibility on the part of the individual for the total life of the community: 'priesthood' meant individual believers being priests to each other, which in turn required each to seek an understanding of the nature and application of God's word and will in terms of the actual situation pertaining in Korea.

Two further fundamental tenets were believed to be essential to genuine socio-political reform by the Protestant community: monotheism and the image of God in humanity.[19] God was not only supreme, he was moral; God not only created humans, he formed them in his own likeness. These doctrines were the basis of the Korean Protestants' concern for human rights and their belief in inherent human dignity—the basis, they were certain, of democracy. The Christianity, democracy and strength of the West were not accidentally but organically joined in history, and therefore the Christian community was regarded as the cradle of the democratic Korea of the future.

Doubtless the distinction between the supernatural and the mundane in monotheism, which distinguishes God from the world of creation, was as radical a departure from tradition in Korea as it had been for Uchimura Kanzō in Japan. Doubtless, too, the conception of the one God's omnipotence being inextricable from his 'holiness' was all the more conducive to reflection on the nature of society when humanity was thought to possess at least the remnants of God's image.[20] Yet it would be forcing a conclusion to claim that the Korean church was on to the absolute transcendence of the Puritans', let alone Kierkegaard's, concept of God. The Korean church historian and philosopher Han T'aedong identifies the failure of Korean Christianity to appreciate fully the distinction between God and created humanity as its basic flaw.[21] The same view may have been behind Yun Ch'iho's complaint in 1945 that Koreans were still not ready for democracy,[22] though both cases reflect the lingering differences between the intellectuals and the less literate believers. For, though few Korean Protestants may have attained what Max Weber described as the 'inner isolation of the individual', the church community knew what it meant to respect individual conscience and personhood and drew its egalitarian ideals therefrom.

The Christian schools, which were mostly boarding schools, were at least as important as the churches in providing the plausibility structures of Protestant ideals, and more important as vehicles of self-reconstruction thought. Though Taesŏng College was closed down during the Conspiracy Case, Yi Sŭnghun's Osan College in Chŏngju remained open and resisted pressure to register under the new education laws after 1915. While Yi was in gaol, the school was run by Yi Kwangsu and Cho Mansik, who had returned from his study of law at Meiji University in 1913. National figures who taught or studied at Osan College during this period include Sŏ Ch'un, Kim Tot'ae, Kim Chihwan, Chu Kich'ŏl, Han Kyŏngjik, Ham Sŏkhŏn (later leader of the Korean Quaker movement) and, of course, Cho, Yi Kwangsu and Yi Sŭnghun. Han Kyŏngjik, who later organised a social–democratic party in northwest Korea before fleeing south to found the famous Young Nak Presbyterian Church in Seoul, claims that Cho Mansik had a decisive influence on pupils, who left the college imbued with the values of self-reliance and mental, moral and physical training.[23] Like the Songdo compound before Yun Ch'iho's arrest, Osan College was promoted as a pilot scheme for national reconstruction and was founded on the principles of the former Ch'ŏngnyŏn Hakuhoe.

One of the few sources of information on the Protestant community from 1910 to 1919 in the Korean language is the *Sinhan Minbo*, which was published in San Francisco. Because Koreans in America were inclined to regard their compatriots inside Korea with some condescension, removed as they were from the harshly limiting political environment there, even these reports are often less than illuminating. Nevertheless, it was universally accepted that the progress of the church was vital to the future of the nation, and letters and reports from Korea were occasionally printed in detail; these were, of course, the views of Koreans inside Korea.

Early letters smuggled out of Korea painted a desperate picture of the inexorable advance of the Japanese shadow over all aspects of life. One in particular described intense persecution of Christians during the Conspiracy Case and pleaded with Koreans abroad to stay there and to seek some way of restoring independence, since all paths inside Korea were blocked.[24] But towards the end of 1913 the tone of the letters became more positive: patriotic sentiment was growing daily and the church was portrayed as the 'foundation on which our race will obtain unbounded blessings and joy'. 'The religious spirit of the people is steadily progressing,' reads another report. 'Their courage is being strengthened, their civic spirit is developing.' In the end, it was said, the gruelling Conspiracy Case only added prestige to the church and harmed the reputation of Japan.[25]

In March and April 1914 there occurred a 'revival' among Christians in P'yongyang which prompted renewed efforts to spread Christianity in Korea. Its effects began to surface in 1915. A report published in September 1915 suggests that the church had regained its confidence after Japanese failure to destroy its influence:

> Compared to several years ago, our people have progressed remarkably. . . If the Church of Christ becomes fully established there will be no need ever again to call into question the Koreans' level [of enlightenment]. . . In terms of the world of spirit, our people are definitely alive, not at all dead. They possess an independent, no longer a slavish, character.[26]

The P'yŏngyang revival stimulated considerable interest in the Christian Bible throughout Korea. The Korean Bible Society reported that in 1917 it 'had an average of more than 150 Korean colporteurs at work throughout the year, and they sold 660 000 books—most of them Gospels'. The colporteurs were more than travelling salesmen. In an unobtrusive, but evidently effective, way they formed a team of evangelists who penetrated regions otherwise beyond the reach of churches. The Rev. F. G. Vesey of the Bible Society recorded that the colporteur's travels took him '. . . along the high road to big towns and country seats, or over the mountain passes and rough hill-paths to villages and hamlets scattered here and there. He visits the markets, meets the crowds gathered to barter and sell . . . and he goes from house to house in sparsely populated places, speaking heart to heart with the lonely farmer. . .'[27]

To Protestant nationalists, the bible was full of political implications, and the colporteurs became involved in activities of which the Rev. Vesey was unaware. 'To me the Bible and the whole Christian religion pointed the road to freedom from the Japanese and to a better life with peace for all mankind,' wrote Yim Louise. 'God never meant slavery to be the destiny of man.'[28] In Ch'ŏnan, South Ch'ung-ch'ŏng province, Yim came across a colporteur early in 1918 who carried leaflets from Christians in Seoul concerning the creation of an underground network. She informed him of her own and nine other cell groups in southern areas and so became linked up with the secret network. It was this network, serviced by colporteurs, which enabled the Protestant churches to distribute copies of the Declaration of Independence and prepare for the March First Movement with such speed and total secrecy that the Japanese initially refused to believe that the operation was carried out without missionary involvement.

The rising tide of confidence emboldened some ministers to focus in their sermons on the actions of Moses and Nehemiah in leading and rebuilding the Jewish nation. But the authorities had not relaxed in their efforts to contain the faith. The exhausting education controversy was underway, and from 1916 the increased boldness of the churches provoked even stricter scrutiny and obstruction of their activities. The Protestants had to adopt great caution lest they fell for 'Japanese provocations' and filled the 'waiting prisons'. Yet it was perceived that the authorities recognised the strength of purpose of the church, and the people were cautiously jubilant that the Government-General had not entirely had its way.[29]

The reconstructive community abroad

The tendency to regard the church as a substitute for the lost state was even stronger among the émigré Protestant communities than in Korea. The political objectives were, understandably, also more explicit. In North America and Hawaii, the Korean National Association was founded, largely directed by Christian nationalists, while An Ch'angho founded the Hŭngsadan (not to be confused with Yu Kiljun's earlier organisation of the same name) in 1913 with the object of developing a community embodying self-reconstruction ideals. In Japan the Korean churches were led by persons of proven 'patriotic' credentials such as Cho Mansik (until 1913), Kim Chŏngsik and the Rev. Chu Kongsam. Yŏ Unhyŏng and Yi Tonghwi requested churches in Korea to send out pastors to form church communities as a means of preserving the Koreans' pride as a nation. Significantly, it was Christian ministers rather than leaders of nationalist societies who were requested: the church was the nationalist society.

Among exile communities, where the choices were not so limited, differences over means were pronounced and in part geographically determined. On Korea's northern borders, where life was difficult and the number of exiles large (about one million by 1917), proximity to the homeland encouraged preparations for direct military action. In the United States, where Koreans were comparatively few, well-fed and distant from Korea, the gradualist approach of advancing knowledge and expertise in commerce, industry, modern political systems and theology was more popular. By the same token, the territories which nationalists chose for exile usually reflected their nationalist allegiances.

Self-reconstruction nationalism was therefore strongest in the United States, where the majority of Korean nationalists were Protestants. Chŏng Yŏsang, an officer of the San Francisco Korean National Association, informed friends on his return to Korea in November 1915 that the movement in America was centred on the churches and attributed the greater political success of the Association in America than elsewhere to the predominance of 'followers of Yun Ch'iho'.[30] Yi Kwanyŏng, the leader of a large organisation linked with Koreans in Peking, Nanking, Shanghai and San Francisco, told interrogators in August 1918 that, whilst a pupil of Taesŏng College from 1906 to 1910, he had 'frequently attended lectures by Yun Ch'iho, principal, and An Ch'angho, teacher, on the protection and preservation of the Fatherland and the establishment of national rights'. After annexation, Yi studied at Sungsil College before travelling to San Francisco to discuss independence strategy with An Ch'angho. In December 1914 he journeyed to China to make contact with Shin Ch'aeho and Yi Tonghwi and to propose a scheme to achieve ideological unity on the basis of An's long-term approach of cultivating 'real strength', 'sound character' and 'unity'.[31] Unity was not attained, and the recreation of national character remained mainly the concern of Koreans in the United States and of groups elsewhere who were loyal to An and Yun.

The Korean community in the United States saw in freedom the opportunity to realise in miniature the ideal pattern of society for the future Korean nation. An Ch'angho, impatient of the habit of looking down on compatriots inside Korea, berated those who failed to appreciate that the police, gendarmes and troops were spread everywhere on the peninsula 'like a great spider's web'. The proper response for American exiles was not to despise their suffering fellows, but to act on the knowledge that the fate of the National Association was the fate of Korea. With its decisive advantages over émigré communities elsewhere, An went so far as to claim that the American Association was Korea's 'motive power'.[32]

This 'motive power', however, depended on 'stepping intrepidly through the gate of righteousness; and the way through this gate of righteousness is belief in Jesus Christ, shouldering the Cross, and treading the path of moral rectitude'.[33] This meant discarding the wrongs and weaknesses that had left Korea defenceless before foreign predation and, as the first stage, reconstructing a new moral framework. The *Sinhan Minbo* supported this view in its editorials and articles. Thoughts bear fruit, 'so one obtains "paradise" when noble thoughts are cherished and suffers ruin when vulgar thoughts are harboured. This is a truth revealed by the Holy Spirit and is the true teaching of the sages'.[34] Since Koreans had a habit of 'bowing the knee to China in the morning and the head to Russia in the evening', the annexation was hardly exceptional. The blame could not be laid at the feet of the monarch or government or 'country-sellers' alone: the tragedy lay on the conscience of 'all twenty million Koreans'. Devoid of courage and perseverance, it was primarily the 'callous unconcern of the people that opened [the door] to Terauchi Masatake's militaristic policy'.[35]

The new moral framework was self-reliance founded on civic responsibility. From September 1916 the *Sinhan Minbo* printed its aims on the top of its front page. One of them read: 'To strive unceasingly to quicken the public's sense of civic duty.' So important was this principle that an editorial on the subject on 5 April 1917 concluded that the 'resurrection of the twenty million Koreans lies solely in this civic morality'. The belief that nationhood was first and foremost a matter of morality was spelt out in April and May 1916 by Kil Ch'ŏnu as the 'Theory of National Reform':

> The basic purpose, as is well known, of those enterprising people presently engaged in projects committed to the fields of religion, education, politics and industry, is simply to inform the people's minds, improve their physiques and thereby create useful persons. Hence the most pressing and important problem in our present social policy is reform of the people. . . . It is impossible to establish a pure national structure and a virtuous society without reforming the citizens in whom resides that nation's and that society's energy. . .
>
> Bearing an important relation with social planning, 'reform of the people'—that is, reforming the faults of the citizens, the components of society—involves studying ways to reform humanity in all its aspects: biology, anthropology, sociology, psychology, hygiene and education.[36]

The influence of utilitarian ethical philosophy via American evangelicalism on this theory is evident in its premise of social planning. J. S. Mill argued the *consensus* of all social phenomena: 'There is no social phenomenon which is not more or less influenced by every other part of the condition of the same society, and therefore by every cause which is influencing any other of the. . . social phenomena.' Once the laws or causes of social phenomena are understood, it becomes possible to 'surround any given society with the greatest possible number of circumstances of which the tendencies are beneficial, and to remove or counteract. . . those of which the tendencies are injurious'.[37] The Koreans adapted this type of

thinking to their own religious viewpoint. Human nature was conceived of as a composite of evil characteristics inherited from Adam
and Eve—sickness of body and mind, criminal instincts, etc.—and
good properties remaining from the original created state. Reform of
the people therefore required attention to both aspects, 'to destroy
this hereditary evil and so pursue reforms that [people] will follow
their good [inclinations]'.[38]

An Ch'angho identified lack of national unity as the most serious
consequence of the enfeeblement of the people's spirit under the
Chosŏn dynasty, alongside fatal neglect through self-indulgence of
the practical foundations of viable statehood. Since the consequent
loss of nationhood, various bodies had sprung up, but had disappeared
by themselves or through persecution. The only body remaining as
a united national group was the Korean National Association, but
even this was threatened by the old evils of parochialism and
individualism.[39]

Quick solutions were a threat to unity, and An insisted on a
'national evolutionary process', on 'taking justice and humanity as
our standard and rising one rung at a time'.[40] Like the English historian, Sir Herbert Butterfield, An seems to have believed that democracy derives not from events like the French Revolution, but from a
'slow growth of reasonableness' among citizens. 'Gradualism' was not
just a tactic or temporary phase; it was to be understood as a realistic
perception of the dynamics of life itself, attunement to which was
essential to generating lasting strength and quality. So, although An
called for unity, he warned against a type of 'union-ism' which
ignored its true roots—the sound formation of individual members—
and reminded National Association members that, without such
training, unity, if attained, would resemble that of the herd rather
than that of well-endowed, responsible citizens.[41]

In a stirring speech delivered to the Los Angeles Branch of the
National Association in June 1916, An Ch'angho gave vivid expression to the Korean Protestant community's self-consciousness as the
new and future Korea. Pointing out that Koreans like himself who
had left Korea before the annexation still retained passports as Koreans, An commented:

> On the face of it, this is because there was no opportunity . . . to obtain
> travel documents from the Japanese Government, but viewed from
> another angle, it signifies that [the Americans] . . . look upon us as the
> image of Korea. This then is our task: To bear upon our backs the shape-
> less form of Korea and to increase the overall strength and influence of the
> National Association so it can act as spokesperson and advocate for this as
> yet unformed nation, till it realises the object of restoring its physical
> reality.[42]

Another émigré community which developed self-reconstruction ideology and which was better placed to influence movements in Korea was the Christian student community in Japan. Although not exiles as such, these students formed an important part of the Korean diaspora. Cho Mansik had left Korea in June 1908 for study in Tokyo where he was joined by other Christians, including Chŏn Yŏngt'aek, Paek Namun, No Chŏngil and Kim Sŏngsu. By 1915 there were approximately 480 Korean students in Tokyo, most of them private students, and in 1916 the Korean Hakuhoe, or Student Association, encompassed seven branches: five in Tokyo and one each in Kyōtō and Ōsaka.⁴³ Cho Mansik returned to Korea in 1913, but by then several more influential Korean Protestants had joined the Tokyo group. Under Yi Kwangsu, Choe Namsŏn, Song Chin'u, Song Kyebaek, Paek Kwansu, Chang Tŏksu and others, the Hakuhoe espoused liberal democracy and became the main organ of Korean nationalism in Japan.

The nation responsible for their colonial status became, when their host, almost a haven for Korean students. From 1915 there arose amongst Japanese students, professors, journalists and some politicians what has been termed the 'mass awakening', a movement for Japan's reconstruction along liberal democratic lines. Pre-eminent among the leaders of this awakening was Professor Yoshino Sakuzō of Tokyo University, who was well-known as a Christian and a contributor to the *Chūō Kōron*. Korean students were greatly inspired by Yoshino's speeches and writings on democracy. They found another ally in the student law society in Tokyo, the Shinjinkai, which was in the main sympathetic to their aspirations.⁴⁴

While Koreans drew theoretical support from the independent Japanese scholars who formed the Reimeikai, it was the Japanese students' impassioned energy that was reflected in the fervent speeches and debates of the Hakuhoe. Even so, the Koreans' speeches were much more strongly marked by the influence of Christianity. Alongside appeals to democracy, Korea's independence was closely linked to the fortunes of Christianity in Korea. Chŏn Yŏngt'aek argued that the religious history of Korea could be stated in terms of Buddhism and Confucianism and their decline. When Christianity, a global religion, was introduced, it took hold rapidly and gave new hope to the people. But the present (1917) outlook was dismal because of the major setback the church had received through the Conspiracy Case and other acts of oppression.⁴⁵ The Rev. Kim Nokjun also lamented the weakened state of the Korean church, but added that 'it actually possesses considerable latent power, and as for adherents, their number amounts to as many as 200 000 people. At any rate, the progress of Christianity in Korea is the most noteworthy development'.[46] Sŏ Ch'un, later a teacher at Osan College, actively supported the view that Korea's future lay in the propagation of the faith among the general populace.[47] The Korean YMCA in Tokyo held receptions for students as they arrived in Japan, at which the newcomers were urged to emulate the Christian church's 'clear aims' and 'dedication to ultimate objectives'. The 'common aim' pressed on the students was 'to build a new Korea'.[48]

Between 1915 and October 1918, the Christian students generally dwelt on the need to cultivate self-reliance, real strength and civic responsibility. Yi Kwangsu, in particular, promoted in his writings a gradualist self-reconstruction program that differed from An Ch'angho's version only in the emphasis he placed on cultural activities. But as Woodrow Wilson's doctrine of national self-determination reached them in late 1918, their speeches became suddenly militant and called for immediate independence. To be sure, Sŏ Ch'un warned that reliance on the allies alone was mistaken and urged Koreans to seek independence through their own strength.[49] But in January 1919 he joined nine other Protestant students to form the committee which organised the February Eighth Tokyo Students' Declaration of Independence, the forerunner of the March First Movement in Korea.

Religious visions and imagined communities

If the promotion of civic morality and a program of thorough human reconstruction premised on the belief that life was fundamentally moral and spiritual was a Christian contribution, the annexation of August 1910 added an ineluctable item to the nationalist agenda which Christianity clearly did not supply. For the recovery of national rights and statehood could not be separated from the expulsion (or exit) of Japan. The Protestants' adoption of gradual reconstruction in Korea, and especially in America, was an attempt to cope with the tension between 'Christian' and 'nationalist' objectives. Inculcating the spirit of Christianity in the people was a Christian, 'cosmic' objective, and the expectation that this would right wrongs, bring peace and create a free community was the 'Good News' of Christianity. In this way the Protestants could offer a course which, while transcending the expulsion of Japan as an immediate objective, could include it nevertheless as a consequence inherently bound up with the Korean people's active adherence to their faith.

The presentation of this solution was, however, open to other interpretations, and it required only a small over-emphasis on the consequences to turn the tension into a virtual contradiction. In a discussion of the benefits of Christianity in Korea in 1917, for example, Yi

Kwangsu dealt solely with elements of a supposedly 'new civilisation' that looked very much like Western civilisation. No doubt Yi was limiting himself to identifying certain desirable developments which he believed flourished within a Christian atmosphere, but the impression is given that Korea's strength was the chief value.[50] Yi also composed the Tokyo Students' Declaration of Independence, Appeal and Resolution of 8 February 1918. The Resolution concluded with the threat of an 'eternal, bloody war' between Korea and Japan. Since Yi's position in the 1920s differed dramatically from the above line, and his later writings reveal serious thought on the appropriate *modus operandi* of a Christian movement for change, it is probable that his expression in the Resolution was only tactical.[51] But he was disappointed with Yun Ch'iho after the latter's release in 1915 because he had expected Yun to be more politically and openly opposed to Japan.[52].

Yun Ch'iho had pondered Korea's and his own position deeply whilst in prison, where through illness he had come very close to death, and he emerged from his incarceration strongly convinced that political agitation scratched only the surface of a deep problem that only religious renewal and practical education could hope to surmount. On his release from Taegu Prison, Yun delivered a speech at the Seoul Central YMCA which was attended by an overflow crowd. In the course of his speech, which treated subjects such as the importance of methodical reading habits, Yun declared: 'Rash, imprudent behaviour can yield no gain. It is strength alone that will save Korea, and strength derives from the youth cultivating themselves morally and mentally; and again after that, from perseverance in education and industry.'[53]

Yun's speech was received with disappointment by many activists, but not, significantly, by An Ch'angho.[54] There was some awareness of the need to respect the tension between faith and nationalistic impulses among the Koreans in America. Kim Hyŏn'gu, a student at Cornell University, affirmed that the expansion of Christianity in Korea was 'our only hope and joy'. But where Yi Kwangsu was concerned lest the faith should lose its political impact through diversion into 'superstitious' activities, Kim was anxious lest it be distracted from its intrinsic spiritual purposes by short-term political schemes or by confusing it with Western learning. Kim also spoke critically of anti-intellectualism and failure to apply Christian beliefs in the present, but he perceived that the greatest danger to Christian progress lay in using it for mundane success: 'If one borrows the name of "believer" in order to do some work outside religion, not only is such a contrivance fraudulent but its object cannot thus be attained. The only result will be harm to oneself, society or race.' Like Uchimura Kanzō in Japan, Kim urged belief in Christianity for its own sake and warned against using it to cover material motives with an appearance of spirituality.[55] But neither in Yun nor Kim did this amount to rejection of ethical utilitarianism (although in Uchimura's case I believe it did): it was a statement that if a conflict of interests arose between Christianity and nationalism, it had to be decided in favour of the former.

Some Koreans were eager to reduce the tension altogether—to deny that there was a tension. Uchimura's call to sacrifice love of country to love of Heaven if need be had no point to those nationalists in America, who took it for granted that 'one who loves his country is one whom God loves'.[56] The Koreans' 'duty, glory and reasonable service', as one obvious biblical paraphrase stated, was 'to keep intact this land until we return to God. . . If we wish to love our country and tend the land of promise God has granted to us, then we must first be baptised in the blood of fervent patriotism and drink of the waters of patriotic zeal.'[57]

This may have been a rather extreme position, but its Psalm-like rhyming of meanings points to what became the most popular justification of Christian nationalism: the symbolic identification of the Korean race with ancient Israel and the Protestant church with the remnant community that brings about restoration. This also provided the conceptual link between the Protestant community and the nation-state. In 1908 the Methodist Yang Jusam (later moderator of the Korean Methodist Church) had already expressed the idea: 'It is Christianity that will save Korea's twenty millions from their sins and restore freedom to our citizens; and it is Christianity that will rescue our Taehan race from the hands of the enemy just as the children of Israel were delivered from Egypt.'[58] The idea gained added force after the annexation. An editorial in the *Sinhan Minbo* on 5 September 1913 attributed the release of the Israelite remnant to rebuild Jerusalem to alleged patriotic statements in the Old Testament during the Babylonian exile. A series of studies on Nehemiah's nation-building activities appeared in the same newspaper in April–May 1916. It was asserted that the Koreans were a holy race like the Jews and would be led to their own Canaan if they turned from their past culpable neglect of the stewardship of their nation's abundant natural and human resources.[59]

This belief was not limited to Koreans in America. In a letter to National Association members in America, Yi Tonghwi expressed his delight in finding thousands of Koreans in China, Manchuria and Siberia who revered God and dedicated themselves to beneficial enterprises in the firm hope of freeing Korea. 'Beloved brothers,' Yi wrote, 'we are a nation sacrificed to God like Israel of old. Wherever we may go, we must make this [self-sacrifice] our proper service [to God].'[60] In Tokyo, a Korean student observed during a speech at the YMCA that the 'situation on the Korean peninsula is truly wretched, bearing close resemblance to that of the Israelites of Judea; and there is no way to save her except through Christianity'.[61]

Just how literally this identification of modern Korea with ancient Israel was taken is difficult to ascertain. The parallel was certainly taken very seriously, along with the inference that God would deliver Korea from Japan. Among the persecuted Protestants inside Korea, the symbolism had considerable potency. Events in Jewish history became favourite themes for drama in Christian schools. Yim Louise recalls the sense of contemporaneity with ancient Israel that she experienced while playing the part of Queen Esther:

> As I walked on the stage and looked out at the audience of girls and parents, I was transformed. The words I had rehearsed so carefully took on new meaning. They seemed to fit the present as well as the past. When I pleaded with King Ahasuerus to save the Hebrews, the words became a plea for Korea. And the meaning of my lines . . . was clearly understood by the audience.[62]

It is reasonable to conclude from the similar (indeed, almost identical) expressions of identity with Israel and of belief that the destiny of the Protestant church in Korea was to reconstruct an independent nation, that Christian leaders in Korea, Manchuria, north China, Japan and the United States, were in contact with each other. Since documents were smuggled out of Korea, one may assume some were smuggled into Korea, and some Koreans were of course moving between Korea and the diaspora communities throughout the decade. Certainly, the information received and published in the San Francisco *Sinhan Minbo* indicates a reasonable communications system.

Their identification as a reconstructive, remnant community was a symbol of the Protestants' determination to resist assimilation, which they equated with national annihilation, and to work out their own future. The intensified police harassment and surveillance provoked by references to Esther, Ezra and Nehemiah in sermons suggest that both sides were well aware of what was happening.

During the P'yŏngyang revival in 1915, a Korean observed that church members had 'discovered' that to enter Heaven one had to walk the thorny paths of this degenerate world and first overcome its evils and find Jerusalem here. The result of this refocusing on Earth, he observed, was an influx of people to dawn prayer meetings.[63] Paradoxical as this might seem, these meetings became the concrete expression of the Protestant community's objectives on Earth. As groups of Koreans prayed side by side, they expressed their solidarity. Vertically related to their God, they were horizontally bound together. The transcendent and the imminent were thus related, and the nation was to be reconstructed according to their image of a future that embodied the transcendental ideals of a Christian civilisation.

5 Cultural reconstruction and the separation of nation and state, 1920–1925

The termination of World War I, the political principles that governed the negotiations at Versailles, the Tokyo students' February Eighth Movement and the March First Movement heralded a new era in Protestant self-reconstruction nationalism in Korea. The leadership and participation of the Protestant community in the March First Movement had so reinforced its image as the restorative remnant that one writer has remarked that, 'especially when infused with the zeal of Wilsonianism, Christianity seemed to many Koreans to be the wave of the future'.[1] The Japanese also observed that Woodrow Wilson's principles were 'received among Koreans like Good News from Heaven'.[2] But not all the changes in the national and international climate were clement, and before long the Protestant identification with 'Wilsonianism' became almost a liability.

When the Protestant Henry Chung (Chŏng Han'gyŏng) announced that the March First Movement had opened the Pandora's Box of Korean nationalism,[3] he asserted a broader truth than he realised. What was released was in fact a multitude of disparate groups and approaches which settled down by 1922 into several opposing movements. The failure of the liberal–democratic Western nations to support Korean independence at Versailles and at the 1921–22 Washington and Pacific conferences, together with the rise of socialism among Koreans, produced a marked ambivalence among Protestants concerning the identification of Christianity with liberal democracy and, by association, with Western culture. The symbolic identification with ancient Israel was also a casualty of the 1920s, since it depended on unity of vision. As it was, self-reconstruction Protestants found themselves in competition not only with non-Christian approaches, but also with organisations whose leadership included influential Protestants. An Ch'angho, Yi Kwangsu and their followers remained committed to liberal democracy, but conceded that many specific political options were ethically neutral and therefore relative. However, they were not only relative to each other, but also relative to the task of creating a Christian civilisation in Korea. In such a civilisation, social and political debate were to be pursued in a climate of mutual respect and the outcome determined in accordance with a central principle of civic morality, the public verdict.

If this suggests the adoption of pluralism, it was not a pure or absolute pluralism; rather, one contemplated only within a framework of unity on essential human values. That these values were to be 'spiritual' was axiomatic. And indeed the Protestant self-reconstruction nationalists retained as an absolute value the creation of a Christian civilisation; denial of exclusive rights to ideologies followed logically. Insofar as the competing ideologies concerned prescriptions for the organisation of the state, which, because it was Japanese, catalysed nationalist politics, the Protestants concerned thought it necessary to separate 'nation' from 'state' and focus attention on the former. Of course, this position was inherent in the pre-annexation approach which gave Christianisation of the nation logical precedence over reorganisation of the state. But the distinction was emphasised in the general context of severe disunity among nationalists in the wake of the March First Movement.

The aftermath of the March First Movement

On 1 March 1919, a public reading of the Korean 'Declaration of Independence' in the Pagoda Palace gardens in Seoul sparked off a nationwide independence movement which, within two months, involved over a million people. Internally, the mass uprising derived from mounting anger at the Government-General's oppressive military rule and a growing consciousness of the need to regain control of the nation. When the ex-Emperor Kojong died early in 1919, rumours abounded that he had been poisoned by the Japanese. The authorities set 3 March as the official day for the funeral, and for the first time in a decade allowed Koreans to travel freely from around the country and congregate in Seoul. The huge crowds that gathered at the end of February were as dry as tinder, fully primed for an explosion of national feeling.

Externally, the movement was a cleverly planned response to the international situation pertaining at the close of World War I. The

victorious nations were gathering in Versailles to deliberate on the
shape of Europe, and what particularly galvanised the Koreans was
the Peace Conference's adoption of Woodrow Wilson's principle of
the self-determination of nations. Here was a chance to persuade the
nations to apply pressure on Japan to return Korea's independence.
Korean students in Japan hurriedly drew up a Declaration of Independence and staged an independence rally at the Korean YMCA in
Tokyo on 8 February. Koreans in Shanghai meanwhile dispatched
Kim Kyusik, a Presbyterian, to Paris to present Korea's case to the
conference delegates. Inside Korea, the proclamation of Korean independence was scheduled for 1 March, when large crowds were expected in Seoul.

Called the March First Movement, this landmark in Korean
nationalism was the fruit of an unexpected alliance between the two
most influential religions in Korea at the time: Ch'ŏndogyo (formerly
Tonghak) and Christianity. Although the movement was planned
in response to Woodrow Wilson's principle of national self-
determination, it was singularly lacking in any long-term policy or
'thesis', so that, in terms of political strategy, the movement has been
dubbed a 'disaster'.[4] The Christian involvement poses a problem:
whereas debates among the Korean Protestants in Tokyo at this time
included many elements of earlier and later Christian nationalist
ideas, the 'Christian' input during the March First Movement cannot
be placed so easily.[5]

That sixteen of the 33 signatories to the March Declaration of Independence were Christian (fifteen were Ch'ŏndogyo and two were
Buddhist) and included such influential leaders as Yi Sŭnghun and
the Rev. Kil Sŏnju may be regarded as contingent on the church's
experience during the 'Dark Ages' of 1910–18. But a well-defined
Protestant position such as that which existed as far back as the 1890s
is difficult to find. It would be extraordinary for such a position to
have suddenly evaporated, and the nature of the movement may
account for the omission. Ch'ŏndogyo and Christianity were serious
rivals in Korea, their collusion having been obtained through inter-
mediaries, so both sides forbore taking any line which might upset an
alliance which had, in fact, nearly shipwrecked on the eve of the
movement during a stormy debate over student involvement. The
movement had been planned only one month in advance under the
inimical conditions of a police state. It was designed to demonstrate
to delegates at the Paris Peace Conference the Koreans' will for independence, which demanded above all else an expression of firm
national solidarity. It was therefore contrary to its objectives to identify with a 'Protestant' or 'Ch'ŏndogyo' cause. If the Buddhist, Han
Yongun, was able to issue an independent statement on the Declara-

tion without endangering unity, this was possibly because Buddhism was not then a strong contender for nationalist leadership.

The haste and circumstances of the planning did leave unclear what was to follow on the movement's euphoric rise and unexpectedly brutal suppression. From Shanghai, nationalists sent an agent to Seoul to ascertain the mind of the imprisoned leaders, only to be instructed to do as they deemed best. They assumed that some form of democracy was best, and so the Shanghai Korean Provisional Government was established under a more or less republican charter. The assumption of democracy was, of course, in line with the political creed of the Protestants, including, at this point, those residing in Siberia.[6] The unanimous selection of the Methodist Syngman Rhee to the position of chief executive underscores the widespread commitment to democracy, since Rhee was considered the foremost interpreter of democracy to the Korean populace through his 'political bible' written in prison between 1899 and 1904.

But this signified agreement only on ends. Dissension over means reduced the provisional government to a faction-ridden, ineffective institution within three years; after 1922 there was little agreement, even on ends. By May 1919, the government already hovered between three strategic courses: diplomatic activity in Europe and the United States; direct military action against Japan; and the gradualist policy of training Koreans at home and abroad in the qualities of independent statehood. Yi Kwangsu, then in Shanghai, described the period as a 'political war', differences being aggravated by the geographical spread of nationalist groups.[7] Attempts to synthesise the three courses in 1920 and 1921 failed, and the alternatives hardened into distinct factions under the leadership of the Protestants Syngman Rhee (diplomacy), Yi Tonghwi (armed action and socialism) and An Ch'angho (gradualism).

Yi Tonghwi was heavily involved in recruiting and training guerillas in Kirin province (Manchuria) when elected the first premier of the provisional government. Syngman Rhee, as president, elected to stay in America to direct diplomatic activities with other Protestant leaders such as Henry Chung and Min Ch'anho. Organisation of the government fell to An Ch'angho, who attempted to reconcile the main factions. His influence waned with the arrival of Yi Tonghwi in September 1919, and by late 1920 the ideal of unity suffered a fateful blow amidst the furore which broke out over Rhee's alleged proposal of a League of Nations mandate over Korea as a step towards independence. Yi vigorously opposed the idea and Rhee was summoned by his cabinet to Shanghai where, on Rhee's arrival in January 1921, Shin Ch'aeho especially took him to task for his 'treachery'.[8]

Some nationalists, such as Hugh Cynn, decried the failure to compromise that had rendered the provisional government impotent by 1921. But there was little ground for compromise. The mandate controversy impinged directly on the question of means. Rhee had earlier held military preparations against Japan up to ridicule, while Henry Chung claimed that the 'saner element of the Korean people saw from the beginning the hopelessness of their cause on the field of military combat with Japan'.[9] The direct action and diplomatist factions had little in common except mutual antagonism. Only An Ch'angho could mediate, and even he soon fell out with Yi and Rhee. Rhee's proverbial charisma failed him and there ensued a spate of resignations up to May, including those of Yi, An, Shin, Yŏ Unhyŏng and Kim Kyusik.

The first real ideological complication was the rise of revolutionary socialism in 1922. The watershed in both the fortunes of the provisional government and the move towards socialism was the refusal of the 'democratic' nations to table Korea's case at the Washington (Pacific) Conferences of 1921–22. 'After the Pacific Conference,' a Japanese report noted, 'the reputation of the Provisional Government plummeted.'[10] Among the Protestants, the most dramatic indicator of this change was the abrupt turn to Moscow by the sorely disillusioned Presbyterian Kim Kyusik, chief campaigner at Versailles. However, these early Protestant socialists, including Yi Tonghwi and Yŏ Unhyŏng, were not committed to communism in any exclusivist or even strictly ideological sense,[11] and did not share Lenin's zest for whittling down the faithful to a core group of revolutionaries: unity was still a desideratum.

When tendering their resignations on 12 May 1921, both Yŏ Unhyŏng and An Ch'angho claimed they did so in the interests of restoring unity. Yŏ submitted that the 'crisis' in Korean nationalism was caused as much by internal strife as by Japan's suppression.[12] An berated the provisional government for falling away from its foundation in the public will to operate on systems of personal and group loyalties, appealing to emotion over reason and currying favours and sowing suspicions in an underhand way[13]—in fact in exactly the terms Yun Ch'iho and his colleagues had used to describe the politics of the late Chosŏn dynasty. Furthermore, the conflict over whether to look to Moscow, the United Kingdom, America or China for support revealed to An the old dependence psychology. With Yŏ, Shin Ch'aeho and Kim Kyusik, An organised the Kungmin Taep'yohoe (National Delegates' Conference) to return the government to the processes of public opinion. The Kungmin Taep'yohoe failed in its objectives, and may have hastened the demise of the government, which was perhaps bound to follow the fate of the diplomatists after the Washington Conference rebuff. For the Korean Protestant diaspora, the incessant feuding created sharp divisions within their own ranks, and although churches abroad remained strongly nationalistic, it is impossible to speak of a Protestant consensus abroad after 1922.

Reform and resistance in Korea, 1919–1921

The relative isolation of the nationalists inside Korea did not prevent the development of divisions parallel to those abroad. As high spirits yielded to bitterness at the brutality of Japanese suppression of the March First Movement and to disappointment at the unconcern of the Western powers, reactions in Korea corresponded in the main to those which had disrupted the provisional government. But the context of these reactions was naturally quite different. The March First Movement caused the Japanese government to review its colonial behaviour, introduce limited reforms and pursue the so-called 'cultural' or 'conciliation' policy on the basis of 'Nisen yūwa' (harmony of Japan and Korea).

The assimilative policy and the organisation of the Government-General were reviewed in the Japanese Diet, and proposals ranged from calls for the repeal of the whole policy to the military faction's advocacy of an even stronger hand. Master of compromise that he was, Premier Hara Kei guided opinion towards a tempered application of assimilation and assented to having Baron Saitō Makoto, a retired military man who emphasised cultural assimilation through education and gradualism in politics, succeed General Hasegawa as Governor-General. It is doubtful the Premier could have prevailed over the militarists had Saitō's proposed reforms not been so innocuous from the Japanese point of view; indeed, in the process of annexing Manchuria in the early 1930s, the military administration was revived and Saitō's cultural policy was terminated as a grudgingly tolerated interregnum.[14]

When Baron Saitō disembarked at Pusan in September 1919 bearing promises of his conciliatory policy, his landing was greeted by a pointed merchants' strike; in Seoul he was welcomed by an attempt on his life. Saitō's reforms were, as a modern Japanese publication notes, 'extremely narrow in scope and did not satisfy the Korean people'.[15] In the central administration, the Education Department was upgraded to an independent bureau, the gendarmerie was abolished and the Police Bureau was transferred from the Governor-General's direct control to the Government-General proper as a civilian bureau.[16] In terms of local administration, a limited franchise was granted to Koreans to elect, in specially chosen villages and under restricted conditions, members of new 'advisory councils' under the provincial governors' supervision. Chǒng Han'gyǒng regarded these councils as an 'espionage system' and expressed the

general scepticism of nationalists: 'The only reforms that have been
introduced are the changing of the name of the "military" administration to that of "civil", and the "gendarmerie" to "police".'[17] Yun
Ch'iho also opined that the only people to benefit from the reforms
would be the Japanese.[18]

Up to 1920 at least, the Protestants, who had borne considerable
material and human loss during the uprising, were determined to
maintain unity and to keep the issue of independence alive and visible
to the world. The Presbyterians and Methodists, in particular, continued to agitate, and a number of Catholic resistance groups also
appeared in P'yŏngyang and Ŭiju. There is some evidence that the
Presbyterian and Methodist assemblies contemplated official patronage of the cause.[19] The churches did officially organise relief funds for
the families of those in prison, and among the Methodists Yun Ch'iho
was the major contributor.[20] Many Christians were committed to the
support of the provisional government, especially as the Rev. Kim
Pyŏngjo, one of the 'Thirty-Three' signatories to the Declaration of
Independence, had escaped to Shanghai to assist in its organisation.

In P'yŏngyang, Presbyterians associated with the P'yŏngyang
Theological Seminary reorganised the Taehan Kungminhoe (Korean
National Association) in August 1919 with the intention of incorpor-
ating all Presbyterians as the first step towards a unified, representative organ for the whole nation on the peninsula. In September it
won recognition from the provisional government. The Constitution
and Manifesto of the Taehan Kungminhoe invoked the self-
reconstruction tradition. Article Two of Chapter One in the Constitution equated reflection on and obedience to the common law of God
with joint deliberation on administrative affairs by both citizen and
official; Article Three of Chapter Four granted voting rights to all
members aged 25 and over, for regional representatives who were to
possess 'patriotism, religious faith and general knowledge'. The Manifesto reinterpreted traditional wisdom in terms of civic rights and
duties and the utilitarian concern for national efficiency and social
happiness:

> The Ancient Texts say that the People are the foundation of the State.
> This saying is indeed the great maxim and reference of political economy
> of every age. Whichever the nation, the people preceded the birth of its
> government, and so the people do not exist for the government but the
> government for the people . . . [Real] citizens must not lose the rights
> belonging to citizens. They should bear the nation on their backs and
> themselves choose and commission state officials, small and great. In co-
> operation and harmony, the officials and the people should deliberate on
> all national affairs, daily increase the strength of the state and preserve
> forever the happiness of the people.'[21]

Concurrently, several other groups with similar aims and links with the provisional government formed among Protestants in Seoul and P'yŏngyang, including the Patriotic Women's Society, the Independence Youth Corps and the Youth Diplomatic Corps. But by the end of the year their leaders had been arrested and imprisoned, together with members of the Taehan Kungminhoe.[22]

The earliest surviving record of a specifically Christian perspective on the foundations of unity and civilisation after 1918 is a police report of a speech delivered by the Rev. Kim P'ilsu before a crowd of some 1500 at the Seoul Central YMCA on 14 November 1919. National welfare, the Rev. Kim preached, rested on the principle enunciated by Christ that a house divided against itself cannot stand. This principle flowed through village, district, province and nation to finally encompass the whole world. The irreligious and ignorant denied that righteousness united and exalted a nation, as Mencius also taught, and instead resorted to militarism, as in the Three Kingdom Period of Ancient Korea and in the Germany of that time. But the breakdown of barriers to unity had already ensued in Korea in the (pre-1919, pre-annexation) move away from distinctions between *yangban* and commoner, and Koreans awaited only democracy to achieve full oneness. The true inspiration of democracy was Christ: Korea's welfare depended on Christian youth 'making the Lord Christ the goal of our unity'.[23]

This line was not immediately popular among the greater part of Korea's Christian youth. The general bitterness observed by Saitō in September 1919 continued throughout 1920 in the form of secret youth societies dedicated to agitation, funding and training guerilla units, and the support of the provisional government. But by early 1921 a number of factors engendered more respect for the Rev. Kim's approach among Protestants. Firstly, disappointment at Versailles and Washington and the discord within the provisional government, together with continual Japanese interception of funds, considerably dampened the spirit of sacrificial donations to the cause which An Ch'angho and Yŏ Unhyŏng had lauded in Shanghai. Secondly, the intense 'mopping up' operations directed towards Korean guerillas by Japanese troops in Hunch'un, Manchuria, from October 1920 rendered a military solution even more remote. Thirdly, the arrest of prominent, moderate Christian leaders like Kim Maria and An Chaehong from late 1919 demolished hopes that, after all, the new administration might create some space for political activity.[24]

In January 1920, Governor-General Saitō did, however, issue publishing permits to three newspapers, two of them in reality Japanese organs and one, the *Tonga Daily*, belonging to the nationalists. The *Tonga Daily* was founded by a respected group of nationalists, most of whom were Protestants. The chief editor was Chang Tŏksu, formerly an organiser of the Tokyo students' independence movement of 8 February 1919. Pak Yŏnghyo, veteran of the 1884 Kapshin Coup, was made manager, while Yang Kit'ak, former editor of the *Taehan Maeil Sinbo* and victim of the Conspiracy Case, was editorial supervisor. For the *Tonga Daily's* first edition on 1 April 1920, Chang composed a dramatic editorial in which he announced the 'resurrection' of the 'Rose of Sharon [Korea] of East Asia', almost at the same time as his fellow Protestant Shin Hŭngu (Hugh Cynn) released his *Rebirth of Korea* in America. The 'progress of liberty' was the journey on which the nation was now embarked, and the newspaper pledged itself to three major tasks:

1 to serve as the people's voice;
2 to champion democracy;
3 to advocate culturalism (*munhwajuŭi*).

The first point may be regarded as a shibboleth. The second was also virtually mandatory at the time. But, as will become clear, the task was not so much to confront the Government-General with demands for democracy (though this was done) as to train Koreans in the meaning of the term, and in the national characteristics which were supposed to be necessary for its growth and implementation. This, in fact, was the import of the third point. 'Culturalism' meant commitment to constructing a new culture as the necessary foundation for independent statehood and democracy.[25]

The shift to culturalism was dominated in its early stages by Chang Tŏksu. From June 1920 Chang began gathering together the numerous youth societies that had mushroomed since 1919. In December he succeeded in forming no fewer than 113 groups into the Korean Youth Association (Chosŏn Ch'ŏngnyŏn Yŏnhaphoe), which he placed under the umbrella of the Seoul YMCA. Chang campaigned for a return to the pre-annexation task of 'cultivating real strength and ability'. The Japanese described the progress of Chang's movement as 'extraordinary' and noted that affiliated youth groups had 'sprung up everywhere throughout all regions and served as the mainstream of the nationalist movement'.[26] As the movement expanded, 'self-cultivation societies' (*suyanghoe*) proliferated. To the slogan 'real strength' was added the cry for 'cultural politics', while, through a system of circuit lectures, students carried self-strengthening programs to rural districts.[27]

The conviction the culturalists brought to their campaign was strengthened by reflections on the ineffectiveness of political agitation. On 20 April 1921, the Christian Youth Federation was formed, representing groups from Sinŭiju in the north to Mokp'o in the far south. Upon election of the federation's officers, Shin Hŭngu, now secretary-general of the YMCA, addressed the delegates:

For about a decade, we Koreans lived our lives in silence, but stimulated by the culture brought in from abroad over recent years we launched an uprising. Yet nothing was gained as a result, and in the end the Korean people incurred only harm and loss.

In future, we must put a stop to this blind activity and exert ourselves fully on behalf of our nation and society. The young are stronger in body than the old. They excel also in vigour of mind and pursuit of learning, and in courageousness of spirit.

Even so, you young men are apt to lose heart and do not relish sound, persevering work, and so it is my hope that you will put short-term considerations behind you and grasp hold of the long-term, lend your strength to this Federation and through it strive to build Heaven in Korea.[28]

Evidently the culturalist stream was appealing to the diagnosis of and antidote to Korea's national plight that had gained currency among Protestants in the first decade of the century. Yet it would be misleading to suggest that the Rev. Kim P'ilsu, Chang Tŏksu and Shin Hŭngu had entirely persuaded the younger Protestants against 'short-term' political action in favour of 'long-term' cultural enterprises. To Yun Ch'iho, whose influence on the younger Shin Hŭngu is plain, the political failure of the March First Movement was a foregone conclusion, and he had refused to be persuaded to join.[29] Its failure, the ethico-spiritual origin of nationhood and the priority of cultural reconstruction were all of a piece for Yun—but this was not necessarily so for the new generation which lacked his experience of the condition of the country before annexation. It was the impracticality of political confrontation which encouraged the favourable response to culturalism among the younger generation.

The most indefatigable proponent of 'nonpolitical', cultural nationalism was the influential but controversial Yi Kwangsu, who returned to Korea in March 1921 determined to spread the reconstruction ideology of An Ch'angho throughout the land. Yi immediately threw himself into the cultural movement with his former colleagues from Tokyo days—Kim Sŏngsu (Principal of Seoul Central Middle School and founder of the Kyŏngsŏng Textile Company), Hong Myŏnghŭi (novelist and later Marxist), Ch'oe Namsŏn, Song Chin'u and Chang Tŏksu. Yi was, and still is, counted among the prominent Christians of his day, but his eclecticism and obvious attraction to Buddhist spirituality upset any facile religious labelling. While teaching at Osan College until 1913, Yi drew criticism from some for teaching 'Tolstoyism' rather than Christianity, and dissatisfaction over the purity of his Christian faith remains. Yi himself spoke reverently of the Presbyterian founder of Osan College, Yi

Sŭnghun, as his mentor and claimed his example had turned practi-
cally the whole population of Chŏngju to Christianity. To Yi Sŭnghun he attributed his own dedication to the self-reconstruction principle that inner strength was the well-spring of social and national
progress.[30] By 1917 at least, Yi Kwangsu apparently regarded Christianity as the source of the highest civilisation. One of Korea's greatest
modern writers, Yi wove Christian themes into his novels and, more
than any other, openly premised much of his nationalist argumenta-
tion on Christian doctrines and the sayings of Christ. Most pertinent
of all, Yi became the foremost apologist and communicator of the
gradualism of An Ch'angho to Koreans on the peninsula.

Though he wrote on several facets of nationalism, Yi's real influence lay in promoting the concept of the cultural roots of a nation,
or the definition of nation as a cultural entity. The kernel of this
concept had appeared in December 1917 in an article contributed to
the Tokyo student journal, *Hak Chi Kwang*. Yi put forward the axiom that the political and cultural histories of a nation, though usually
related, were in fact sometimes, and conceptually always, distinct.
Far from being subordinate, a nation's cultural history determined its
worth. Taken this way, 'Korean history' did not exist: Koreans could
claim no share in world cultural history. Belonging to Chinese culture
was no comfort:

> That we have soaked ourselves in tens of thousands of readings of the
> Chinese Classics over the past 500 years does not ascribe any value to the
> existence of the Korean race and neither does the appellation 'Little
> China' or the boast that we have perfected the philosophy of the Chu Hsi
> [neo-Confucian] School . . . There is one, and only one, way to acquire any
> value for the existence of our race, and that is to create a new culture which
> we can call our own.[31]

There is some awkwardness in Yi's position, since he was advocating a new, Christian basis for culture which was hardly more an indigenous creation than the neo-Confucianism it was to replace. The inconsistency diminishes if the statement is interpreted (as no doubt
it should be) nationalistically. Such an interpretation of participation
in neo-Confucianism implies slavish imitation of and vassalage to
China, an imperialist power which had so shackled Korea that it was
unable to respond to nineteenth-century changes. By contrast, the
adoption of Christianity and Western ideas signifies the development
of a nation-state free from vassalage to any other nation. In any case,
Yi proclaimed production of the new culture to be the new national
ideal. Like Yun and An, who both placed Korea's national maturity a
century in the future, Yi warned that this new culture and nation
would only appear after one or two hundred years' perseverance. But
unlike An, who saw no opportunity to work in Korea, Yi became

convinced that Korea was the place where the doctrine was most relevant. Yi recognised that the influence of exiles on events in their
homeland was severely limited and began to look upon the
'emptying' of Korea by its leaders as a great mistake.[32]

Yi opened his campaign in Korea with a long message to the country's teenagers which was serialised in a culturalist journal, *Kaebyŏk*
(Creation) from November 1921 to March 1922. Yi argued that
Korea's present position was a penalty for the long bankruptcy in her
learning, morality and economy, and devoted by far the most space
to an account of Korea's ethical ruin. But his major piece, 'Discourse
on National Reconstruction', appeared in *Kaebyŏk* in May 1922. Yi
had penned the introduction on 11 November 1921, the very day the
Pacific Conference was convened. The contents, he acknowledged
with a nod to An Ch'angho, had been worked out by Koreans
abroad. 'Reconstruction', he continued, was the watchword for the
present, replacing other slogans such as 'reform' and even 'revolution.' It signified something more profound than these, for it encompassed the worldwide move from imperialism to democracy, competition to co-operation and male chauvinism to equality of the sexes.
For the Koreans it was a summons to reconstruct the national character, economy, environment, religion, morality—in short, Korean
civilisation in its entirety.[33]

It was in this 'Discourse' that Yi introduced the most controversial
element in the creed: its relegation of politics to a position subordinate to moral reconstruction and education. Almost all nationalist
organisations from the late nineteenth century on had run themselves
out on the sands of politics, heedless of the crucial lesson that the
nation's collapse had been caused by moral and spiritual sickness.
Only the Ch'ŏngnyŏn Hakuhoe (1908–11), the forerunner of the
Hŭngsadan, had understood this and thus determined not to have any
political colouring. Since it was not moral ignorance but moral
powerlessness that led Korea to ruin, the need was for new wine-
skins—that is, the national character had to be renewed. Through
just twelve disciples Jesus had launched a nonpolitical movement
which in time produced a whole new civilisation. Thus, however
long it took, cultural reconstruction, 'an eternal, all-embracing
movement', had to be kept free of any political connection lest it be
interrupted by government interference.

A self-civilising enterprise, cultural reconstruction required serious
attention to education, which itself required an ethical foundation.
As the demand for schooling among Koreans soared, culturalism
appeared poised to win the allegiance of the people. Increasing numbers began studying in Japan in obedience to the principle that they
must 'first establish firm foundations of national self-reliance and
lay plans for adequate cultural development and real strength in

readiness for some future opportunity'.[34] In Korea, Chang Tŏksu promoted schooling funded and staffed by Koreans in his home province of Hwanghae, while Song Chin'u and Kim Sŏngsu upgraded the Seoul Central Middle and High Schools. In Chŏngju, North P'yŏngan, Cho Mansik was back at the helm of Osan College following his release from a term in prison for his part in leading the March First Movement. Perhaps the best indicator of the breadth and intensity of this commitment to the 'new' education lies in the records of the hitherto-unexamined Australian Presbyterian Mission which concern the traditionally less responsive southern provinces. 'All schools are overcrowded,' reported Dr William Taylor from Chinju in 1922. 'There is a perfect craze for education all over the peninsula.'[35] In Pusan, another Australian, Ms Withers, perceived the nationalistic impulse behind the surge:

> Throughout the whole country there is a tremendous thirst for learning and the people are beginning to realise that their present position is a good deal due to lack of education in the past . . . Our schools are overcrowded. Last Spring in Fusanchin [Pusan district] over 100 were turned away, and in Chinju, Masanpo and throughout the whole country large numbers had to be refused admission.[36]

There is no doubt that the education movement made good mileage out of Saitō's slight liberalisation of schooling and his permission for Christian schools to include religious instruction in their curricula. But the Japanese were anxious to supply the increased demand themselves, and when late in 1922 a movement to establish a Korean university was launched, their fears of a '*mombusho* [education ministry] within a *mombusho*' were renewed.

The Preparatory Committee to Establish a People's University is sometimes regarded as just one expression of Korean nationalism in the 1920s. It was, in fact, the first action of many of the Protestant signatories to the Declaration of Independence immediately following their release from prison. It is only recently that the Committee has received even brief analysis, from the standpoint of its critics.[37] As part of the culturalist movement, however, the university campaign, and especially its manifesto, demonstrate the currency and influence of the definition of the nation as culture distinct from the political state.

The idea of a university was not new. After a movement to repay Korea's national debt was frustrated shortly before annexation, Yun Ch'iho and others had discussed using the money collected for the debt to establish a university. With six million *hwan* in hand they petitioned the Governor-General, but were rebuffed. In 1920 Yun approached Saitō, but with no more fortune. When the March First leaders were released, and in view of the enthusiasm for education, the time was judged right to recruit more support. By March 1923, 1170 persons from throughout Korea joined the 47 founders of the Preparatory Committee, and on 29 March, 462 delegates gathered at the Seoul Central YMCA to discuss strategy and compose the Manifesto.[38]

An elegantly phrased composition, the Manifesto opened with a rhetorical question: 'How shall we work out our destiny?' It then proceeded to exalt education as the true foundation of 'secondary' enterprises such as industry, diplomacy and politics. Tertiary education had a 'tremendous connexion with the evolution of mankind', ensuring 'cultural progress' and raising the quality of life of nations. The universities which were established in Italy, France, Germany and England in the twelfth and thirteenth centuries were the cradle of Europe and America's grand civilisation and the source of their religious renewal and political revolutions. Everything of importance that Korea needed in the modern world required or attended university education.[39]

This appraisal of the role of education had been introduced into *Kaebyŏk* in June 1920. 'What a man knows, that he is,' quoted one contributor. 'Therefore education is our life, the life of the nation and society, the life of the whole universe . . . Where there is education there is life, well-being, civilisation, happiness and victory.' In proportion to the population, schools were woefully few and there was still no university, the contributor lamented.[40] The Australian missionaries shared the culturalists' vision. Observing that the 'young people are thinking deeply of their future service of their country', they concurred with the view that the 'coming new nation is in the hands of the present students'.[41]

The importance of this viewpoint is that it defies the central political principle of nationalism: that a nation has no reality except in its political institutions and that the prior congruence of nation and state is the necessary condition for the development of national culture. In its context, the 'coming new nation' referred not to a politically independent state of Korea, but to the character and ethos of the civilisation that would be moulded by the generation then imbibing the new education and religion. The culturalists were arguing, in effect, that the battle was profoundly cultural; politics were secondary and political resistance should be relinquished when the returns were too small, or counterproductive. The Japanese were culturally vulnerable, for they could only evolve a Japanese nation-state, and this was impossible in Korea: it would never work; the Koreans would not be assimilated, as indeed a Japanese scholar had argued in 1910.[42] Cultural nationalism would in time undermine Japanese rule, but it was in any case a moral imperative whose validity could not be cancelled by the issue of who ruled. For many Protestants, this removed the offence of particularism from nationalistic activities. Thus a form of nonpolitical nationalism was advanced which immediately drew both enthusiastic support and bitter opposition.

The defence of culturalism, 1923–1925

Despite detailed work on a comprehensive curriculum, the venture to establish a Korean university ground to a halt in 1925. The immediate causes of its failure are clear enough: they were primarily the failure to attract sufficient funds and Government-General counteraction. At first, contributions came thick and fast, but with this the limits of indulgence had been reached and the authorities began to obstruct the project in various ways.[43] In 1922, Dr Mizuno, of the Education Bureau, announced the Government-General's intention of opening a university in Seoul. Potential contributors to the Korean venture were discouraged by this pre-emptive action, but when Keijō Imperial University opened in 1927, entry for Koreans was restricted to one-third of the total enrolment and Korean lecturers were excluded except for the provision of instruction in Chinese and Korean literature and occasionally in mathematics.[44]

But among the Koreans, growing disillusionment with liberalism, and misgivings over the political philosophy of the culturalists, contributed to the failure of the movement. From 1922, significant numbers of Protestants also began to develop an interest in socialism. In 1922 a split occurred in Chang Tŏksu's youth association as Kim Myŏngsik seceded to publish a moderate leftist journal, Shin Saengwhal, with Pak Hŭido, a YMCA leader and recently released member of the 'Thirty-Three'. As the Leninist doctrine of imperialism became known, many of the younger Protestants, such as Han Wigŏn, turned with high hopes to Marxism. While the Shin Saengwhal attacked Tonga Daily and Kaebyŏk culturalism, the more radical left dismissed the university movement as an élitist hobby.[45] Culturalists also faced hostility from the right. The fact that Yi Kwangsu had been allowed to re-enter Korea a free man had given rise to rumours of a dishonourable understanding with the Japanese. When, in an article in July 1921, he urged Koreans to reject political plots and instead form a key class of intellectuals to spearhead the cultural revival,[46] the counsel against resistance appeared suspicious.

This opposition may not have been sufficient reason for the failure of the university movement, which would probably have succeeded but for Japanese intervention, but it called into question self-reconstruction nationalism in its culturalist form. The ascendancy of socialism by 1924 not only ended the numerical dominance of the culturalists, but also put them at a psychological disadvantage. Socialism offered sharp definitions and a clearcut program; culturalism seemed vague, ambiguous and even insipid. Socialism was on the rise and held promise; culturalism had been tried and found wanting. Further, by attracting numbers of important Protestants, socialism deprived culturalism of a consensus of support among the very group which had originally inspired it.

It is important not to exaggerate the division. Socialism had not been adopted by church congregations and was at this stage a creed which was even more restricted to the educated élite than culturalism. No section of Korean society could claim greater involvement in primary education, rural and urban, than the Protestants, and Japanese documents state that the idea of deliverance through education continued to strike a responsive cord among 'ordinary' Koreans at least up to 1930.[47] In fact, the presence of Christians within the socialist and communist movements actually mitigated the effects of the division. Yi Tonghwi maintained positive relations with Song Chin'u, manager of the *Tonga Daily*, while Han Wigŏn, a reporter for the *Tonga Daily*, facilitated mediation between Song Chin'u and leftist critics in Tokyo.[48] Nevertheless, there was division, and the culturalists were obliged to rise to their defence.

Yi Kwangsu claimed he was simply following the precedent of the Ch'ŏngnyŏn Hakuhoe, which no-one had criticised. In February 1922 he and his fiancée Pak Hyŏnhwan had formed a Hŭngsadan branch in Seoul with about ten other nationalists, including the Protestants Kim Yun'gyŏng and Chu Yohan. To hide its connection with An Ch'angho, the branch was given the innocuous title of Suyang Tongmaenhoe, the Self-Improvement League. A similar body arose in P'yŏngyang among graduates of An's Taesŏng College: Cho Myŏngsik, Kim Sŏngŏp and the Presbyterian Elder and colleague of Cho Mansik, Kim Tongwŏn.[49] Then, in 1923, Cho Mansik, Kim Sŏngsu, An Chaehong, Song Chin'u and the Ch'ŏndogyo leader Ch'oe Rin met to discuss a unified, nonpolitical body to promote self-reconstruction. It was decided to commence with the serialisation of Yi Kwangsu's 'National Statecraft' theses in the *Tonga Daily* over the period 2–6 January 1924.

In the opening section, Yi openly rejected the 'socialistic' idea of determinism of the individual will in history, classing it along with Hegel's historical philosophy as 'superstitious and arbitrary'.[50] He next rejected the notion that Koreans could be properly involved only in political movements which made Japan's expulsion their immediate or even primary aim.[51] Finally, Yi asserted that education was still the most urgent and formidable task of all, the means whereby Korea's fourteen million farmers, with whom the nation's destiny lay, would be equipped for the task of the material construction of the new Korea.[52] In view of the negative reaction from right and left to these articles (Cho Mansik may not even have been at ease with them himself), organisation of the intended national body was deferred. In March 1924 Yi Kwangsu went to Peking to consult with An Ch'angho on future strategy. On his return he published his 'Ŭigi Ron', in which he set Christian doctrines against materialistic concepts of history and methodologies of class struggle.

The composition of society was spiritual: 'A person's most precious possession is public spirit. . . If there be such things as high and low classes, they can be divided only with reference to public spirit.' St Paul's cry, 'Ah, I am a wretched being!' suggested that the line separating good and evil ran not between classes or nations, but through the heart of each individual, where the primary and decisive battle had to be waged. Christ's expression on the Cross, 'It is finished,' was his final song of victory over the evil in human nature. His command to all who follow was therefore: 'Be perfect as your Father in Heaven is perfect.' The process of history was thus quite other than economically determined:

> We believe in evolution in history. We believe that humanity has been steadily evolving from ancient times in a good direction, and that it is the blood of the many righteous, or public-spirited people who have fought from of old, that is the force driving human history in this direction . . .
> Do not mourn our lack of political freedom. Mourn not our state of economic insolvency. Neither mourn should some fearsome disease strike us down. Not that these are not grievous things; but they are nothing compared with the lack among us of righteous people.

Public spirit was altruistic action towards neighbour, district, nation and all humankind. Yi proposed a program which would not only deliver Korea, but also Japan and the rest of the world, from the forces of enslavement—which were derived from within the individual. On this view, he argued, 'making myself, as one person, perfect, is the greatest of works on behalf of humanity'.[53]

The writings of Yi Kwangsu reflect the dilemma faced by Protestants inside Korea after it had become obvious that neither Japan nor the democratic West was sympathetic to their aspiration for political independence. He spoke for those who perceived the old reliance on outside powers in the new turn to Moscow (possibly influenced by An Ch'angho) and also for those who concurred with Yun Ch'iho's and Shin Hŭngu's dissatisfaction over heroic but counterproductive political agitation. That Yi should draw criticism from both the socialist and rightist camps was natural, but his position vis-à-vis the latter was ironic since, for all his commitment to the anti-toadyist, self-reliance tradition, his position was labelled by many of his opponents as a compromise with Japanese power. By the end of 1923, the sudden burst of enthusiasm for education, though by no means over, had been eclipsed by the rise of political ideologies of left and right. When it had become least feasible, the demand for the upper ceiling—immediate, unconditional independence—was pressed most strongly, and any hint of a political armistice with Japan was interpreted as compromise. The culturalists' separation of nation as culture from nation as sovereign political entity clashed with the sacred cow of political nationalism, which had no time for subtlety. The nationalist right was interested not in the evolution of the state, but in its recovery. Where a decisive nationalist strategy was looked for, the culturalists gave a theory of civilisation.

Although wholly consistent with the philosophy of change he and others had espoused from before the annexation, Yun Ch'iho's position during the 1920s has also been construed as passive collaboration. Yun, Pak Yŏnghyo and former 'patriotic' politicians such as Han Kyusŏl had been approached in January and February 1919 about joining the March First organisation, but all had declined. Yun's refusal has been interpreted as the shame-faced reluctance of a 54-year-old man of letters, still frail from his former imprisonment, to court arrest, torture and incarceration once again.[54] There may be some truth in this, but with the recent release of the seventh and eighth volumes of Yun's diary, it is no longer necessary to speculate.

Yun's objection to the March First uprising was that to succeed it required the strength Korea lacked. As early as 1893, Yun had spoken of the 'absurdity' of appealing to America's conscience against its self-interest,[55] and in 1919 he foresaw that the hopes placed in the Paris Peace Conference would be dashed, and that nothing but harm would follow. It should be noted that Yun's opinion of the political folly of the March First Movement was soon shared by socialist strategists and has been supported by modern scholars, though from different perspectives.[56] By joining the movement to establish a Korean university, Yun reaffirmed his commitment to his original vision.

In many respects Yun was a classical bourgeois nationalist, but he was not really typical. In an earlier chapter it was mentioned that Yun was an enigma to Koreans who adopted Christianity as a politically useful proposition, since his own conversion followed a personal search for truth and the spiritual power to follow the demands of his conscience. In his diary, Yun had early confessed to a growing admiration for St Paul's unwavering commitment to his mission amidst political resistance by Israel to Rome: 'I admire the character of St Paul more and more. In his life time Judia went through all the national agonies of vassalage and dissolution. It must have been an exciting time for a high-spirited young Jew. Yet Paul stuck to what he saw to be the true mission for which he was elected.'[57]

Yun realised that, had Paul offered his faith to the cause of Jewish zealotism, Christianity would not have become a world religion but at best a successful Jewish heresy or sect. He laid his finger on the crucial factor whereby Christianity became universalistic and burst free from racial, national and political boundaries. This may have been the most critically Christian aspect of Yun's rejection of a nationalism premised on racial confrontation and a Christianity identified with anti-Japanese political ideology. In the final analysis, strict nationalists could not approve Yun's 'authentic' Christianity, just as Yun likewise could not approve their definition of nationalism. Yun regarded himself as a missionary in his own land and, taking Paul as his example, refused to be diverted.

On several occasions, Yun was urged by Yi Sangjae, Kim Chŏngsik and Shin Hŭngu to go abroad, where he would be free to work for Korean independence. Yun rather regarded the idea as escapism and insisted that 'Korea is the Korean's battleground'.[58] He was also pressured by the Japanese to encourage a benign view of the reforms among Koreans. This, too, he resolutely refused to do, at least until 1937.[59]

Though the Japanese attitude towards the Koreans incensed him (as did the high-handed manner of the Western missionaries), Yun saw little alternative to their rule for the time being. This did not mean he thought the situation hopeless, however; on the contrary, independence remained the object: 'The Koreans have shown they are willing to die for this ideal . . . As water will never rest until it has found its level; as fire will never rest till it has found its upward current, so the Korean race will never rest until it has found its independence.'[60] What it did mean was that political agitation was not the proper course for the present. Yun criticised the idea that politics was the only patriotic action as 'one of the superstitions of the Korean'.[61] His own view was that politics was the end result of a number of more fundamental factors: 'Religion and morality are the soul of a race; knowledge, its brain; wealth, its body; while political status is only its clothes.'[62] This was vintage culturalism, self-reconstruction ideology founded on personal spirituality, ethics and learning. Yun was optimistic that this would in due course triumph; it was his conviction that 'no nation has ever succeeded in keeping down the intellectual growth of another race'.[63]

The socialists, however, were concerned specifically with imperial power and so regarded the 'nonpolitical' nationalism of the culturalists as tacit acceptance of imperialism. At best, the cultural apologetics of Yi Kwangsu seemed to suggest naively that the economic and political machinery of the Japanese empire would be overcome by a combination of learning and Christian character. This was not strictly accurate, but it highlights the obvious disagreement over the cause of Korea's subjection to Japan. The socialists and communists of this period perceived a necessary connection between capitalism and imperialism and concluded that Korea was the victim of impersonal historical forces. The culturalism of the Korean Protestants was based on the view that, even if imperialism worked according to its own laws, it was Korea's own 'sin' of national decay that had allowed these laws to operate on her own territory. (There is a parallel here with Yun Ch'iho's resolution in the 1890s of the conflict between social Darwinism and Providence.) According to this critique, the designation of Japan as the principal enemy for whatever reason was regressive. Hence, although political resistance was then deemed unfeasible, culturalism was not merely a tactic for the times but the antidote to the nation's 'real' problems. After 1925, when the ranks of the socialist and 'pure' nationalist movements were reduced by imprisonment and desertion, Protestant self-reconstruction nationalists reorganised and sought once more to effect the spiritual revolution of the Korean nation.

6 National repentance and civilisation, 1925–1937

The appearance of socialist and communist organisations in Korea by 1923 alarmed the Government-General. In 1923 Pak Hŭido and Kim Myŏngsik were sentenced to six months' imprisonment for calling for a political revolution, and their journal, *Shin Saenghwal*, was banned indefinitely.[1] In April 1925, the three main communist factions in Korea secretly formed the First Korean Communist Party in Seoul. A reckless flag-waving incident in Sinŭiju, North P'yŏngan, exposed the party and led to the arrest of 30 prominent leaders in November. This incident provoked a factional struggle which threatened the young communist movement, especially after the Second Korean Communist Party was crushed in mid-1926 amidst the arrest of many more members.[2]

Meanwhile, the non-communist nationalists suffered reverses of their own. In September 1924, the struggling pro-Japanese *Chosŏn Daily* was bought by Yi Sanghyŏp and the Protestants Yi Sangjae, An Chaehong and Paek Kwansu, and was soon regarded as the organ of the moderate nationalist left. For a time, *Chosŏn Daily* articles criticised the *Tonga Daily*'s non-resistance stance. However, the *Chosŏn Daily* staff also suffered from the exposure of the communists at Sinŭiju, whereupon Yi Sanghyŏp accepted responsibility and resigned. In 1925 also, staff of the *Tonga Daily*, *Kaebyŏk* and Ch'oe Namsŏn's *Sidae Ilbo* suffered fines and imprisonment. Thereupon the management of the *Chosŏn* and *Tonga* dailies sought solidarity against the Government-General's attempts to stifle the press. In December 1925, Song Chin'u and An Chaehong came together to found a Reporters' Support League in order to protect press freedom and human rights.[3]

Despite this collusion, the two newspapers remained at odds over the political issue. When the weakened communists approached the nationalists concerning the formation of a united front, the *Chosŏn Daily* management concurred enthusiastically. In February 1927 the united front was formally launched as the Sin'ganhoe, with Yi Sangjae elected as its first president. The continuance of the political disagreement was marked by the initial absence of any members of the staff of the *Tonga Daily* and by the pointed claim of the *Chosŏn Daily* that the Sin'ganhoe was a firmly non-compromise organisation.

General Protestant support of the Sin'ganhoe, which soon attracted a membership of some 30000, was crucial if the church was to remain a force in Korean nationalism. Numbers of important Protestant figures, including members of Yi Kwangsu's Suyang Tongmaenghoe, did therefore join the united front. Self-reconstruction nationalists were not opposed to political activity within legal limits (since political training was integral to citizenship), and the Sin'ganhoe had been formed with Japanese permission and existed on Government-General sufferance. There was therefore a gap between image and reality in the *Chosŏn Daily's* description of a political organisation that rejected all 'opportunism' outright. As soon as it stepped beyond the bounds of legality in its clandestine sponsorship of the 1929 Kwangju Student Uprising, turning it into a nationwide movement, its leaders and several hundred members found themselves behind bars. The Japanese refusal to grant permission to reorganise after its internal dissolution in May 1931 underlined its former dependence on official tolerance. The Protestants among the Sin'ganhoe leadership were generally opposed to any engagement in politically provocative acts, not only on principle but because they foresaw that such actions would splinter the front and so postpone further their ideal of national unity. The breakdown of the experiment was blamed by its last president, the Christian lawyer and Tongmaenghoe member, Kim Pyŏngno, on excessive and self-defeating politics.[4] Cho Mansik, one of the sturdiest protagonists of self-reconstruction ideology and non-resistance, kept the P'yŏngyang branch of the Sin'ganhoe out of the Kwangju uprising and succeeded in maintaining the coherence of his branch up to the final dissolution (which the P'yŏngyang delegates voted against).

In the midst of these political vicissitudes, the self-reconstruction ideals were maintained by two main Protestant organisations: the Suyang Tonguhoe (the renamed Suyang Tongmaenghoe) and the Hŭngŏp Kurakbu. The former drew its inspiration from An Ch'angho, as the Korean branch of the Hŭngsadan. The latter, a more conservative group whose leadership included Yun Ch'iho, Shin Hŭngu and Yu Kiljun's son Yu Ŏkkyŏm, was dedicated to the development of Korean industry and modern education and tended to identify with Syngman Rhee in America and with the *kiho*, the mid-western provinces, in Korea. While both organisations grew out of the Protestant self-reconstruction tradition, it was the Suyang Tongu-hoe which strove more visibly and actively to keep the torch burning and which is the subject of this chapter.

The sociology of repentance

The setback suffered by revolutionary politics encouraged the Seoul Suyang Tongmaenghoe and the P'yŏngyang Tongu Kurakbu to amalgamate in January 1926 as the Suyang Tonguhoe. Chu Yohan, the son of the Rev. Chu Kongsam (who led the Korean Presbyterians in Tokyo) and a former leader in the Far Eastern Bureau of the Hŭngsadan in Peking, founded the Tonggwang Company in Seoul and in May commenced publication of a monthly journal, the *Tong-gwang*. As the mouthpiece of the Suyang Tonguhoe, the first issue committed itself to the promotion of the 'Three Categories of Educa-tion' first enunciated by the Ch'ŏngnyŏn Hakuhoe in 1908, and of the concepts of individual reform and public virtue.

The leading article concerned ethics: 'Above all else, we must rec-ognise that morally we have far greater flaws than other peoples. By "moral failure" we by no means refer to a lack of fidelity or filial piety or any other moral item. Rather, we refer to a fundamental lack in the very foundations of our morality.' Korean morality needed to redirect itself towards honesty, good faith, perseverance, unselfish-ness and the priority of public over private and family concerns. It had to grasp the underlying spirit of universal ethics: love, forgive-ness and mutual encouragement. Training in such was the 'essential ingredient of national revival', the 'greatest duty of every individual member of the Korean race'. As Koreans committed to self-reconstruction 'increase one by one, two by two, so our race's shrivelled roots will send forth new, sharply pointed shoots'.[5]

The Tonguhoe's methodology of change was explained in the same issue under the pseudonym Changbaek Sanin. 'Magical' ideas of in-stantaneous change were opposed with the argument that all real change follows the same principle of 'graduality'. Revolution was therefore not a sudden event created by *fiat*, but the 'consummation of a gradual process of factor piling upon factor'. Koreans were sup-plied with ten areas of need for improvement in personal and social life, with the concluding challenge: 'Before plotting any revolution, accomplish a revolution within yourself.'[6]

The stage was thus set for the public dissemination—for the first time for most Koreans on the peninsula—of An Ch'angho's polished doctrine of gradualism. From 1926 to 1931 the *Tonggwang* carried as much of An's writing, usually pseudonymously, as the Japanese censors permitted. Writing in the style of a religious prophet, An subjected the Korean race to a hard-hitting analysis of its moral and spiritual dissipation. Koreans were summoned to create a new civilisation founded on the practical ethics of Protestantism as An conceived them. Among other failures, An charged Koreans with irresponsibility towards their society, allowing it to be ruled by foreigners, destructive envy of any who achieve good or become leaders, vainglory, unreliability, mendacity and chronic disunity.[7] The remedy was to work at the apposite virtues: stewardship, mutual encouragement and trust, singlemindedness, hard work, honesty and co-operation. An harshly criticised the tendency, still prevailing after the 'vanished dream' of support from Versailles and the League of Nations, to cast about for aid among the strong nations. 'To believe only in another's strength and to live in reliance on another's strength is slavery.'[8]

The principle of national repentance had been expounded in Shanghai in an important speech titled 'Reconstruction'. Culture, or civilisation, appears in this speech as an idealist concept, almost a final cause drawing and directing human endeavour everywhere to itself. Its ethical make-up is supposedly Protestant. The 'supreme hope and end' of humankind is universal happiness, a happiness whose mother is civilisation (*munmyŏng*). Civilisation in turn is the offspring of effort put into reconstruction (*kaejo*). Though Christianity did not first introduce 'reconstruction' to humanity, for it is the 'sum of all the teachings of Confucius, Buddha, Socrates and Tolstoy', Christ had given it its sharpest expression, and had pointed the way to its fulfilment:

> What was the very first word John, who came just before Jesus, cried out to the people? 'Repent!' After that, what was the first thing of all Jesus cried out in a loud voice? Again, 'Repent!' This 'repentance' is exactly what I mean by reconstruction.

Civilisation, An continued, was 'beauty and light' set in antithesis to 'darkness and filth'. Accordingly, there was an urgent need to renovate everything in Korea: education, religion, agriculture, commerce, public works, food, customs, clothing, cities, villages and even rivers and mountains. Fully forested hills and clear running streams were necessary for housing, farming and the environment; barren hills and polluted rivers caused erosion, floods and material and spiritual impoverishment. The whole cultural edifice, and therefore the whole task of reconstruction, rested upon individual reformation. 'A reconstructive animal is my definition of a human being . . . Any who claims to be unable to undertake the work of reconstruction is not a human being, or at least only a dead one.'[9]

Although An seems to have subscribed to the not-uncommon

psychological theory that people can transform their characters by a process of deliberate repetition of good actions until the will gladly and habitually falls in line, he was sensible of the indispensible spiritual quality of 'divine love' that, according to the teachings of Christianity, must inspire the process. Where Yun Ch'iho and Yi Kwangsu defined this mainly in terms of altruism, An likened it to self-denying philanthropy; and all praised it as the slayer of egotism. In a sermon first delivered to Koreans in Shanghai, An turned to the theme of the first chapter of John's Gospel, of Christ entering the world as light shining into darkness, bearing the 'life that was the light of men'. An preached that the self-sacrificing love expressed in God's sending his only son to die for men at the hand of men was the fountainhead of all true happiness.[10] Since happiness was at once the definition of civilisation and the fruit of Christian love, the nation An envisaged was a 'Christian civilisation'. An's position may be expressed as a sylogism:

A. Christian love is the source of happiness.
B. Happiness is the mark of true civilisation.
C. Therefore Christian love is the source of true civilisation.

In that God demanded this love of all people, obedience at this point became the entrance of God into human souls, and this was the meaning of Christ's words that those who followed his commands would be in him and he in them. Hence, while in an immediate sense human survival and happiness depended on material support, as soon as the question of the knowledge necessary for the acquisition and proper use of materials was raised, it became evident that such knowledge had to be sought in a spirit of selfless love. A loveless knowledge would become a curse.[11]

An's description of the 'happy' society recalled the enthusiasm of the earlier Protestant reformers for the civic ethics they witnessed in Europe and America. Societies could be reduced to two basic types: the pitiless and cruel and the warmhearted and humane; these represented opposite poles. Korean social relationships were cold and hard as stone in family, school and the administration at all levels: 'The suffering of the Taehan race, devoid of all good will is truly worse than Hell. Taehan society is a field of thorns. There is no joy in it.' Furthermore, it was among the worst societies in the world: 'Having lived without ever a taste of a warmhearted society, we have the strength to endure an inhuman society. But let people who have lived in some other, humane society suddenly enter a cruel society like ours and they feel mortally done for.'[12] This society was then contrasted with Western societies whose greatness An attributed to harmony and goodwill. Drawing on his direct experience of American social and family life, An described a society where marriages were founded on genuine affection, children and women were treated with dignity, individual freedom was respected and where in all public life, from local administration to standing in queues, citizens acted with mutual consideration (!)[13]

The object of the Hŭngsadan, the Suyang Tonguhoe in Korea, was to become a model community of individuals united in reforming themselves and their relationships according to the above description of a warmhearted society. An Ch'angho had in mind the construction of a pilot village that would serve as a pattern for all Koreans, much the role Yun Ch'iho had envisaged for his Songdo settlement in 1907. Such a community was to attract membership from the common people and so become the instrument of national renewal. It was no accident that An fashioned the Hŭngsadan after the Presbyterian Church, requiring candidates for full membership to be sponsored by two members and to undergo training for up to six months in its principles before admission after a strict 'catechism' examination.[14] The Protestant church still bore the future Korea within it, and truth, goodness and love were to be its pillars.

Such a society required unity. Just as the Rev. Kim P'ilsu had warned that a nation divided against itself could not stand, so An Ch'angho predicted that a divided society would suffer a 'fundamental death', and appealed to the motto of the American independence movement: 'United we stand; divided we fall.' Earlier, in 1919, An had insisted that 'unity is the absolute',[15] and later advanced St Paul's comparison of communal unity with the functioning of a human body.[16] How then did this absolute of unity fit in with respect for individual liberty and conscience?

An's position on liberty was closely wedded to his notion of the spiritual origin and nature of true unity, which he had emphasised when leading the Korean National Association in America. He argued that room for the free expression of individual opinion could only be guaranteed where there existed unity on fundamental norms of human society. Such unity was spiritual and would create the atmosphere within which human liberty could breathe and social and political pluralism thrive.[17] But this pluralism was not, of course, itself an absolute: An was nowhere near accepting the type of pluralism described by Isaiah Berlin, which is premised on the non-existence of any universal or eternal value.[18] An had great faith in the processes of public opinion in a society that was educated and morally healthy. As each member of society, after consulting reason and conscience, advanced his or her own views, a body of public opinion was formed from which issued the public verdict, the nation's 'will, cry and command'. In short, spiritual unity was the source of national unity, not directly, but *via* the public opinion it enlivened.[19]

The common will had to be pursued through a concrete organisation, which in sovereign states was ideally the government headed by a chief executive. Koreans had to create their own national guardian and executor of the common will, but this touched a raw nerve: the issue of leadership. An Ch'angho's treatment of this issue reveals his idea of the relationship between liberty and unity. Realising that amongst Korea's youth a contradiction was sensed between egalitarian ideals and submission to a leader, An sought to dispel this 'misunderstanding' with the analogy of an orchestra, the beauty of whose musical harmony depended on each skilled player following the conductor. Any 'individual freedom' that conflicted with the interests of national unity was to be dismissed as 'self-centered and egotistical'.[20] Thus was the Pauline metaphor of the human body to be understood. There is, of course, some ambiguity here, characteristic of attempts to combine an individualistic ethic with utilitarian social thought, over which was the 'ultimate beneficiary' (as Benjamin Schwartz expresses it) of individual labour and perfection—the individual or the social (or national) unit.[21]

An Ch'angho was obviously interested in creating a 'good' society in both the ethical and material sense, and his analogy of an orchestra recalls L. T. Hobhouse's view that a person is properly free 'when he is controlled by principles and rules which all society must obey'.[22] But an important qualification must be made. An would not have been altogether happy with Hobhouse's statement that freedom is 'not so much a right of the individual as a necessity of society'.[23] His exhortations also reflect his belief that Korean society was rotten precisely because traditional social thinking had not respected the rightful freedom and sanctity of the individual. To be sure, freedom was necessary for a happy society, but social reality was a whole: at the centre of the whole was the individual, whose rights and dignity were inherent because they had been given by God. Where methodology of change and social reconstruction was concerned, An was an individualist, and from the mid-1920s to his death in 1938 he maintained a consistent viewpoint on such issues.

The determining feature of An's individualism was the ethico-spiritual theory of the origin of human liberty which, from the 1890s, he shared with Yun Ch'iho. He was therefore opposed to the 'immoral' idea of utilising egotistical drives to create a well-ordered society. Even if efficient, a society so engendered could not be happy—that is, the individuals of the society could not be happy—because the source of happiness and true civilisation was Christian love, which was at the opposite pole of egotism. A striking and rather surprising omission in the nationalist literature of all streams is any consequential reference to Rousseau. The Protestants themselves had valued Western 'Protestant' individualism from the outset as the antithesis of the selfishness they detected in Korea's family-centred society. Even capitalism had been envisaged, rather eccentrically, not as a motive to personal gain or as enlightened self-interest, but as service to others. The Korean Protestants' concept of liberty had no place for an untrammelled freedom, since true freedom was constrained by self-denying love. As such, at least in An's view, it did not threaten, but actually ensured, unity. The individualism he described for *Tong-gwang* readers was conscious of individual responsibility and involved sacrifice, compassion, fidelity to conscience and reason, respect for others and commitment to social welfare.[24]

Agreement on the spiritual foundations of unity did not entail uniformity among Protestants of opinion on the question of the relation between individual and society. Not all were methodological individualists, and from August 1926 *Tonggwang* serialised the writings of Kim Yun'gyŏng, who gave the subjects of liberty and national culture an Hegelian twist. Soon after his return from doctoral studies in philosophy in Japan in 1922, an Hegelian Society was formed, and it briefly appeared that certain lines in An's thought would be transformed into an all-embracing doctrine of the state as the highest manifestation of national spirit, the supreme representative ot the Absolute Ego. But Kim stopped short of portraying the state as the father of culture which, besides playing into the hands of the Japanese, would have reversed the self-reconstruction tradition on the relationship between the nation and the state. Instead he concentrated on the individual and society, national unity and universal civilisation or cosmic consciousness. Much of Kim's argument dealing with philosophical categories is abstruse and probably had minimal impact on Korean nationalism. But Kim also gave strong support to ethical nationalism; he was rivalled only by Yi Kwangsu and Chu Yohan as a communicator of Hŭngsadan ideals.

Kim Yun'gyŏng implicitly repudiated the former Protestant nationalist subscription to a social Darwinist definition of social and national life as survival of the (morally) fittest, and heralded the adoption of an organic conception of society as mutual aid. Since Kim reasoned that all 'concepts are reflections of the world outside the ego', the essence of the self embraced social factors. All reality was thus interrelated and social misery was the result of disunity caused by individuals attempting to live without reference to society. Social conflict was a disease, not the source of evolutionary progress in history, whereas national unity produced a healthy civilisation, the grounds of all liberty. Hegel's teaching that the moral quality of an individual increases according to the extent to which one favours the absolute over the relative ego 'contains a profound truth', for the relative world is akin to Hell. Those who realise the absolute ego within themselves, who identify with and live for society, have found their true self and true freedom.[25]

Although Kim portrayed society as a moral structure, he adhered to the view of the individual as a cell whose only possible fulfilment was in its belonging to the social organism. In this he appealed to the British idealist philosopher, T. H. Green.[26] By suggesting that the individual was not an ontologically independent member of society, Kim proposed a different solution to the problem of social relationships from An Ch'angho's vision of a 'humane society'. Kim's monistic society consisted of humans related to each other by virtue of their ultimately indistinguishable identity with the Absolute Ego of the social organism. An's vision was of a society of distinct, indivisible personalities united by the only power capable of relating such individual beings, namely spiritual or divine love. The body was only a metaphor to convey a message; it was not intended to imply that society was a literal organism. An rejoiced in the distinct identity of persons, wherein lay their inviolability and their opportunity to 'deny' themselves, and his unambiguous monotheism makes his position more authentically Protestant.[27] But, although the Hegelian terminology was later dropped, An's approach temporarily lost ground to a collectivist liberalism among Protestants.

Inasmuch as the Japanese drastically limited the scope of nationalistic activity, this divergence of viewpoint had little immediate practical effect. Kim Yun'gyŏng, in any case, enthusiastically advanced An's 'Four Great Principles' of truth, ability, loyalty and courage. Moreover, the two were allies in a crucial area: both repudiated race as the grounds of national unity and reconstruction. An Ch'angho regarded the belief in racial grounds of unity to be the 'ruin of humankind'.[28] Kim Yun'gyŏng struck out against the 'narrow militarist' view of nationalism that defined itself in terms of an enemy. Although for the present 'the nation is the greatest manifestation of united, common consciousness', Kim yearned for the realisation of the Stoic and Christian ideal of a higher consciousness embracing all humanity. This ideal, he complained, was frequently misunderstood by narrow nationalists as anti-nationalism. But 'just as family life is not inconsistent with national life . . . so the common, united life of all humanity is not a contradiction of national life and neither is national life inconsistent with the common life of all mankind'. The health of one nation contributed to the health of the whole world, and this, rather than racial hatred, had to inspire Korean nationalism.[29]

The influence of this position inside Korea is certain, but it is difficult to quantify. The Japanese noted that Hŭngsadan ideas had already made considerable inroads among the 'rising, progressive youth' in the P'yŏngan and Hwanghae provinces by the end of 1920.[30] It might be expected that the rise of socialism and the levelling off of culturalism by 1925 would have diminished this support to some degree. Yet by that common but irrational law of nationalism, An

Ch'angho's fame was only enhanced by his extended absence from his homeland, so that as his words appeared in print they were devoured hungrily, nourishing a modest revival of self-reconstruction ideology among Koreans. Until it was banned in February 1933, the *Tong-gwang* attracted supportive articles on ethical nationalism, personal perfection and national unity from many influential Protestants, not all of them members of the Suyang Tonguhoe. Contributors included the Protestants Kim Chihwan, Kim Ch'angse, Yi Yunje, Mun Ilp'yŏng, Kim Ch'angdŏk, Sŏ Chaep'il, Chŏn Yŏngt'aek, Yi Sangjae, Yun Ch'iho and the Osan College director Myŏng Ihang, and also Christian socialists such as Yi Sunt'aek, Pak Hŭido, Kim Yŏngje and Paek Namun. The support of Cho Mansik, fast emerging as the most influential Protestant and nationalist in Korea, was well known, while the basic concurrence of Ch'ŏndogyo and Buddhist leaders such as Yi Chongnin and Han Yongun extended the movement's influence even further.[31] The Christian church itself had been growing steadily since 1920, as prominent Christians such as the Rev. O Hwayŏng, a Methodist member of the 'Thirty-Three', attracted large crowds to the evangelistic meetings the Rev. O commenced on release from prison late in 1922.[32] By 1935 the Christian population approached half a million out of a population of twenty million and was the only religion recording growth among the Koreans.[33]

$= 2 \%$

The move to collective liberalism

Political non-resistance was susceptible to manipulation by the Japanese. The Japanese *Seoul Press*, for example, had represented Yun Ch'iho's argument against the practicality of the March First Movement as counsel to the weak to submit to the strong and forget about independence.[34] In November 1924, the head of the Government-General Police Affairs Bureau, Mr Maruyama, had delivered a speech in support of the then pro-Japanese *Chosŏn Daily*, in which he acknowledged the threat posed to the administration by the belief that steady, peaceful advancement of Korean culture would achieve independence. It was imperative that a way be found to harmonise cultural movements with Government-General objectives. The Japanese, too, were anxious that Koreans be persuaded against racial particularism: 'We must instil in the Koreans an awareness of the need to subscribe to a higher idea than subservience to a feverish search for the Fatherland.'[35] As the number of industrial labourers virtually doubled over the decade, from 55000 in 1920 to 102000 in 1930, the Japanese became even more anxious that the educated classes favour political non-resistance tactics.

Opponents of the non-resistance strategy were quick to notice this

vulnerability, and accused its apologists of lulling national consciousness to sleep on behalf of the Japanese. The most sensational attack
was delivered in a short story written by Shin Ch'aeho in Peking in
1926. Shin, a leading intellectual of the time, presided over the rise of
anarchist thought in Korea.[36] Since he had been an active supporter
of the pre-annexation Sinminhoe and Ch'ŏngnyŏn Hakuhoe, his
attack, which included a bitter repudiation of Christ's teachings, was
all the more important.

In Shin's allegorical story, *The Great Battle of the Dragons*, there
are two dragons, one named Miri and the other simply Dragon. On
one level Miri represents subservience, which Shin found in traditional Eastern philosophy and in Christianity, while Dragon personifies
the revolutionary, anarchic spirit flowing from the West. Miri arrives
on the scene in 1868, the year of the Japanese Meiji Restoration, and,
by soft talk about security and survival, seduces the people to accept
colonial rule. Suddenly, Christ appears in a village church and begins
spreading the 'fraud and trickery' by which he had already deceived
the West. An evil sorcerer, Christ bewitches people's minds:

> By lies, 'Blessed are they that suffer, blessed are the poverty-stricken', he
> deceives those who had lost their nation and the unpropertied masses into
> thinking they were holy, thus making them forget their real enemy and
> dream of a sham heaven, and so granting every convenience to the power-
> holders and rulers . . .[37]

The Dragon slays Christ on behalf of the people who rise up and
demolish all structures of society and administration and religion,
proclaiming 'all things on earth to be the common possession of all'.
The people thereupon 'named the whole globe the Kingdom of Earth
and announced the total severance of all intercourse with heaven'.[38]
The 'diehards' who remain searching for God are mocked as 'faithful
slaves'.[39]

By the mid-1920s, Shin Ch'aeho was moving away from a statist
form of nationalism, for he desired to free the nation—and all
nations—not by installing a Korean government in place of the
Japanese regime, but by destroying all 'states' without exception.[40]
He saw in Christianity, however, a double obstacle to freedom, for it
not only prevented resistance to the real enemy of state power but
also taught that the people's 'real' enemy was the evil that was in
them—a 'superstition'. In a back-handed way Shin acknowledged, as
had Mr Maruyama, that Christianity and the self-cultivation movement were a force in Korean society to be reckoned with. Combined
with criticism from the right and left wings, Shin's charge that the
self-reconstruction movement was an effectual prop to the Japanese
regime fuelled debate within the Suyang Tonguhoe over the ever-
present problem of its political philosophy.

During the latter half of 1926, Cho Pyŏngok, a Presbyterian who
had earned a doctorate in economics at Columbia University, strongly urged that the Suyang Tonguhoe should reorganise as an explicitly
political movement.[41] Cho had been an active member of the Hŭngsadan in the United States and his views reflected the move there, led
by one Kwak Imt'ae, for more radical and direct action. At the same
time, Chu Yohan's brother Chu Yosŏp led a faction within the Far
Eastern Bureau of the Hŭngsadan in Shanghai which campaigned for
the adoption of socialism. The Far Eastern Bureau almost split over
the issue, while in Nanking the Hŭngsadan's Tongmyŏng Institute
was on the verge of collapse due to conflicts between Sŏnu Hyŏk and
Ch'a Risŏk.[42] In Manchuria, the Hŭngsadan leader, the Rev. Kim
Pyŏngjo (one of the 'Thirty-Three') was afflicted by a temporary ban
imposed on his church school in Hsing-ching and on cultivation
rights,[43] while the unsettled political climate in China and the 1925
Mitsoya Agreement severely limited Korean nationalist activities
from Nanking to Manchuria. In Korea, Chu Yohan himself concluded that the emphasis on self-cultivation was a grave hindrance to
attracting youth, and suggested it was time to wind up the 'cultivation
of real strength' line and commence political training for direct
revolutionary manoeuvres.[44]

Dismayed by the theoretical division of the Hŭngsadan, An Ch'angho called Chu Yohan to Nanking for discussions in September 1926.
An shared with Chu his unease lest the Hŭngsadan become a politically partisan body. As individuals, members would naturally hold
their respective political views, but should the Hŭngsadan nail its col-
ours to any single political mast, there was a serious danger of it
disintegrating in the wake of any change in the direction of the
ideological wind. Its fate must not be linked to the fortunes of any
political faction. The Hŭngsadan had a distinct, indispensible role in
the independence struggle, An insisted, but allowed that when a
broad revolutionary party was formed–a united front?—it could
positively aid the revolution as one section of the larger movement.
Chu seems to have consented to this, and he returned to Korea.[45] An
himself toured the branches in North China and Manchuria in 1927
and then wrote to the American branch on the issue. 'I have already
said this time and again,' he chided, 'but placed as we are in a revolutionary era we shall inevitably have to engage in some revolutionary
movement. But for this there will need to be a special revolutionary
organ distinct from the self-cultivation organs.'[46]

In January 1927, the Suyang Tonguhoe leaders resolved on a campaign to increase membership and reassert the timeliness and relevance of their approach. The *Tonggwang* issue for that month carried
an announcement under a revamped prospectus of the creation of
the Tonggwang Support Group. The vision was to expand its

membership 'to many tens of thousands', and to achieve a secure economic base. But there may have been a strategic consideration behind this move. It is probable that the leaders had got wind of the united front movement which would declare itself as the Sin'gan-hoe the following month, and wished to be able to consider Tongu-hoe policy towards it from a position of strength. In July 1927, Chu Yohan published a report on the movement which suggests the response to the membership drive was positive.

Chu's reassertion of Tonguhoe principles, however, involved a definite change of emphasis away from individuals to engagement in social structures. Whilst affirming that 'Koreans fighting for the construction of a new destiny must first possess sound personalities', Chu also argued that the social environment decisively determined individual character. Indeed, he charged the self-cultivation movement with forgetting the social dimension. In a leading article in July, Chu stated that the people's way of life:

> has been socialised to the extent that it is now recognised that since the individual cannot depart from society, it is not a matter of an individual's society but of a society's individual. Leaders of cultivation movements must therefore never forget that any individual reconstruction that does not involve social reconstruction is totally ineffective . . .
>
> Since it is difficult for individuals in an unhealthy society to become healthy themselves, it is only after a society is made healthy that individuals can be made genuinely healthy . . . The essence of our movement then, is to prepare sound combat units for the construction of this healthy society.
>
> Our path is in this direction alone. From makeshift personal reconstruction to social reconstruction![47]

On the theoretical level this is not particularly well thought out. It shares the ambiguity common to all attempts to blend the abstract with the concrete in social theory. On the practical level, it proved even more confusing. How were Koreans supposed to conceive of movements to change social structures if not as political activity? And if political, it had to be political in a specific sense. It was not sufficient to explain, as Chu quickly did, that the basis of change was still ethical and that the only allegiance asked for was to truth and goodness.[48] For whatever the dynamism behind change, social change itself was inescapably political, and what political platform did Chu propose? But of course Chu was purposely not proposing a political platform, and the result was an uncertain compromise.

Amidst the ambiguity, one thing at least emerged with some clarity: the Tonguhoe movement, for all its moralism, was to be understood as a movement that was directly related to the struggle for independence. Social reconstruction was the means. To be sure, this social reconstruction meant neither Shin Ch'aeho's demolition of its formal structures nor the Marxist program of social power passing to the proletariat. It was still a matter of philanthropy. Chu issued a call to all citizens supposedly already equipped—specialists, skilled workers, scientists, businessmen, ministers and teachers—to band together and create the new social environment. If 'sound' were substituted for 'free', Chu's principle might appear similar to the Marxist doctrine that the 'free development of each is the condition of the free development of all', for both are collectivist in methodology. But any similarity between Marxism and Chu's position stops here. In the former, development supposes a material base; in the latter, it assumes an ethical base. In the former, being becomes aware of itself when it produces; in the latter, it does so when it grasps its ethical relation to the social organism. Aware that it was this ethical stand which had been the cause of misunderstanding, Chu was determined to demonstrate that his movement's ethics were not accomplices of the ruling powers, as its critics claimed. Ethics were a vehicle of resistance:

> We must discard the morality of obedience and adopt the morality of resistance. Obeying one's parents is 'filial piety'; well, we shall have to throw filial piety out. And if obedience to the king be called loyalty, we shall have to throw out loyalty also. If obedience to seniority, to power-holders, to the rich be called morality, then we cannot but do away with morality.
>
> This is a time for resistance. Today is the time to rise up under the banner of revolt.[49]

Chu's call for resistance and ethical radicalism was an attempt to endow the self-reconstruction movement with backbone, to restore the cutting edge which the reconstruction movement, with its Protestant values, had formerly owned, to sound out once more a prophetic note to Koreans to break free from their past. It was also a challenge to colonial power (and it is surprising the censors allowed the article to be printed), which would also be swept away before an ethical fervor implacable in its loyalty to truth and goodness. It was designed to dispel doubts over the relevance of self-reconstruction 'moralism' and to present it instead as the centre of uncompromising resistance to the very values—shared by Korean and Japanese alike—which were keeping Korea enslaved. This was the Korean 'satyagraha,' the force of truth no power of evil could extinguish.

Chu's articles appeared all the more radical to many Koreans because the ethical focus had shifted from the individual or human nature to the social system. Chu was not advancing the notion of a model community as a 'plausibility structure' so much as the theory that the social milieu was responsible for the privations of humanity. The connection of the Tonghuoe with pertinent Protestant doctrines on the nature and origin of sin, for example, was at this juncture at best tenuous. But this failed to elicit discussion. The practical effect of Chu's 'reassertion' of Hŭngsadan principles was, in conjunction with Kim Yun'gyŏng's Hegelianism, to popularise methodological collectivism with a liberalist stamp. Although Chu himself hesitated here, others came quickly to the logical conclusion that initiating change at the level of structure was really direct political intervention and therefore required a common political stand.

Whereas the Hŭngsadan branches abroad remained relatively weak, in 1928 the Suyang Tonguhoe grew in strength and numbered among its supporters members of several political organisations and many socialists, albeit 'ethical' socialists.[50] In 1929 a reorganisation occurred. 'Suyang' (meaning moral cultivation) was withdrawn from the title of the organisation, which thenceforth was known simply as the Tonguhoe; the words 'Chosŏn new culture movement' in the Constitution were changed to 'new Chosŏn construction movement'; and an article was inserted describing the body as one detachment of the whole revolutionary forces.[51] The Central Committee set about consciously focusing on independence and in February 1931 agreed upon a four-year plan directed to that end which bore the imprint of leftist political ideology. It was further agreed that any articles advocating home-rule or political accommodation and any critical of socialism would be barred from future *Tonggwang* issues.[52] The view that national society has meaning only in relation to its political institutions and that, therefore, independent statehood is vital to national reconstruction, came to enjoy dominance among Tonguhoe members.

But only temporarily: the reorganisation had come at an inopportune time. The Great Depression weakened the Tonguhoe's economic base, and the Japanese operations in Manchuria were accompanied in Korea by the termination of Saitō's 'cultural' politics, accelerated industrialisation of northern Korea, and renewed suppression of nationalist and communist movements. 'Circuit lectures' were banned, and the February 1933 issue of *Tonggwang*, its 40th issue, proved to be its last. The united front movement, which had in part inspired the politicisation of the Tonguhoe, had folded already in May 1931 amidst charges of heedless and divisive politics. Some on the political right resorted to terrorism, while the communist movement, having failed in its three attempts to reorganise a party inside Korea between 1929 and 1932, centred itself once more on Koreans in exile. Among Protestants in general the pendulum swung back to non-political options. Self-reconstruction nationalists returned to their former conviction that the revolutionary struggle began with personal renewal. At the same time, they began to distance themselves from socialism and opposed the Marxist–Leninist form of revolution.

A Christian theory of revolution

In February 1931, *Tonggwang* published An Ch'angho's 'Plea to Youth concerning Perfection of Character and Training in Unity'. An reiterated that the 'fundamental cause of all our failures is the feebleness of our national unity. This was the cause, too, of our initial collapse.'[53] In May, in response to the splintering and fall of the Sin'ganhoe, An published a second letter. Surely the cause of Korea's tragedy was now abundantly clear: 'If we act together we shall survive; if not, we shall perish—that is our situation!' All else was secondary, and all else secondary could be achieved only after unity was attained.[54]

Ironically, in April 1932, An Ch'angho was seized by Japanese police in Shanghai during a raid on Koreans there in retaliation against terrorist activities directed by Kim Ku. An was extradited to Korea, and although no connection was established with the terrorist Aegukdan in Shanghai, he was sentenced to penal servitude in Taegu Prison, where he remained until January 1936. Four months after his arrest, Chu Yohan composed a leading article for *Tonggwang* which revealed renewed commitment to An's position on the nature of the Hŭngsadan's mission.

> There are many who consider the Tonguhoe to be a political organisation. This is fundamentally in error. All criticism which ensues from this mistaken view must necessarily miss the mark . . . Though one part of our national power, it would be a departure from the facts to identify it as a force of 'nationalism' where that signifies certain *fixed essential political features*. [Emphasis added.]

Whilst some might mock it as an 'Everlasting Retirement Centre', Chu was convinced the Tonguhoe creed was vital to Korea's future, for two reasons:

> First, the record of Korean social life over the last 300 years or even the last four decades, shows there is historical value in 'establishing trust', 'inculcating the spirit of unity', 'unity in quality before quantity' and so on . . .
> Second, under the present circumstances in Korea, there is major cultural–historical significance in the Tonguhoe enterprise . . . Depending on one's point of view, one may regard this as the root and trunk of all other movements.

The reason for the Tonguhoe's insistence on rejecting political colourings was not that politics was downgraded, but stemmed rather from a recognition of the importance of politics as a distinct field of action in its own right. Moreover, was it not self-evident that in Korea an overt, legal body such as the Tonguhoe could not become politically active? Reiterating the Tonguhoe objection to 'narrow' views of nationalism, Chu concluded:

> The political inclinations of a Tonguhoe member will be decided at that point when he or she participates in some political activity . . . And that activity will be pursued not through the Tonguhoe but through a separate, political body . . . To judge and criticise a program professing to be just one part as though it were the whole is, whether intended or not, a kind of demagoguery.[55]

Likewise, it was demagoguery for any particular political camp to claim exclusive rights over the nation, and so the Tonguhoe and Protestants in general finally expressed open opposition to the Marxist–Leninist doctrine of revolution. The self-reconstruction emphasis on social reconciliation was, of course, a 'political' viewpoint that was antagonistic to any class-conflict theory. In January 1931, Yi Kwang-su had already urged awareness of the distinctiveness of the Tonguhoe's philosophy of change. He attacked the Korean communists in Manchuria for bringing terrible suffering upon innocent Koreans, women and children, through their methods, and he opposed the violence of their spirit with Christ's command not to hate but to love one's foes.[56] In the YMCA journal, *Ch'ŏngnyŏn*, Yi drew a sharp distinction between the Christian and Marxist–Leninist revolutionary methods. Concerned that the term 'revolution' was used by many to mean only a violent class confrontation, and aware that even Tonguhoe committee members were swayed by political radicalism, Yi urged that the 'Christian' definition be accepted as the genuine one. Yi presented the differences between the two forms of revolution as four major contrasts:

1. Christianity prescribes prayer for those who hate you and love towards enemies. Marxist–Leninism demands hatred of the 'bourgeoisie'.
2. Christian revolution is founded upon meeting class power and antagonism with love and upon suffering oneself to be killed. Marxist–Leninist revolution means violent destruction of the opposing class.
3. Christianity binds its army to a cross, Marxist–Leninism to guns.
4. The eyes of Christian revolutionaries are filled with tears of love and forgiveness, those of Marxist–Leninists with fires of hatred and vengeance.[57]

Far from being original, the Marxist–Leninist theory of revolution was merely faithful to the dismal pattern of revolution throughout history, a pattern that always failed to make good its promises because the ends were ruined in advance by the means. Yi cited Gandhi as one pursuing the example of Christ, yet he questioned whether even he attained the full Christian attitude, which went beyond non-violent resistance to positive prayer for one's enemy. But how and what was Christ trying to revolutionise? Not bourgeois or proletarian society, or any other society based on violence, strife and evil, but rather: 'He purposes to root out, exterminate and commit wholly to the flames all thoughts, desires and habits of malice, belligerence and violence residing in the heart of humankind.' Since this demanded unyielding determination, it implied a far-from-peaceful revolution. But whereas Marxist–Leninists filled rivers with the blood of their victims, Christians had to fill them with their own blood.[58]

Yi Kwangsu's reverence for Tolstoy was known in Korea since at least 1912, and his novels, such as *Chaesaeng* (regeneration, or resurrection), reflect direct Tolstoyan influence. In 1932, aged 40, Yi wrote his novel *Hŭk* (Mother Earth), which was serialised in the *Tonga Daily*. The hero of the novel was a peasant youth named Hŏ Sung, who had left for university training and later 'returned to the land' to live among and enlighten the rural people. By another author of his day, Hŏ Sung might have been portrayed as a fiery socialist revolutionary, but Yi's character embodied the ideals of the self-sacrificing 'friend of the people,' a mystical lover of the land and its sons.

From this point onwards, a note of resignation, almost of passivity, can be sensed in Yi's writings, which may reflect his growing enamourment with Buddhist spirituality, as well as the low morale of nationalists in general in the mid-1930s. However that may be, although he dwelt on much the same themes as Tolstoy, his writings lack Tolstoy's toughness and vigor. Nevertheless, Yi Kwangsu's writings on 'Christian' revolution were part of a conscious return by Protestant leaders to the spiritual roots of their ideology, prompted by the failure of the united front.

During the final one and a half years of the Sin'ganhoe movement, there had occurred an unexpected rapprochement between such Protestants as the 'bourgeois' Yun Ch'iho and the 'socialist' Pak Hŭido.[59] Between 1931 and 1933 a number of groups formed under the leadership of Yun Ch'iho, An Chaehong, Yi Kwangsu and Cho Mansik, all aimed at the elusive ideal of unity. These attempts were mostly frustrated by the old rivalries between the radical left and the culturalists and between the Christians and Ch'ŏndogyo adherents, and the only groups to get off the ground were those organised by or in conjunction with Yun Ch'iho, being the least 'political' of them all. But a united, successful stand against the political–revolutionary and rightist tone of Shin Hŭngu's Positive Youth Corps from 1933 to 1935 by the Tonguhoe, Hŭngŏp Kurakbu and the YMCA enlivened hopes for Protestant nationalist unity.[60] On New Year's Day 1936, Cho Mansik wrote an article for the *Shin Tonga*, the cultural journal of the *Tonga Daily*, on the reconstitution of a central organisation. After outlining a comprehensive program of urban and rural reform in industry, education, culture and social welfare, Cho proposed the formation of a central organ to co-ordinate these activities in country

and city. He insisted that all such activity be based on 'reform of
lifestyle'.[61] In a further article, Cho reaffirmed that repentance was
the only foundation of worthwhile social change and called upon
young people to dedicate their talents, possessions and energy to the
reconstruction of the nation.[62] Cho deliberately forwarded an ethical
basis for revolution and denied that present action found justification
only in immediate, visible historical results. At the same time, Yun
Ch'iho added his summons to 'throw away all factionalism and adopt
a common, united stand'.[63]

In January 1936 also, An Ch'angho was released from goal. At a
gathering of nationalists, An immediately launched into a defence of
self-reconstruction principles:

> I am aware there is much to do at this time . . . But whatever we may do, I
> believe that revolution of character is the key to it all. I mean the trans-
> formation of the people . . . You may mock this as some Ch'unwŏn [Yi
> Kwangsu]-style 'national reconstruction theory,' but even so, I believe that
> revolution of the personality is what is needed most just now . . . I agree
> that unless the evil system is abolished it is impossible to produce this good
> character. But who is it that will rid us of the evil system if not 'character'?
> And what sort of social revolution is achieved by good-for-nothing charac-
> ters? It all goes back to revolution of the personality . . . Without revolu-
> tion in character, even if one does abolish an evil social system, it will be
> followed by another bad system . . . If the soil is bad, no matter how good
> the seed, it is still bad.[64]

An then sought out Cho Mansik, Paek Kwansu, Yi Kwangsu, Kim
Sŏngsu, Kim Pyŏngno, Yŏ Unhyŏng (now back in Korea) and other
Protestant colleagues to discuss action on Cho's proposals.[65]

Since An was associated with the Tonguhoe and Yun Ch'iho and
An Chaehong with the Hŭngŏp Kurakbu, Cho Mansik, formally
affiliated to neither, was the ideal focus for Protestant unity. In
February he again wrote on the formation of a central co-ordinating
body[66] and followed this up with a speech at the Sŏnch'ŏn YMCA
which was reported in Ch'ŏngnyŏn in April. In the latter, Cho
stressed that the proclamation of the Gospel was not just one among
other conditions but the alpha and omega of national revival. He
urged wholehearted support for the 'one district, one church' campaign, which he expected would give great impetus to the task of
Christianising the social life of the nation. He appealed for large-scale
evangelisation and for Korea's Protestants to take the lead in uniting
the people in social holiness. The Korean nation was to be founded
on a common allegiance to the 'ideal Great Man', who was Christ.[67]
In the midst of despair and loss of ideals, the church once again had
to stand at the centre of national life to unite the nation around the
task of 'seeking first our people in righteousness'.[68]

Cho acknowledged that, standing in the way of ideals, there were various material and circumstantial problems which had to be taken seriously. But he expressed confidence that the human spirit could surmount these obstacles if individuals, through prayer, were empowered by God. Cho took issue with the Marxists here:

> According to the Marxist view where the material life controls the mental or spiritual life, there is, they say, some possibility of changing [people's ideals]. But in fact, people change their ideals very easily for any reason: the propertied due to their property, the unpropertied due to their lack of property, the learned because of their learning and the ignorant because of their ignorance.[69]

Since true, stable ideals were spiritually inspired and maintained, of all legacies, Christian faith was the greatest that the present generation could pass on to its descendants.[70] The change that would ensue in social relations was the meaning of 'saving people from their sins'.[71] Cho's message was supported also by a number of independent Christians, including the disciples of Uchimura Kanzō, Kim Kyoshin and Ham Sŏkhŏn, a graduate of Osan College who is today the foremost Quaker leader in South Korea.

As a leading exponent of the ethical self-reconstruction ideology and the most widely respected and least tainted with parochialism of the Protestant nationalists, Cho Mansik revived the belief of the Protestant church in its role as the reconstructive community. But Cho was principally a man of action, and his popularity and influence derived less from his rather infrequent appearances in print than from his demonstration of the practicality of the self-reconstruction ideal by applying it to a practical area of existence: economics. Culturalism was only a part of the self-reconstruction program, and it was in the economic field that its position in the nationalist landscape of the 1920s and 1930s emerged most clearly.

7 Economic reconstruction: The ideal on trial

Economic reconstruction shared equal place with education and political training on the 1896 Independence Club and 1907 Sinminhoe platforms. It absorbed much of the attention of Yu Kiljun and Namgung Ŏk before the annexation in 1910, and industrial education surrendered priority only to religious instruction in Yun Ch'iho's Songdo Han-Yŏng College. Both Yi Sŭnghun and Cho Mansik had first celebrated their discovery of the new faith and learning by embarking on commercial enterprises, while trade, industry and economic mobility became emblematic of the Protestant communities in the northwestern provinces in particular.[1] In accordance with the earlier Ch'ŏngnyŏn Hakuhoe approach, Yi Kwangsu had likewise emphasised that both economic and cultural reconstruction were equally urgent in his "National Statecraft" theses of 1924.

The most tangible economic reminder of the Koreans' colonial status was, of course, their exclusion from the economic direction of their society. Faithful to their ethico-spiritual analysis of Korea's subjection, Protestant self-reconstruction nationalists reminded their compatriots that it was the absence of a sound economic national base which first invited foreign economic predation. Self-reliance or self-sufficiency became the watchword of their economic programs, and the Korean Products Promotion Society inaugurated by Cho Mansik in 1922 was the largest and most explicit embodiment of their principles. As such, the society engendered considerable debate among nationalists and socialists of all shades. Before the movement itself is examined, we must turn briefly to its economic context.

Economic background

The Japanese Oriental Development Company, a semi-official agency of the Government-General, began acquiring Korean farmlands in 1907. Its land holdings increased dramatically between 1910 and 1931 from approximately 11000 hectares to 123000 hectares; by 1920 it already owned 77000 hectares.[2] There is some disagreement about how much was eventually owned by the Japanese, but a recent study estimates that total Japanese holdings peaked at a little over 25 per cent of arable land.[3] Given that the Japanese in Korea at the time numbered only 3 per cent of the total population (of between seventeen and nineteen million, about 80 per cent were rural), and that these were mostly bureaucrats, patrolmen and soldiers, it is evident that a small number of Japanese directly controlled a sizeable share of Korean agriculture.

Until the operation of the Yen Bloc economy of the 1930s, priority was given to agricultural industry. The most intensive agricultural development occurred during the 1920s, when the Rice Production Expansion Plan was implemented in the wake of the 1918 and 1920 rice riots in Japan. This plan was designed to achieve imperial self-sufficiency in rice and to solve the problem of rising food prices following World War I.[4] Hence although rice output in Korea almost doubled between 1910 and 1938, export of rice to Japan in the same period rose twenty-fold, accounting for 40 per cent of Korea's annual yield. Korean rice consumption, on the other hand, declined by almost half; rice was replaced mainly by millet imported from Manchuria.[5] In 1913 the Japanese noted that Korean farmers even in the capital province of Kyŏnggi often subsisted on 'the roots of grasses and the tender bark of trees',[6] and Governor-General Ugaki observed a similar situation in the 1930s. As agricultural development moved apace, the proportion of farmers tilling their own soil declined, and tenancy increased between 1922 and 1933 from 40.6 per cent to 55.2 per cent of rural households.[7] Excluded from land and labour opportunities, from the 1920s farmers were obliged to emigrate in large numbers to Manchuria, Mongolia, North China, Hawaii and Japan. Nearly 140000 Koreans emigrated to Manchuria between 1920 and 1929, while the number of Korean labourers in Japan (mainly in Ōsaka) rose from less than 30000 in 1920 to over 230 000 in 1933.[8]

Non-agricultural industry showed a steady quantitative increase from pre-annexation levels, with the construction of railways and the development of mining. Zaibatsu firms—Mitsui, Mitsubishi and Nagoya—established themselves in Korea in the mid-1920s to augment beer, paper, flour, cement, magnesium, tungsten, nitrogen and hydro-electric industries, as well as to develop the existing textile, iron and coal industries.[9] On the heels of the Great Depression the Government-General implemented rapid industrialisation through its North Korea Exploitation Plan; thus social dislocation derived from structural change in industry became a feature of the later 1930s.

The overriding economic grievance of Korean nationalists in the 1920s was the Government-General stranglehold on enterprise, both rural and urban. The only large-scale Korean enterprises which succeeded without openly pledging loyalty to Japan were the Protestant Kim Sŏngsu's Kyŏngsang Textile Company (Seoul), the Kyŏngnam Bank (Pusan), the Paeksan Trading Company (Pusan) and the Honam Bank (Southwestern Korea). Even the latter two were forced to dissolve or merge with Japanese enterprises in 1927 and 1941 respectively.[10] (Small and medium enterprises fared somewhat better in Seoul and P'yŏngyang.) Grievances were exacerbated at employment level by a discriminatory wage system which left Korean workers at least 40 per cent poorer than their Japanese counterparts in Korea.[11] Korea's economic dependence on Japan is evinced by the fact that by 1931, 95.1 per cent of Korean exports went to Japan whilst 80 per cent of her imports came from Japan to absorb zaibatsu surplusses.[12] In short, the Korean economy was a colonial economy: its determining features were controlled by and for the Japanese, while Koreans supplied relatively underpaid services and labour.

Yet a distinction vital to any analysis of Korean economic nationalism must be drawn between the grievances of the rural and urban labourers and those of the new Korean entrepreneurial and industrial capitalist class of the 1920s and 1930s. The labourers' grievances related to specific issues: wages, working hours and conditions, job security, tenants' rights and taxation burdens. Such grievances concern worker exploitation, and are what one finds in periods of industrial and commercial modernisation in any society, whether colonial or not. The frequency of labour disputes in Korea increased hand in hand with industrialisation. Whereas only six strikes occurred in 1912, the 1930s witnessed an average of 170 strikes per year.[13] Especially after 1919, these strikes were directed against both Korean and Japanese industries, including the aforementioned Kyŏngsŏng Textile Company, whose owner, Kim Sŏngsu, was a prominent cultural nationalist.

The grievances of the new industrial capitalists, however, arose from frustration at having to compete with the Japanese for control of the economy. Up to 1919 the Government-General had deliberately hindered private capital investment and denied Koreans the opportunities afforded Japanese settlers.[14] After 1919, partly in response to the March First Movement and partly due to industrial capital surplusses in Japan and increased overseas market opportunities after World War I, crucial changes were made in the colonial economy. In his study of Korean capital formation, Carter Eckert argues that the abolition of most tariff barriers and the repeal of the 1910 *Company Law* in 1920 'substantially reduced' the political barrier to capitalist activity among Koreans.[15] A number of Koreans saw in this their opportunity to challenge Japan's industrial paramountcy on the peninsula.

There was a serious political difficulty here. Governor-General Saitō's 'conciliatory' policy was designed to create harmony between Koreans and Japanese, and assistance was not offered disinterestedly to budding Korean capitalists. Koreans who desired both to take advantage of the economic opportunities and to retain nationalist credentials found themselves playing the same unequal game against the colonial authorities as the culturalists we examined in the previous chapters. To succeed to the point where they could share in the development of Korea's economy, they sometimes found it necessary to co-operate with the Japanese, and this appeared inconsistent with nationalism. It is hardly surprising that the labourers became inclined to tar them with the same brush as the colonial oppressors.

The crux of the problem was the relationship between capitalism and imperialism. Korean industry in the 1920s and even more in the 1930s was part of the structure of a consciously expanding Japanese economic and political empire. The claim of the Korean industrialists was that they were fighting Japanese imperialism by creating independent 'national capital'. But to those in the Korean left who considered that capitalism and imperialism were inseparable, this claim appeared contradictory and cynical. Whether or not the workers readily connected their exploitation under Korean industrialists with imperialism, making this connection was central to the left's attack on the rising Korean bourgeoisie.[16]

Economic issues understandably focused ideological debate more sharply than the rather amorphous issue of cultural identity. But we must be careful not to exaggerate or claim to find a black and white situation of two clearly and consistently defined camps throughout the two decades. Such a finding rests on reading the later division of Korea back into the past or on a selective and face-value citation of the harshest polemics of the time.

The involvement of Protestants and self-reconstruction nationalists in general in the economic movements of the 1920s and 1930s is very important to our understanding of the debates. In a negative sense, it makes it very difficult to draw the clean lines one would like between opposing camps. This is partly because of the untidiness of the debates, but also because there was more than just a single axis along which positions could become polarised. In a positive sense, it indicates there was a third way, between the 'national capital' and 'capitalism equals imperialism' arguments, offered to the people.

This third way accepted that Japan's invasion of Korea involved a capitalistic invasion without arguing a necessary relation between imperialism and capitalism, and affirmed the validity of Koreans endeavouring to wrest back control of the national economy. The ideological basis for this alternative was the self-reconstruction principle of the moral and spiritual foundation of the nation. 'Self-reconstruction' translated into 'economic nationalism' as the call to 'self-reliance', a corrective to toadyism among the élites and indifference among the commoners. As we shall discover, an argument was being put forward which some leftists, as well as traditional nationalists, felt able to support and which closely resembles *juch'e*, the official ideology of self-reliance in North Korea. The man who came to symbolise this form of economic resistance to Japan was Cho Mansik, a Presbyterian elder in P'yŏngyang and the founder of the Korean Products Promotion Society.

The Korean Products Promotion Society: Formation and activities

The Korean Products Promotion Society (Chosŏn Mulsan Changnyŏ Hoe) was born in P'yŏngyang amidst a widespread growth of numerous smaller movements such as temperance societies and savings clubs, mostly initiated by Protestants. These promoted frugality, self-sufficiency and ethical lifestyles. The idea was not entirely new to the region. A 'Love Korean Products' movement had arisen in P'yŏngyang in 1909 to promote a national economy based on native industry.[17] Indeed, the northwestern provinces were commercially far more active and socially mobile than the conservative, *yangban*-dominated southern areas.

Cho Mansik was a Presbyterian elder, general secretary of the P'yŏngyang YMCA, an organiser of the 1919 March First Movement and Principal of the Christian Osan College in Chŏngju, North P'yŏngan province. He was the son of a medium owner–cultivator in a relatively poor and strongly Protestant village in Kangsŏ-gun near P'yŏngyang and a graduate in law of Meiji University. Having recruited support from colleagues and Christian youth, Cho had proclaimed the formation of the Korean Products Promotion Society as early as 1920,[18] but it was not until mid-1922 that the society was firmly established in the P'yŏngyang YMCA, with the support of Korean businesses in the area.[19]

Although generated among the P'yŏngyang Protestants, Cho intended the society to be a national movement supported by all social groups and religious organisations. Above all, Cho desired it to encompass 'ordinary' Koreans, and accordingly described its purpose in simple terms, claiming it was a commonsense response to their plight:

The present indigence among Koreans is due to mindless contempt of and failure to cherish their own goods. So without realising it, Koreans are suffering under foreign economic invasion. Beginning with trivial daily merchandise, Japan's capitalistic economic invasion has now ravaged our very centre. The way to block this invasion is to increase production of native goods and to develop and elevate products to a high level of excellence. These goods must then be constantly patronised in order to promote further production.[20]

Cho retailored the traditional male costume to simplify it for an active working life, shod himself in straw sandals and shaved his head. He dwelt in P'yŏngyang city in a two-room bungalow which an acquaintance described as being 'like a peasant's in frugality'.[21] As people from all walks of life, from regional personalities to failed examinees and distressed labourers, made their pilgrimage to visit Cho, he became a symbol of the 'new Korea'. In his blending of traditional commoners' values with the practical elements of the Western religious and scientific outlook, Cho Mansik was able to communicate directly to the people the essence of self-reconstruction ideas which in their 'culturalist' form had been less accessible or less acceptable. In particular, his practice of seeking to influence people through personal moral example rather than political or social authority gained him respect even from critics, and earned him the title 'Gandhi of Korea'.

Cho was not disappointed in his expectation of the national appeal of his movement. Within months, an enthusiastic lobby had formed in Seoul where, in mid-December 1922, 50 students under YMCA leader Yŏm T'aejin organised a Self-Support Association (Chajak Hoe). After presenting statistical evidence of the serious trade imbalance caused by the importation of daily necessities, the association published a three-point program and announced plans to form 'large, English guild-style industrial co-operatives to produce and supply goods Koreans eat, wear and use, and to make these the organs of production and consumption for the whole of Korea'.[22] This development stimulated debate in the nationalist newspapers, especially the *Tonga Daily*, while lecture tours organised in the provinces to propagate the concept attracted reported crowds of up to 6000.[23]

Chang Tŏksu's Korean Youth Association spearheaded the movement in Seoul from November 1922. An article which appeared in the *Tonga Daily* on 1 December, commemorating the Youth Association's second anniversary, stressed the urgency of support for a Korean-based economy. Three weeks later, the Youth Association published an appeal for a 'national contract', a 'sacred covenant' of the Korean people to practise the principles of 'self-support and self-sufficiency' (*chajak chagŭp*).[24] The Government-General reacted quickly. Lecture tours were disrupted and one campaigner was arrested in the northwest border town of Ŭiju.[25] Forewarned, supporters in Seoul decided to establish branches in Seoul and other districts in order to present the Japanese with a *fait accompli*. In some measure the strategy succeeded.

On 9 January 1923, ten or more people met to form a preparatory committee. Within eleven days, 20 'directors' were elected from among 160 interested persons and an interim policy of buying Korean clothing, foodstuffs and other native goods was publicised.[26] From here, the Japanese later conceded, the movement 'mushroomed'.[27] Early in February, the socialist Presbyterian Yi Kapsŏng and the Methodist Minister O Hwayŏng lectured with two others before about 2000 people at the Seoul Ch'ŏndogyo Hall on the importance of Koreans developing respect for Korean products.[28] Within a week, a concerted membership drive added 400 financial members to the Products Society, which brought the Seoul branch total membership to 817.[29] A week later, regional branches sprang up in all the larger provincial cities, in addition to some smaller towns: Pusan, Taejŏn, Masan, Hamhŭng, Kwangju, Miryang, Taegu, Yangsan, Tongnae, Anju, Yŏngdong, Yŏnghŭng and Kŭmje.[30] Despite immediate Government-General harassment, the movement continued to spread to the smallest rural villages from February to October 1923.[31] Support came from youth groups, the Christian, Ch'ŏndogyo and Buddhist groups, women's clubs, businessmen and industrialists, while in P'yŏngyang the unusual nationalist unity of the society was demonstrated by the support of the P'yŏngyang Labour League.[32] Support also came from an unexpected quarter. In Miryang (South Kyŏngsang province), the *Kisaeng*, or entertainment women, adopted the slogan 'Korea for Koreans' and made a pact to wear only simple, native Korean clothing. In Masan, in the same province, 40 *Kisaeng* women formed a league and declared that since they too were Koreans, forced into their present occupation by poverty, they were well aware of the need to live frugally and patronise native products.[33]

Encouraged by this response, the Seoul, P'yŏngyang and several other provincial branches prepared to hold highly visible rallies on the approaching Lunar New Year holiday (16 February). But on 13 February the Seoul directors were summoned to the Central Police Station and threatened punitive action on the basis of laws regulating assembly and public peace.[34] Alternative arrangements were promptly made. A 'social' gathering took place at the Ch'ŏndogyo Hall at 2 p.m. on Lunar New Year's Day, attended by several thousand people, all in plain Korean costume. The eight provinces were represented by special flags depicting their local products, manifestos were distributed and Kim Pyŏnghŭi of the *Chosŏn Daily* and Song Chin'u, manager of the *Tonga Daily*, made plenary speeches. From 7 p.m.

lectures were given at the Central YMCA and Youth Association buildings by noted nationalist figures and religious leaders on the theme: 'The Self-Support Movement will be accomplished by the united strength of our twenty million people'.[35]

In P'yŏngyang, the streets had served host to pre-New Year rallies of up to 7000 people. The police complained about the excessive size of the rallies and ordered Kim Sŏngŏp, chairman of the P'yŏngyang branch, to limit the New Year's Day parades to two separate corps of no more than 50 marchers each. The parades took place as instructed, but a large crowd representing over 60 community groups gathered afterwards in the P'yŏngyang Christian College grounds to hear the Rev. Kim Tongwŏn speak on the subject of self-sufficiency.[36] Rallies were held also in Sŏnch'ŏn, South P'yŏngan, Suan in Hwanghae province, Talsŏng and Yangsan in South Kyŏngsang and Sunch'ŏn in South Chŏlla. In Kunsan in North Chŏlla province, and in Pusan, large parades were led by the *Kisaeng* women.[37]

In the midst of this resounding success, a Seoul director, Na Kyŏngsŏk, a bright student fresh from studies in Tokyo, proposed immediate action on two fronts: formation of consumers' co-operatives and propagation of the movement's theoretical basis.[38] The Seoul Board of Directors met on 22 February and commissioned Na, Yi Sunt'aek, an economist trained in Japan, and the Youth Association and YMCA leader Kim Ch'ŏlsu to examine the co-operative movements of a variety of countries.[39] A month later they reported that in Korea's situation it would be advisable initially to establish co-operatives from above and steadily encourage mass participation until the movement became spontaneous. A tax on members was proposed to raise the 5000 yen it was estimated would be required to initiate the co-operative venture.[40] But since insufficient financial support was pledged, the Seoul directors perceived that education would have to come first and concentrated instead on Na Kyŏngsŏk's second proposal.

Despite considerable Government-General opposition, the Seoul branch launched a journal, the *Sanŏp Kye* (Industrial World), in November 1923. With some lapses and several changes of name, the journal remained in circulation until Japanese pressure and the strain of the Great Depression forced it to cease publication late in 1932. In January 1925 Kim Ch'ŏlsu urged that the journal turn from theory to practice,[41] and by 1929 the journal, renamed the *Chosŏn Mulsan Changnyŏhoe Hoebo* (Journal of the Korean Products Promotion Society), attracted wider readership by carrying articles on the practical operation of national industries.[42]

Reports on the society continued to appear almost weekly in the nationalist press until late 1924, when enthusiasm began to flag. Lecture rallies held in the Ch'ŏndogyo and YMCA headquarters in Seoul and at P'yŏngyang Christian College on Lunar New Year's Day (5 February 1924) appeared to be the last big events the society could muster in face of rising Japanese intolerance.[43] One disappointed contributor to the culturalist journal *Kaebyŏk* indignantly demanded to know how it was that 'this fervent movement which so shook the whole country has become desolate within six or seven months'.[44] The leaders of the society were apparently not so surprised. In February 1923, the chairman of the Seoul Board, Yu Kiljun's brother Yu Sŏngjun, had predicted that the movement would not be able to maintain its present feverish energy nor accomplish its aims in a matter of a few years.[45] The Ch'ŏndogyo youth leader, Yi Chongnin, also stressed the need for perseverance, while Kim Ch'ŏlsu expressed his hope that Koreans had by now overcome their tendency to latch euphorically on to a new thing but desert the cause when the initial noise died down.[46] But despite these warnings and pleas, support for the movement continued to slump. Japanese harassment was probably the most important external factor, but the radical left's criticism of 'culturalism' and related movements from 1923 caused internal debates and defections, a subject which is treated further below.

In 1925 the Seoul directors attempted to revive the former support. Kim Ch'ŏlsu severely criticised the 'inexcusable' habit of following emotional surges without thought for the practical steps required to attain an objective, and estimated that only a tenth of the 2000 members in each province were at all conscientious.[47] In July the Board of Directors drew up a plan for revival:

1. Visit each of the 3000 [Seoul?] members, clearly outline the situation and form a support group of consenting members.
2. Should the number of supportive members reach 100 or more, announce a revitalisation meeting and entrust the arrangements to members elected for the purpose.
3. Encourage non-members who are in accord with our objectives to join the Society.[48]

Although 120 indicated active support, only 37 attended the meeting convened on 3 October 1925 at Tongdŏk Girls' School in Seoul. Nevertheless, a promotional campaigned ensued which enabled the society to clear its debts and to operate once more from its own premises.[49]

The society struggled on for another two years without great support. At the Seoul annual general meeting of April 1927, the board of directors was given one month to submit its opinions on the causes of failure and its proposals to remedy this. Accordingly, a questionnaire was despatched to 300 leading members throughout the nation. The reasons advanced included suppression by the Japanese, threats against members and supporters, the critical stance of a section of the

Youth Association, factionalism, resignation due to destitution among the common people and the refusal by importers to co-operate.[50] It was imperative some means be found to give the movement greater visibility.

The Seoul branch finally received clearance from the authorities to hold a bazaar at the Central YMCA in April 1928. Designed to rectify the ignorance among Koreans of what was produced from province to province, the bazaar was preceded by publication in the *Chosŏn Daily* of an extensive list of items of local produce. The newspaper was to have carried an editorial warning that Koreans were fast losing even nominal participation in the economy and urging all to promote 'the maximum growth possible under the various actual political and economic conditions now prevailing'.[51] But the Government-General judged this too subversive and censored the editorial comment.

The bazaar did, however, mark an upswing in the Korean Products Promotion Society's fortunes. The Seoul annual general meeting in April 1929 adopted a six-point program which essentially concerned practical steps towards founding industries through commercial and industrial leagues or guilds. A newly elected director, the architect Chŏng Segwŏn, acquired new premises for the society and arranged free printing of the journal.[52] Another very successful bazaar was held in the Seoul YMCA in April 1930, attended by unprecedented numbers.[53] That Yun Ch'iho presided over this bazaar is a measure of the healing of divisions which was taking place among the less extreme nationalist groups. The P'yŏngyang branch was no less vigorous at this point and had enjoyed far greater unity and freedom from its inception. New Year parades were scheduled most years: a successful parade in 1928 was followed in 1930 by an enthusiastic march of some 600 people led by Cho Mansik. Again the YMCA served as the centre of operations.[54]

It is probable that regained solidarity among self-reconstruction groups and the levelling off of the earlier wave of radical socialist enthusiasm, rather than economic factors, were responsible for this renewed activity by the Korean Products Promotion Society. The economic indicators themselves were hardly encouraging, as the impact of the Great Depression began to be felt in East Asia towards the close of 1930. In any case, the nationalist newspapers and journals such as *Tonggwang* maintained lively interest in economic issues, especially co-operatives and tenancy reform, throughout the Depression years,[55] despite the fact that the Government-General's industrialisation program involved even tighter control over the economy and so deprived the heightened economic consciousness of any satisfactory outlet. The society did, however, influence or establish a few medium and small industries in P'yŏngyang, Seoul and some other provincial centres, while co-operatives began to form more or less independently in some numbers from the late 1920s, peaking at 38 major co-operatives formed in 1931 alone.[56] In short, the society's activities enjoyed relative success in limited ventures such as bazaars and parades, while its accomplishments diminished dramatically in proportion to the scale of its practical industrial ambitions, particularly wherever such ambitions conflicted with Japanese interests or required sizeable capital outlay. Yet the modesty of these economic results should not obscure the importance of the society as a focus of nationalism inside Korea.

Self-sufficiency and national survival

The explicit rationale of the Korean Products Promotion Society was self-support, self-sufficiency, self-reliance (*chajak chagŭp*; hereafter 'self-sufficiency' will be italicised when it occurs as a translation of this expression). This principle was almost an article of faith among Protestant self-reconstruction nationalists, inasmuch as it was regarded as the application to economics of 'stewardship' as propounded by Yun Ch'iho and Sŏ Chaep'il since the 1890s. Moreover, the principle had by the 1920s gained currency among other religious groups as well. The leading Buddhist nationalist and reformer Han Yongun subscribed to it explicitly, together with a prominent Buddhist member of the Korean Products Promotion Society, Kim T'aehyŏp.[57] The Ch'ŏndogyo leader Yi Chongnin, who had maintained an active association with Yun Ch'iho since pre-annexation times, was also a society member. In economic terms, then, stewardship meant self-sufficiency or at least preparations for such—not, in the foreseeable future, the overthrow of Japanese imperialism or the destruction of capitalism.

Cho Mansik laid the blame for the 'Japanese capitalistic invasion' squarely on Korean ignorance born of thoughtlessness concerning the basic conditions of economic survival. In December 1922 the Korean Youth Association adopted Cho's theme in an article titled 'My life by my means'. The article stated, in accord with the familiar utilitarian doctrine, that morality, instincts and the like had to do with the universal human task of creating a secure social environment. Contrary to this impulse, Koreans had allowed themselves to be 'buffeted by wind and wave', living 'lives without foundation'. Taking the bull by the horns, the article emphatically declared that economic activity was 'the most direct and most vital' means of ensuring Korea's survival; politics could come later.[58] Early in January 1923, a member of the nationalist Minuhoe society, Sŏl T'aehŭi, wrote a bold article for the *Tonga Daily* on Korea's 'slavery'. Not even masters of their own food and clothing, he complained, Koreans were reduced to playing games with 'movements for the right to political participation'. Yet what was urgently needed was concerted action to reverse the process of borrowing money in order to eat and relinquishing land in order to live. In one aphorism, Sŏl encapsulated the mood of the mounting economic nationalism: 'At present we live off others' labour and goods; before long we shall be living off their rubbish tips.'[59]

The Manifesto of the Korean Products Promotion Society spelled out these ideas for the general public:

> If there is nothing for us to eat and nowhere secure for us to dwell, then our very livelihood will be destroyed. Then what rights, freedom or happiness can we expect and what hope may we entertain for any truly human development? The first condition of life is food–clothing–shelter, which is, to put it another way, our industrial base. If through the destruction of this industrial base nothing remains to our name, it is only to be expected that we should become utterly impoverished and fail to enjoy a livelihood worthy of human beings . . .
>
> Food, clothing, and shelter—that is, the industrial question—is the most urgent problem we face . . . Simply take a hard look at the clothes we wear, the food we eat and all the goods we use. Are any of these wrought by our own hands or produced by our own efforts? . . . Can we possibly sell our houses, land and even our own bodies for things other hands supply, and still lay claim to our rivers and mountains and manage our households as before? If the destruction of one's industrial base incontestably involves the destruction of one's livelihood . . . the present economic condition of the Korean people will certainly consign us all to the dark pit of ruin . . . '
>
> In order to promote Korean products we must make it our aim to buy and use goods made by Koreans, and also unite to manufacture such goods as we need. Unless we thus come to our senses and exert ourselves, how can we expect to maintain our livelihood and develop our society?[60]

The 'Three Policies of Action' under Article 2 of the Seoul by-laws confirm the program of mental and moral enlightenment implied in the Manifesto:

1. promotion of industry through cultivating industrial knowledge;
2. promotion of love and use of Korean products; and
3. economic guidance through investigating the people's lifestyles and circumstances with a view to reforming their economic customs.[61]

Although the annual general meeting held in April 1929 resolved to focus its activities more on practical issues, the society by no means dropped theoretical discussion from its journal, and the contents differed in no important respect from this initial position. Self-sufficiency remained the guiding principle. One society member, Yi Kŭngno, published an explanation of the concept in February 1930.

Since Korea was not some Robinson Crusoe cut off from the international market, *self-sufficiency* was clearly a relative concept only. It was not an ideology of 'primitive' economics or a refusal to engage in the modern world. But nor was it a temporary expedient. It had to become the permanent rationale of Korean economic activity. *Self-sufficiency* implied constant development of skills and technology: it was profoundly practical and dynamic. Yi then turned to the moral theme. The former *self-sufficiency* of the home unit had vanished before the rise of a short-sighted, suicidal opting for present convenience. It is easier, at first, to let others produce goods and simply buy them—but after that, the deluge: no land, no nation. *Self-sufficiency* meant being master of one's own and the nation's economy.[62]

Articles continued to drum out this theme up to 1932, attacking the 'underlying hedonism' of Koreans, their fatalism, short-sightedness and disdain of movements that required stamina or that were not 'political'.[63] Sŏl T'aehŭi opined that the Great Depression underlined the urgency of *self-sufficiency* by demonstrating the utter resourcelessness of industrially underdeveloped peoples in such cases. With some sarcasm he asked whether Koreans imagined that four or five hundred horse-power engines were necessary to produce any of Korea's daily requirements, transport and electricity excepted.[64] The Buddhist Kim T'aehyŏp asserted that Koreans could choose between self-extinction and self-survival ultimately only on the basis of spiritual health: 'If we lack the inner resources of *self-sufficiency*, no additional factor introduced from outside will be of any avail.'[65]

The theoretical position of the Korean Products Promotion Society placed it firmly in the tradition of self-reconstruction nationalism. It enjoyed much wider support than the university scheme and in general succeeded in uniting persons and groups otherwise divided. The Tonguhoe, Hŭngŏp Kurakbu and YMCA all officially backed the movement, which also attracted united support from the *Tonga* and *Chosŏn* dailies. Although its active membership was not very great after 1924, not all or even a majority of supporters could be expected to be financial members. Kim Ch'ŏlsu seems to imply the society enjoyed a membership of over 10000 in January 1925,[66] which is not inconsiderable for a subsection of the wider self-reconstruction movement. Its representation can be clarified to some degree by examining the leadership as a social group.

Details on Cho Mansik have already been given: a 'self-made' man, he was a natural leader of an economic self-sufficiency movement. On the 20 directors elected by the Seoul branch in 1923 we can put together the following details.[67] Paek Kwansu, Kim Ch'ŏlsu, Yi Kapsŏng, Pak Tongwŏn, Chŏng Nosik and Yi Sunt'aek were prominent Protestant leaders, all but the last having been involved in the organisation of the February Eighth or March First Movements. Kim

Ch'ŏlsu, a close associate of Yi Tonghwi, was among the first Koreans to turn to socialism (in 1919 or 1920) and was a leader of the leftist faction of the Seoul Youth Association from 1922. In 1930 Kim attempted to establish a Communist Party in Seoul, but was arrested.[68] Yi Sunt'aek studied economics in Japan and in 1923 lectured at the Presbyterian Yŏnhŭi Special School in Seoul. He was a critic of capitalism, publishing a series of ten or more articles on its contradictions in the *Tonga Daily* during January 1923. Na Kyŏngsŏk was a theoretician for the society who had studied Marxism and Kantian social thought in Tokyo: he became one of the most articulate devotees of ethical socialism.

Sŏl T'aehŭi, critic, journalist and educationalist, had been involved in the 'enlightenment' movement as a member of the Sŏbuk Hakhoe (1907–10), the Taehan Hyŏphoe (1908–09) and Yun Ch'iho's Self-Strengthening Society (Taehan Chagang Hoe: 1906–07). A scholar of some depth with a background in classical (Korean) studies, who had early introduced Western legal and economic thought and liberalism in detail to the literate classes,[69] Sŏl was also activist enough to have participated in the March First Movement. Yi Chongnin had also been an active member of the Taehan Hyŏphoe and with Im Kyŏngho represented the Ch'ŏndogyo religion on the board of directors. Yi Tŭngnyŏn, Kim Tonghyŏk and Yi Siwan likewise belonged to the enlightenment tradition. Kim Yunsu and Kim Tŏkch'ang were businessmen.

The chairman of the board of directors in the early years was Yu Sŏngjun, brother of the famous politician and liberal reformer of the late nineteenth century, Yu Kiljun. Arrested for his involvement in the Independence Club, Yu Sŏngjun had emerged from prison in 1904 a committed Protestant and became a founding member of the Korean YMCA alongside Yun Ch'iho, Syngman Rhee and Yi Sangjae.[70] During the Protectorate, Yu had served as chief of the Educational Bureau and held other posts in the Ministry of Education,[71] and became councillor of North Ch'ungch'ŏng province under the Government-General in October 1910.[72] Yu later became vice-governor of Kyŏnggi province, but was dismissed from all service by the Government-General on 5 April 1921. Yun Ch'iho attributed Yu's dismissal to 'his Christian faith and ill-disguised Korean patriotism'.[73] His nephew, Yu Ŏkkyŏm, was an accomplished lawyer, protégé of Yun Ch'iho, YMCA leader and a conservative Christian nationalist who played a leading role in the Hŭngŏp Kurakbu.[74] Yu Sŏngjun was thus a member of an illustrious and well known aristocratic family.

The Korean Products Promotion Society was managed by a well-educated group of proven national leaders with some influential connections and a good representation of religious, especially Protestant, groups. The two businessmen on the board of directors, together with the numerous business establishments which supported its activities in Seoul and P'yŏngyang, demonstrate definite commercial representation. But there was also substantial representation on the left, which makes it impossible to position the membership on one plane: to bring one group into focus is to blur the other, and vice-versa. Indeed, as revolutionary socialist groups in the mid-1920s began to attack the society, Kim Ch'ŏlsu and Yi Sunt'aek grew uncomfortable with its more conservative leaders and left the movement altogether in the late 1920s. With some notable exceptions, the membership of the society by the end of the decade was of much the same character as that of the Tonguhoe and Hŭngŏp Kurakbu. For this reason, some historians have been inclined to portray the movement as nonpopular, irrelevant to and rejected by the masses. The reality seems to have been more subtle, and an examination of the debate between the society and its contemporary critics reveals its complexity—and produces some surprises.

The ideological debate

Shortly after the Korean Products Promotion Society was established in Seoul, the ideological debate was opened by a member of the Seoul–Shanghai communist faction, Chu Chonggŏn, in a number of articles published in the *Tonga Daily* from 6 to 23 April 1923. The main thrust of his criticism was that the venture was impossible: native industry could not develop under colonial rule, and certainly not without political power. Any commercial development that did take place would be plundered by Korean capitalists, which meant exploitation in the end by foreign (Japanese) capitalists. Chu dismissed earlier assurances by his former fellow-student in Tokyo, Na Kyŏngsŏk, that the masses would win out in the long run.[75] If the process began wrongly, that is, in reliance on bourgeois and capitalist activity, then there was no guarantee the proletariat's sufferings would be rewarded later. (Chu became a founding member of the First Korean Communist Party in Seoul in 1925 and was imprisoned in November the same year.)

Other critics attacked the class composition of the society leadership. The split in the Youth Association involved this very issue. As a 'product of the leadership class' the society was judged incapable of tapping 'the central strength of the Korean people.'[76] One Yi Sŏngt'ae wrote an article in the leftist journal *Shin Saenghwal*, imputing corrupt motives to the society's organisers: they were after all the intelligentsia and so their activities were simply a plot to maintain their leadership and support bourgeois society.[77] There was more to this than flinging mud, for it was feared that any success of the society could only weaken the revolutionary spirit of the proletariat. The Youth Association members involved in the criticisms were objectively in the same 'leadership class' of intelligentsia they impugned, even if they were not landlords or businessmen. Hence, in their response, society defenders were concerned more with Chu Chonggŏn's treatment of the issue on its own merits.

Cho Mansik's biographer claims he treated the criticisms with disdain.[78] This is unconvincing, for Cho regarded Marx as a great thinker. No record of Cho's response, however, has been discovered. It is possible that the criticisms had less effect in northern Korea, where social conditions differed in important ways from the south and where Christianity was strong and radical socialism weak. L.-G. Paik, who knew Cho well, recalled he was a practitioner rather than a theorist and that among society members there was general agreement on the validity of its aims and methods.[79] But there was the wider audience to take into account, and in Seoul two society members leaped to the defence: Yun Yŏngnam and Na Kyŏngsŏk.

In an article of some 10 000 words,[80] Yun Yŏngnam took the critics to task for vague use of terminology: capitalist, proletariat, bourgeois and so on. He pointed out that Korean society differed clearly from the social situation such words had been coined to describe. In Korea they were mere words and one could not inspire genuine class-consciousness by opposing phantoms. Since Chu argued that there was no true capitalist class among Koreans, he ought to have concluded that there existed no real proletariat, that is, a class defined in contrast and opposition to capitalists. Or if the proletariat was taken (erroneously) to mean the impoverished, then almost all Koreans belonged—or very soon would. Yun proceeded with a 'heads-I-win-tails-you-lose' argument:

> To be really consistent, one should say that apart from a minority group of workers (the proletariat?) all Koreans are 'idlers' (petty bourgeoisie and above?). Surely then, any means of wiping out the idlers would be welcomed by that minority group of workers who pour out their blood and sweat. It is not certain whether these idlers, after displaying all-round improvement in efficiency, will change into a [true] propertied or unpropertied class. Yet if they become unpropertied, that is well; and if propertied, that should cause no harm . . . For to the degree they may become a propertied class, they will become material of a substance worth contending against.

Not surprisingly, Yun feared he might be accused of twisting the Marxist argument. He pleaded serious-mindedness and argued that though some proletarian ends must be pursued by proletarian means, according to Marxist method the desired end could not be attained without travelling through each stage of the journey.[81] He challenged his opponents to do some real research into the Korean situation, to pay heed to the material context of thought and harness theory to reality. Consciousness had to be practical, and the society was able to produce this for it would 'more or less clarify the distinctions between the propertied and productive classes'. The reality (he claimed) was that 60 per cent of land and at least 80 per cent of wealth was in Japanese hands. Since statistics indicated that this trend was accelerating as Korea's overall wealth increased, it was here that action had to be taken. In effect, Yun appeared to be stating that the classic Marxist prediction that economic misery of the proletariat must increase as the capitalist economy advanced was being fulfilled in Korea between Koreans and Japanese, and that this was the origin of the society.

Na Kyŏngsŏk, who seems to have been active in the YMCA whilst in Tokyo studying, published his reply under the name Kongmin in four articles printed, again, in the *Tonga Daily*.[82] He opened his defence by countering Chu Chonggŏn's charge that the society's aims were impossible. The society was a 'movement generated by the undeniable actual problems in Korea', whose urgency Chu failed to grasp. The movement did exist, and the fact that Koreans had rallied to resist approaching economic extinction could not be irrelevant to the question of the possibility of success. Despite the obvious and severe limitations imposed by political powerlessness, doing nothing was not an adequate response. Na implied that this economic movement was not just one but the only alternative and an incontestable duty.

Na admitted that the movement could be construed as an alliance imposed by a bourgeoisie threatened with ruin on a proletariat lacking clear class-consciousness. But, like Yun Yŏngnam, he believed that the Korean bourgeoisie had perforce become proletarian in effect. Endowed with relatively good intellectual training, they could be the heralds of a real proletarian movement even if as a bourgeois swansong. The unpropertied class was always the most vulnerable, but it was a *non sequitur* to conclude that the Korean Products Promotion Society was therefore harmful to proletarian interests. For one thing, Korea had to progress from manual, cottage and non-diversified rural industries to mechanised industry to survive, and this did not violate any socialist principle. For another, the society was not simply a boycott movement, but aimed to awaken consciousness of economic facts and issues. The practice of selling one's labour to industry was one of the real defects of the basic social structure but was a problem as yet remote from the common people's present plight: corpses could not unite. If the critics would only take seriously the formulae of historical materialism, they would realise that the suffering of the proletariat and the intense development of the productive forces were expressly stated to be necessary phases. Proletarian consciousness could not develop in solo; that would not be dialectical. (This seems to involve a misunderstanding of Marxist dialectics. Neither Marx nor Lenin believed that the revolutionary potential increased in proportion to the poverty of a class, though Mao Tse-tung may have. This idea was evidently widely accepted in these early days of Marxism in Korea, and helps account for some of the Marxists' tactics of the time.)

Finally, Na accused Chu of confounding social and political revolutions. Russia experienced a political but not a social revolution because the conditions of the latter did not exist. Therefore Russia had to impose state capitalism to generate the missing necessary productive power. All three of Trotsky's requisites of a successful social revolution[83] were also lacking in Korea, where a growth in consciousness accompanied by an increase in productive power was needed. Na failed to see how a movement to use and produce native goods would threaten this growth rather than promote it. The greatest threat to the proletariat lay in proposing political confrontations when it was in no position to carry them through.

To summarise, Yun and Na argued that political, not economic, action was impossible in Korea's circumstances; that, in any case, political change did not equal or guarantee socio-economic transformation; that since Koreans had lost virtually any semblance of an economic base, the society was a direct and most relevant response to Korean realities; and that rather than undermining the consciousness of an as yet hardly existent proletariat, the movement was the only hope of such consciousness appearing at all. Thus the primary tasks were to encourage people to use native goods where practical and to transform the 'idlers', those with capital and skills, into producers.

This defence of the Society is somewhat puzzling. What does one make of an organisation that was not officially socialist yet defended itself with Marxist analysis, and not anti-socialist yet to all intents encouraged capitalistic economic relationships? The arguments of Na and Yun do suggest the following solution of this anomaly. It is erroneous to imagine that true, capitalistic, bourgeois and proletarian classes existed in Korea in the 1920s. It is likewise erroneous to conceive of capitalism and socialism as two distinct alternatives leading in opposite directions: they are part of the same process and the capitalist phase must, according to Marxism, precede socialism. This is the point of Na's contention that Soviet Russia was *compelled* to institute state capitalism rather than immediately implementing socialism. Both Yun and Na appear to have seen in Marx the justification for a period of industrial capitalism in much the same way as Russian social–democrat leaders like Peter Struve did. Like Sun Yat-sen, they were trying to make capitalism create socialism. However, three other practical factors fashioned the Korean Products Promotion Society: the demand for unity; anti-nihilism; and religious convictions.[84]

Cho Mansik intended the society to be a truly national movement supported by all classes. Unity had been the one grand positive achievement of the 1919 March First Movement which nationalist leaders were anxious to maintain. An Ch'angho ranked the struggle for unity among the highest and most urgent tasks of the nationalist movement, while reserving the strongest condemnation for the chronic lack of this quality among his fellow Koreans. From the mid-1920s this theme featured large in *Tonggwang* articles. The Korean Products Promotion Society shared the self-reconstruction belief that, under the circumstances, conflict between ideologies, classes or anything else was a recipe for extinction. Hence Na Kyŏngsŏk declared that the only 'ism' of the movement was 'death-escapism'.[85]

Although Na and Yun professed a type of socialism, they attacked the radical left for the strong current of nihilism they perceived in it. Much of their counter-attack can only be understood in the light of the popular nihilism which began to emerge as one reaction to the failure of the March First Movement and the continuing intransigence of the Government-General. Shin Ch'aeho in Peking espoused the principle that 'without destruction there can be no construction',[86] a clear disagreement with the gradualist reconstruction movement in Korea. Against a background of despair expressed in Korean drama, novels, poetry and songs, a short-lived Nihilist Party (Hŏmu Tang) was formed in southern Korea in January 1926.[87]

Within the leftist movement this nihilism took on a more serious and practical form. Nihilism, or 'destruction', was posited as a negative phase in revolutionary tactics, a necessary program of sabotage of the existing order. This possibly accounts for the initial lack of involvement by the radical left in co-operative movements, in favour of supporting rural tenants' disputes. Yun Yŏngnam attacked this position as muddled thinking. If anything was impossible in colonial Korea it was this nihilistic tactic. Revolution in Korea had to be launched from a position of genuine strength and by some real means: For the desperately vulnerable Koreans, economic nihilism meant self-annihilation and destruction meant destruction full stop.[88] Na also took Chu Chonggŏn to task for offering no alternative to economic nihilism: 'to say "it cannot be done" is to command a race without means of future livelihood to sit and wait for death.'[89] Ironically, the radical left was accused of being a negative force, of being reactionary in Metternich's sense of the term.

The attack on nihilism had strong ethical inspiration, and here the religious background of the movement is evident and throws light on the problem of the society's relationship to socialist ideology. The reasons for the strength of religion, particularly Protestant Christianity, in Korean nationalism are complex. But the historical cause of interest in Christianity was similar to the cause of interest in socialism or communism: both were viewed as rallying points for opposition to Japan and as sources of a new Korean civilisation. Christians had been excited by Woodrow Wilson's principle of national self-determination because it seemed to own legal and moral grounds. Now socialism seemed to have scientific grounds—and moral grounds too, for socialism was a response to oppression. Hence Christians were naturally attracted to socialism after the disappointments of 1919–22. Indeed, some South Korean Buddhists today blame Christians for opening Korea to communism.

This affinity between the causes of interest in Christianity and socialism explains one aspect of the particularly Korean flavour of economic nationalism in the 1920s and 1930s. Cho Mansik illustrates the blend. Among politicians, thinkers, scientists and novelists, Cho wrote that he most admired Bismarck, Marx, Darwin and Victor Hugo.[90] Here we have the synthesis: Bismarck, the nationalist unifier; Marx, the anti-imperialist and preacher of economic dignity; Darwin, the (supposed) source of a social concept of the struggle for survival; and finally Hugo, the believer in Christian compassion as the most powerful influence for beneficial social change. This might appear to be a confusion of contradictory positions,[91] but, if one steps from the realm of theory into the Korean historical arena of the 1920s, it is not difficult to see that it was the moral factor which made working sense of the synthesis.

However, the affinity must not be pushed too far. As a movement, the society rejected a political–revolutionary approach. Indeed, within the self-reconstruction tradition, it was the counterpart of the culturalist movement. Where the culturalists sought the creation of national culture before and as a means to the political state, the society members (who were often the same people) sought the creation of a national economy as a necessary condition of retrieving statehood.

The very moralism behind the adoption of socialism by many Christians was at the same time a hindrance to their accepting a strict Marxist or communist form of socialism. As we have seen, this moral viewpoint extended to the origins of Korea's colonial occupation, which was attributed to moral and spiritual decay. Given such a divergence between the religious and the communist explanations of the causes of Korea's problems, incompatibility between their respective solutions was inevitable. Open political confrontation with the Government-General was a solution most self-reconstruction Protestants opposed.

The position of Yun Ch'iho illustrates the point. Although not a member of the Products Promotion Society, Yun was deeply involved in economic matters. In October 1919 he had already heartily endorsed a plan to establish a Society for the Promotion of Industry (Siksan changnyŏ hoe), led by Pak Yŏnghyo and Yi Sangjae through the Seoul YMCA.[92] Retaining and using land was more important than organising political movements: 'As sure as man cannot live on bread alone, so sure no race can live on politics alone . . . In this city of Seoul not a Korean photographer, and not a Korean public bath.'[93]

Yun Ch'iho was not unaware of the political aspect of the economic problem, nor unmindful that ultimately a political change would be necessary. He had no illusions concerning the Government-General's reforms after 1919. He observed that the Japanese aimed at 'the utter economic exhaustion of the Korean', and characterised colonial economics as a 'diabolical national policy' of 'exploitation and expropriation'.[94] His diary during the 1920s resounds with the theme of the impoverishment of the Korean people through deliberate Japanese policy. But without acquiring industrial know-how and its material base, politics was fruitless, a scoundrel's resort. It was at bottom still a moral issue.[95]

Yun also dismissed the rising popularity of extreme socialism, or what he called Bolshevism as opposed to non-revolutionary socialism, as a lack of moral fibre. He attributed its popularity also to merciless Japanese economic policies,[96] but regarded the hope that socialist politics would drive Japan out as a vain illusion and a seductive alternative to hard work.[97] In any case, he did not consider that the 'Korean version' of socialism was the real article. Yun actually looked upon Marxism and Leninism as systems requiring 'the highest degree of co-operative civilization,' and judged that Lenin had plunged a great nation into chaos 'for the sake of carrying an academic ideal to its impractical conclusion'.[98] If only Yun could have once suspended his moral contempt for his fellow Koreans, he might have made some worthwhile contribution to the debate.

But distrust of strict communism among Protestants grew out of experience as much as theoretical differences. A Government-General police report of 1928 reveals that once they began to gain support, Korean communists attacked religion harshly as they thought they were obliged to do.[99] This needs some interpretation. In that they wanted not clarification but rejection of much of the Korean tradition, the Christians had been the first modern revolutionary force in Korea. Yet what characterised the Christian nationalists from early on was the axiom that genuine social reform derived from reform of the inner self. However, the political failure of the March First Movement and diplomatic campaign in the West cast considerable doubt on that axiom. The materialist approach of Marxism owed its appeal to its confronting a more or less established Protestant nationalist orthodoxy with something that was again iconoclastic. For their part the radical communists regarded their ideology also as a break with tradition: one had to convert to it or be conquered by it. Yet in opposing religion these communists found themselves taking on much of nationalism itself, and they were directed, too late, to tone down their attacks.[100]

The communist attack on religion in Korea was a strategic blunder. The religion, if it can be called such, which had bolstered the Korean monarchy and supported the social *status quo* was Confucianism, and this had lost its dominance among Koreans as early as 1905. In the colonial context, Christianity was valued by many nationalists for being antipathetic to Japanese rule, and Ch'ŏndogyo shared a similar image. Moreover, Ch'ŏndogyo claimed its membership was 99 per cent rural,[101] while Protestantism had begun as a village movement penetrating the remotest areas of the land. The Protestant church was also strong in the cities, especially in the north. In 1930 it was estimated that 10 per cent of P'yŏngyang attended Presbyterian churches alone, while in Sŏnch'ŏn to the west fully half of its 13000-strong population was reckoned to be at church on Sundays.[102] The communist attack on popular religions, which so visibly inspired much of the nationalist leadership, could not have greatly impressed the ordinary Korean.

But for all their moralism, the self-reconstruction Protestants hardly took into account the fact that the most common motivation of industry was possibly greed—or would become so, once things improved. Like Yu Kiljun earlier, Cho Mansik and his colleagues relied on Christianity to inject altruism into Korean social and economic relations. On their own showing, perhaps this was not entirely unwarranted. Cho Mansik often worked without any remuneration and lived in humble circumstances; Cho's wealthy colleague O Yunsŏn funded national and public enterprises, as did Kim Sŏngsu, founder of Chungang School; the merchant Yi Sŭnghun had put his money into founding Osan College; Yun Ch'iho supported numerous young Koreans in higher, 'useful' education; and under Cho's influence a library, community hall and an orphanage were established in P'yŏngyang, mainly through the fruits of the commercial initiative of two widows. The possibility of using private capital for the public good seemed vindicated.

Nevertheless, these were individual instances which could not guarantee the behaviour of a whole economic system. Could issues of justice realistically wait upon a voluntary exercise of Christian love which Korean Protestants expected from a Christianisation of their land that might never be achieved? One is reminded here of the dictum of a Christian economist, Henry George, a half-century earlier:

'That which is above justice must be based on justice, and include justice, and be reached through justice.'[103] To be sure, at least one contributor to *Tonggwang* did give thought to the operation of greed: 'So long as God does not remove the lust for possessions the realisation of pristine Christianity's communal idea through the spirit of Christian love alone is impossible.'[104]

But the Korean Products Promotion Society failed to address the issue of economic justice in these terms. During strikes at Kim Sŏngsu's Kyŏngsang textile plant in 1925, 1928 and especially in 1931, it was evident that Korean workers were little better off under Korean capitalists than under the Japanese. The *Tonga Daily*, in contrast to its treatment of strikes against Japanese industries, played down these strikes against an illustrious member of the Korean Products Promotion Society.[105] There was some point to the radical left's concern that the society's approach, if successful, would not be in the interests of the majority of Koreans. Accordingly, some Christian leaders did consider that a genuine form of socialism and even communism might avoid the ravages of economic individualism.[106] In 1929 the former society director, Yi Sunt'aek, joined his fellow teacher at the Presbyterian Yŏnhŭi Special School, Paek Namun, in a campaign to 'turn the campus red' and opposed the school's Hŭngŏp Kurakbu faction led by Yu Ŏkkyŏm.[107]

The end of the experiment

From 1932 the Korean Products Promotion Society began to suffer strict containment by the Government-General. The architect Chŏng Segwŏn was prevented from funding the society, members were threatened with reprisals and the journal had to cease publication. The society itself managed to survive until 1937, when it was ordered to dissolve. At the same time, its supporting organisations were destroyed by the police and the core of the self-reconstruction nationalist leadership was arrested or otherwise compromised.

Upon the discovery of subversive documents in May 1937 calling upon Christians to 'deliver the people', the Japanese moved against the YMCA and Tonguhoe personnel. After 'earnest' interrogation of Chu Yohan and others, the police arrested 55 Tonguhoe members in Seoul in August and a further 93 from Sŏnch'ŏn and P'yŏngyang in November. In March 1938, 33 more were arrested in Anak, and therewith 181 leaders from the traditional centres of Christian resistance were arraigned for trial. The majority were lawyers, physicians, teachers, Christian ministers and 'propertied' people who held positions of influence in their respective regions. 'Above all,' the police reported, 'the Christian ministers concerned have secured a firm foothold within the Northern Presbyterian denomination which embraces over 200000 members throughout Korea.' In P'yŏngyang and Sŏnch'ŏn, 'all the real power of Christianity is involved in the Tonguhoe'. The Japanese estimated those influenced by the movement to be in the order of tens of thousands.[108] The arrested included, needless to say, Yi Kwangsu, who for fourteen years had successfully hidden the true identity of the Tonguhoe from the Japanese police.

In March 1938, in his 60th year, An Ch'angho died, under guard, of pulmonary tuberculosis. Within months of his death, Yun Ch'iho, Yu Ŏkkyŏm, Shin Hŭngu, Chang Tŏksu and other members of the Hŭngŏp Kurakbu were arrested, and several staff members of Christian colleges were forced to resign.[109] At this point the Japanese government advised the Government-General to seek a political solution, with the result that the Tonguhoe and Kurakbu members were freed on condition of good behaviour.[110] The authorities then moved rapidly to bring the Protestant denominations under direct supervision. After a bitter struggle which exhausted the churches, the Japanese in 1939 proclaimed with relief and triumph that at last the 'stubborn' Presbyterians, the strongest single group in the land, had submitted and renounced their 'dependence' on Western Christianity in order to conform to 'Japan-style Christianity'.[111]

In reality, not all Protestants had so submitted, and the struggle continued through to the end of the Pacific War with a number of martyrs among the Christians, including Chu Kich'ŏl, pastor of the same Presbyterian church in P'yŏngyang in which Cho Mansik was an elder. But by this time the focus of resistance had shifted to refusal to 'worship' at Shintō shrines. Although this essentially theologically inspired resistance was also a political defiance, organised Protestant nationalism, cultural and economic, was over.

Conclusion

On 6 December 1945, Baron Yun Ch'iho, former president of the first 'modern' nationalist organisation in Korea, the Independence Club of 1896–99, died at his home in Kaesŏng at the age of 80—a suicide, some publications claim, in despair over charges of having been pro-Japanese.[1] Among the mourners at his funeral was another Protestant veteran of the Independence Club, Syngman Rhee, who became the first president of the Republic of Korea. During the next eighteen months a number of Protestant nationalists fell victim to assassins: Song Chin'u, Kim Ku, Chang Tŏksu and Yŏ Unhyŏng. In the north, the Soviet Command confined and presumably executed Cho Mansik, together with colleagues such as the Elder Kim Hyŏnsŏk. An Ch'angho, of course, had already died in a prison hospital.

The deaths of these and other figures associated at some point with Protestant reconstruction ideology certainly did not mark the end of their thought and labours, for others stood up where they were struck down and strove to keep the tradition alive. The occurrence, after the liberation by foreign powers, of precisely those things Yun Ch'iho and An Ch'angho had warned about—the fateful reliance on other powers, internal division and an undemocratic society—inclined some to regard them as prophetic figures. Nor did their deaths weaken the link between Christianity and Korean nationalism, a link which has survived rather strongly in the south. But in that they facilitated the rise in the south of Syngman Rhee's rather different form of 'Christian' nationalism and encouraged a mass exodus from the north of its large Christian population, these deaths signalled a turning away from the nationalists' spiritual critique and vision.

In politics, their decline attended a preoccupation with the 'glorious' struggles of the Korean patriots in exile which naturally encouraged political leaders in both north and south to subsume the idea of nation entirely under the concept of the state. Nationalism was made official: it was defined as the process whereby each regime came to power; and through their respective definitions they claimed legitimacy.

Although in the north the principle of *juch'e*, often loosely translated as 'self-sufficiency', is strictly and religiously described as a brilliant innovation and contribution to world socialism by Chairman Kim Il-Sŏng, it is manifest that the notion has its roots in the soil of the economic nationalism of the 1920s and 1930s. Several of the leaders in Cho Mansik's Korean Products Promotion Society were, or became, socialists or Marxists. Kim Ch'ŏlsu and Yi Sunt'aek are clear examples, but more pertinently, Yi Kŭngno, who published an explication of 'self-reliance' (*chajak chagŭp*) in the society journal, became a founding member of the Democratic People's Republic of Korea. The religious background to this principle has, of course, been repudiated.

In the south, too, a tradition of 'self-reliance', or *chaju*, was established by the military regime of Park Chŏnghŭi, and was later given concrete expression in the Sae Maŭl Undong, or New Village Movement. But again, this did not imply recognition or favour towards the self-reconstruction tradition. Upon President Syngman Rhee's resignation in 1960, the surviving Hŭngsadan members regrouped in the expectation that the suppression it had suffered under Rhee's regime would be lifted. But when in 1961 General Park Chŏnghŭi took power in a coup d'état, he ordered the Hŭngsadan to dissolve. Its jubilee celebrations of May 1963 were held in the United States. Six months later the ban was lifted and the organisation re-established itself under its erstwhile leader Chu Yohan, who immediately compiled and published An Ch'angho's collected works.

Nevertheless, official perspectives and the legacies and prejudices of resistance groups which operated in exile during the Japanese occupation continue to influence histories of Korean nationalism in the two Koreas (and to some extent elsewhere). An Ch'angho's death in a prison hospital and his prior relatively unfettered activity in northern China and America have been of immense advantage to him in terms of the selective whims of historical memory. The self-reconstruction tradition itself, however, and particularly its history inside Korea, has scarcely been examined. The circumstances of Yun Ch'iho's alleged suicide and the unfortunate suggestion by Yi Kwangsu late in the Pacific War that perhaps the Greater East Asia Co-Prosperity Sphere was itself a triumph over 'narrow' nationalism,[2] cannot wholly account for this lack of sympathy.

That the demands of the present influence the way we look at the past is nowhere truer than in relation to nationalists, whether 'official' or otherwise, writing about national history. Almost by definition, such histories must exclude from their sympathies any nationalist tradition the writers do not wish to remain active in the present.[3] A cultural definition of the nation can dismiss or minimise cultural and other divisions within a national society as effectively as statism, by appealing to a fictional cultural homogeneity. But the deep changes which have been occurring in Korea this decade have created space for some experimental reconsideration of the self-reconstruction tradition, particularly as the desire for national reconciliation intensifies.

The defenders of official, state nationalism in the south appear to see in culturalist principles a means of preventing any further development of sectional and ideological divisions. In 1981 a leading Korean newspaper, the *Han'guk Ilbo*, began printing articles on self-reconstruction ideas. Though An Ch'angho was not mentioned by name (possibly because General Chun Doo-hwan's regime was nervous about it), his Four Great Principles once again saw the light of day. A commendatory article on Yun Ch'iho also appeared.[4] The historian and former president of Koryŏ University, Kim Junyŏp, wrote in 1987 of the need to teach the history of Korean independence movements in such a way as to strengthen the sense of national unity. This involves the assumption that all Koreans can share the same sense of what 'my country' (*nae nara*) is.[5] Dissident nationalism, particularly the *minjung* (people's) movement in the south, seems also to be advancing a basic principle of culturalism by arguing that the transformation of the political structure in the south and the reunification of the nation will be achieved through an expansion of *minjung* culture.

Nevertheless, the charge that self-reconstruction ideology was a compromise with Japanese power, first laid by its opponents in the 1920s, remains generally the orthodox position and there is little indication that a displacement of official with populist nationalism in Korea will alter this. However, this orthodoxy needs to be questioned.

Self-reconstruction and nationalist legitimacy

In terms of immediate historical results it is clear that, in its cultural and economic ventures, the self-reconstruction movement succeeded only minimally. At least one scholar, Chin Tŏkkyu, has attributed this to popular rejection of the movement as both élitist and collaborationist.[6] Defining true nationalism as popular movements, Mr Chin in effect concludes that if a movement fails it is because it is not supported by the people. As an historical axiom, this is questionable in itself, and in the case of Korea one would have to conclude from the lack of success of any movement in the 1920s and 1930s that none at all was supported by the people, *ergo*, that there was no nationalism.[7]

The fate of the movement cannot be explained adequately in terms of the compromise versus non-compromise debate of the period. In their 'theses' of March 1928, the Korean communists themselves pointed to the difficulty of applying such a demarcation.[8] Cho Mansik was affiliated with the 'non-compromise' side, and became head of the P'yŏngyang branch of the Sin'ganhoe as soon as it was launched. The first national president of the Sin'ganhoe was the Christian Yi Sangjae, who as a leader in the university movement in 1923–25 ought to belong to the 'compromise' side, but as an owner of the *Chosŏn Daily* ought to be placed in the 'non-compromise' camp. Founding members of the 'non-compromise' Sin'ganhoe include the following founding members of the 'non-popular' Korean Products Promotion Society: Yi Sunt'aek, Pak Tongwŏn, Yi Chongnin, Myŏng Chese, Yu Okkyŏm and the communist youth leader Han Wigŏn. Han Wigŏn was a reporter for the *Tonga Daily*, while Cho Mansik was at one time manager of the *Chosŏn Daily*. That charges of compromise were directed at some individuals and even the groups they belonged to is not to be denied, but such charges must be interpreted in the light of their polemical intent and context. It is hazardous to try to place groups on either side of a line which at the time meandered untidily through the midst of the groups themselves.

The radical left's charge that 'national capital' could only be established by participating in Japanese imperialism was also a moral accusation that the industrial capitalists were collaborating with Japanese power to exploit Korean workers. Carter Eckert's detailed study of Kim Sŏngsu's Kyŏngsŏng Textile Company bears out this contention, in the sense that Kim, and especially his brother Yŏnsu, made use of the financing procedures made available to Koreans by the Japanese after 1920. In fact, Eckert even judges that, 'Among the least oppressed was the nascent Korean bourgeoisie. Indeed, it is questionable whether the Korean bourgeoisie may be justly considered a victim of Japanese aggression at all.'[9] He further points out that the Japanese deliberately encouraged some development of Korean industrial capital as a strategy to promote class differentiation and thereby weaken the kind of national unity which they witnessed during the March First Movement in 1919. This, and the fact that Kyŏngsŏng Company officials were prepared to employ Government-General labour laws (or the lack of them) and police against striking workers in 1931, is taken as evidence that Kim Sŏngsu and his ilk were not real nationalists.[10] They were cynical or deluded; in either case they were stooges of the Japanese. This requires some further discussion.

There seem to be three lines of reasoning. Firstly, there is an argument that participation in the colonial power's economic structure is incompatible with being a nationalist. This can only hold good if, in the face of history, one has already defined a nationalist in this way. But unless one chooses exile, it is impossible not to participate at some point in the structures imposed by the colonial power. Indian nationalists became involved in British economic, educational and political structures in order to pursue nationalist objectives. Demanding that all Korean nationalists should have openly repudiated the Japanese is not common sense, and leaves little room for the exercise of intelligence or the adoption of a long-term strategy. The point is the use one makes of certain provisions one may or may not be able to avoid. There is no logical inconsistency in a nationalist attempting to turn colonially imposed systems to nationalistic advantage, even where the situation is hopeless.

It may be countered that capitalism is 'logically' internationalist, therefore not nationalist.[11] On an abstract level this may be so, but in the actual world capitalists have made very good nationalists (and in the United States capitalism is the hallmark of one version of nationalism). Capitalism, in fact, has had a great deal to do with nationalism and the creation of nation-states. A global market and national economic policies may exist in tension, but the claim that capitalists cannot be nationalists is dubious. Anarchism may logically imply the abolition of nation-states, but not capitalism.

Secondly, there is an argument that only those who suffer oppression are real nationalists, and the less one suffers, the weaker one's nationalist credentials. To be sure, this works to some extent on an emotional level. But the point of the argument is that the Korean bourgeoisie avoided suffering by playing along with the Japanese, that is, by not being nationalists. Yet those Koreans who suffered economically did not usually suffer in this way because they resisted the Japanese. The assertion that the Korean 'bourgeoisie' did not suffer from Japanese colonialism is also questionable. Yun Ch'iho's diary in the 1920s abounds with bitter denunciations of Japanese obstruction of Korean enterprise and heavy irony towards the economic 'reforms'. It is not the laws but the administrative practices which are pertinent here. If the Japanese decided to show leniency towards the 'bourgeoisie' after 1919, that was their own decision, and as such provided the conditions under which 'bourgeois' nationalists could operate. Again, the point is not how much they were oppressed, but whether they worked or thought they worked for nationalist ends. Formation of national capital was considered a patriotic act, and national capital was after all being formed. To disallow nationalist claims on the grounds that they borrowed from Japanese sources is to define nationalism as strict anti-foreignism.

Thirdly, there is an argument that use of economic and political force against striking workers is contrary to nationalism, since such force depended on the Government-General. But the management of the Kyŏngsŏng Company did not regard a factory strike as a nationalist issue: it was a matter of industrial relations. As one may call for the police when one's private property is stolen or endangered, so it was thought legitimate to call for them when private capital accumulation was hindered. This is normal capitalist rhetoric. Modernising the economy was the nationalist mission, doubly so when Koreans were doing it. In pointing out that the economic practices of Kim Sŏngsu and others were not necessarily in the interests of the workers simply points out what is well known, that they were not socialists. However many and good the reasons one might have for preferring them to have been socialists, the fact that they were not has nothing to do with whether they were nationalists.

We must be careful not to confuse the question with moral issues. Nationalism is not a moral category. There is no contradiction between nationalism and worker exploitation—or between nationalism and political oppression, for that matter. The self-reconstruction nationalists did not aspire towards the liberation of the workers, just as they did not anticipate any thoroughgoing liberation of women. Nationalism was considered generic, something for which all Koreans were to work. Enlightenment of the workers consisted in their understanding that they must work, and work hard, for the nation. In other words they (and Korean women also) were nationalised, and any expression of sectional interest was, as An Ch'angho formulated it, mere egotism.

A brief comparison with the experiences of nationalist movements under peacetime colonial rule elsewhere may shed light on the problem of compromise. In her study of the Constitutionalist Party of Cochinchina, Megan Cook indicates that its leaders, whom she calls 'idealistic collaborators', enjoyed considerable success in the mid-1920s when French policies were 'relatively liberal'.[12] The party frankly admired French culture and expected France to ease the passage of a proud new state of Vietnam into the modern world. But as French policy hardened and the people turned to armed resistance, the Constitutionalists fell between two stools. They could not approve armed revolt both on principle and because they recognised France was too strong, and yet they failed also in attempts to persuade the French against harsh repression. Indeed, for attempting to do so, the French accused them of 'hatred' of France.[13]

In Indonesia, a dramatic swing to 'co-operation' nationalism (i.e. co-operation in municipal, regional councils, etc.) occurred between

1935 and 1942 because the Dutch had severely limited the scope of legal action by the non-co-operating parties. Yet co-operation nationalists proved no more able to move the colonial masters.[14] Co-operation nationalism in India fared better, although the process was very slow. Tilak favoured co-operation on the grounds that it would preserve unity and C. R. Das advocated participation in local councils in order to upset British rule from within, while the Indian Congress always negotiated with Britain and openly participated in provincial council elections from 1935-39.[15] A gradual transfer of power did take place.

None of these three cases, however, compares easily with the Korean experience. The case of Cochinchina has one similarity: the rise of the most severe and uncompromising rhetoric among many nationalists precisely when the rulers became flintlike in their attitude and deaf to even moderate appeals. In Korea the narrowing of the definition of what was acceptable nationalism occurred after the discovery that Saitō's 'conciliatory' policy was fraudulent. But the culturalists did not become unpopular with the 'people' so much as with rival nationalists. The only similarity with the Indonesian case is that Korean 'legal' nationalism fared no better than underground activities in moving the political authorities. Participation in the local 'advisory councils' instituted by Governor-General Saitō Makoto in 1919 was never adopted as a nationalist strategy by self-reconstruction nationalists.

The political and social complexion of India differed so much from that of Korea that a comparison of nationalist streams as such is not helpful. Not only did India lack Korea's ethnic and linguistic homogeneity, but it was not up against a colonial policy of assimilation. However, in terms of ideas, Korean culturalists, especially Protestant culturalists, were close to the gradualist and non-violent approach of their Indian counterparts. They admired Gandhi's emphasis on spirituality and his belief in the power of truth and righteousness. Though unthinkable for the strict nationalists and socialists, Gandhi's early position that he was really concerned that the British Empire be 'founded not on material but spiritual foundations',[16] *may* have drawn qualified assent, *mutatis mutandis*, from Yi Kwangsu and possibly also Yun Ch'iho, had they known of it. As it was, the (non-Korean) intellectual traditions with which the Korean Protestant self-reconstruction nationalists can most validly be compared were the utilitarian social doctrine of American evangelicals and the nation-idealism of the Russian pre-revolutionary religious thinkers.[17] While both are evident in the writings and speeches of Yun Ch'iho and An Ch'angho, the latter is consciously acknowledged in Yi Kwangsu's novels and his sponsorship of a *Narod* movement in the 1930s in conjunction with Song Chin'u and the *Tonga Daily*.

The question of compromise concerns not obvious collaborators (willing agents of Japan against Korea's national interests and so on), but rather a group of committed nationalists who shared three basic convictions. First, there was the idealist notion of the ethico-spiritual origins of nationhood. From this followed the denial that blame for Korea's loss of independence could be laid wholly or even mainly at the feet of Japan: Japan was not absolute villain and Korea was not innocent victim. Secondly, there was the associated theory that nation as a cultural entity logically preceded the political state. On this basis, Yi Kwangsu in particular argued that on the historical plane also it was possible to develop the former where the latter was withdrawn, and indeed, that in this way the two would eventually have to come together. Thirdly, there was the conviction that political agitation was ruinous to the interests of the nation. Whether or not these convictions were understood, they were not well received by the nationalist right or radical left.

Leaving aside the more philosophical question of the merits and demerits of the movement's nation-idealism, Protestant self-reconstruction nationalism can be charged with misjudgment and some inconsistency. In an international climate where the nation-state formula was universal and where Japan, on her own behalf, applied that formula with great energy, the 'non-political' nationalism of the culturalists was certainly caught in a serious dilemma. It was idle to compare Korea with Garibaldi's Italy and Bismarck's Germany, for there the issues concerned unification, or with Washington's America, for that *was* essentially a political struggle, and an armed one at that. In any case, the international order had changed since the first bloom of nationalism, and the nature of Japanese nationalism ought to have been taken more into account.

The problem with Japanese nationalism was not that it was narrow, but that it was not narrow enough. Had it been content merely to impose its political authority over colonial possessions, there would have been fewer barriers to Korean cultural aspirations, and the Korean 'nation' could in theory have survived as it had in earlier centuries under Mongolian and Manchu rule. To be fair, the culturalists envisaged that a period of one or two centuries might be necessary to fulfil their objective. But there was a lack of political realism here. Even in India, where a single nation had not been created, the patient course of its nationalism was giving way to urgent demands. Japan's assimilative policy could not tolerate a 'nation' of Koreans within the state of Chōsen. The culturalists should have conceded the logic of Japan's position, since it was the reverse side of their argument that once Korea became a true nation the Japanese state would become ultimately unviable. The more successful their movement, the more certain it was that Japan would crush it.

Individualism, collectivism and politics

The state is the only entity that can legitimately operate in global politics in the modern world. And a 'society has no reality for us except in its political institutions'.[18] However much the Protestant ethical nationalists disliked and disagreed with this development, it had to be faced. It was, after all, the logic of establishing the provisional government in exile and of trying to gain official recognition at the League of Nations. In construing the struggle with Japan as a profoundly cultural one, they were, of course, correct. But the conclusion that political resistance was secondary and could be relinquished when conditions were unfavourable was perhaps faulty. For it was through its *state* power that Japan was determined to bring about the cultural devolution of the Korean nation. Not surprisingly, there was periodic agitation within the ranks of the self-reconstruction nationalists to engage in political resistance.

The Protestants tended to divide, albeit in a relative sense, over whether to adopt an individualist or collectivist approach. Methodological individualism supported non-political engagement and so favoured the separation of nation and state, in a way analogous to the Protestants' separation of church and state (and the church was, after all, regarded by Protestants as the model for the future nation). Methodological collectivism, on the other hand, was understood by its advocates necessarily to entail political engagement and therefore adoption of an explicit political creed, although Chu Yohan was inconsistent here. The organic conception of the nation which was associated with a collectivist approach seemed to imply that the state was its 'head,' and therefore that rule by a foreign nation could only wither the national organism, or at best thoroughly deform it.

Until 1927 the former generally prevailed. But with the formation of the Sin'ganhoe united front movement in February 1927, the debate became stronger on the other side. The pendulum swung back again when the united front experiment collapsed and the Government-General tightened its political control. Thus are issues often determined and the range of choices limited. Nevertheless, despite the change in mood in the late 1920s to early 1930s, it was the individualist approach that enjoyed most consistent popularity among the heirs of Yun Ch'iho's nationalist theology. To them, the restoration of a nation which had fallen from grace depended on the ethical and spiritual renewal of individuals. While Yi Kwangsu pointed out that just ten righteous individuals would have been sufficient to save Sodom,[19] Cho Mansik reaffirmed that evangelisation and instruction of the people in the way of Christ was the *sine qua non* of national revival. In An Ch'angho's view, individuals who blamed socio-political structures for their unhappy condition and refused to take responsibility for their own lives were actually accomplices in their own enslavement. The environment was a limiting, not a determining, factor. This emphasis on personal ethical self-cultivation refers us back to another complex question: to what extent was the Protestant self-reconstruction movement a restatement of the neo-Confucian position on the roots of civilisation?

Civilisation and the sources of change

Interpretation and evaluation of modern Asian nationalist movements which propose the priority of ideas or the need to establish an intellectual, spiritual and cultural foundation for national change and growth are fraught with difficulty. The literature on the 'culturalist' movements in China from the late Ch'ing period reveals the potential for widely divergent judgments.[20] With the publication recently of studies by Vipan Chandra and Michael Robinson, there is now some literature on the Korean experience to guide debate. The substantial influence of religious systems, in this case of Protestantism, on the quest for a new civilisation may be the variable that gives the Korean 'cultural—intellectual' movement its particular flavour. It also complicates the question of the principle sources of the Korean self-reconstruction tradition.

It is important to recognise that, in reflecting on the source, means and ends of social change, the Koreans were grappling with issues that were universal and that therefore the various alternatives open to humankind are not each the exclusive preserve of any one tradition. Some traditions affirm each other. The idea of moral and cultural transformation and the emphasis on education are present in many cultures. The Koreans' exposure to traditions which include these ideas is well documented. The Russian ideal of *sobornost*, a national-spiritual community which envisaged the solidarity of the intelligentsia with the people (or the peasantry: *narod*), presupposed a spiritual dynamic of change. The American, Australian and other European missionaries who introduced Protestantism to Korea taught that education and cultivation of moral character would transform the Korean nation. The belief that the masses were oppressed by their own ignorance and moral turpitude, especially selfishness, served as the general background to discussion on social reform in the Western nations with which Korean Protestant intellectuals were in contact.[21]

Nevertheless, Korea's Protestants were not Westerners, and the intellectuals among them had been schooled in the Confucian classics. Following Joseph Levenson's evaluation of Chinese culturalists, one might say that Korea's Protestants simply used different terms to express the same ideals. But this presents difficulties. For example, one might judge that the Korean leftist statement, 'The common man, the masses, are the backbone of society',[22] is no doubt a Confucian hangover, a restatement of the maxim that 'The people are the foundation of the state'. But of course Marxism introduced a concept of the 'people' which was not only inactive in Confucianism but also alien to its whole ethos. (This is not to deny by any means that 'communism' in North Korea today may not be heavily influenced by Confucian family and state ideals.)

With regard to the ethical emphases of Korean Protestant culturalists, the problem is intricate, for comparison must be made not only with Confucianism but also with the amorphous assumptions of Western liberalism. An Ch'angho placed great emphasis on moral training and likened moral citizens to skilled musicians. Was this the moral élitism of Confucianism or a reflection of what has been termed the 'élitist assumptions' of liberalism?[23] For, in China's case, the liberal Yen Fü's linkage of democracy to the intellectual and moral quality of the people has been interpreted as a borrowing from Western liberalism's position on freedom and democracy. Yen Fü's position has even been described as a '"change of heart" in an entirely new direction—a thorough transvaluation of values'.[24] In the Korean Protestants' case, we *can* speak of a 'change of heart'. Certainly there was a reorganisation of the moral hierarchy and a deliberate shift of ethical focus.

The Korean Protestants actually made it reasonably clear what they valued in Christian ethics and how they regarded Confucianism. Yun Ch'iho held that morality was objective and universal and therefore approved of Confucian and Mencian ethics where they reflected this universalism. The view that the fate of a nation depends on the quality of its citizens was described in the *Sinhan Minbo* as 'a truth revealed by the Holy Spirit and . . . the true teaching of the sages'.[25] This implies that the sages of the East were inspired by the Holy Spirit since, the latter being God, truth could have no other origin. This position was explicit in Yu Kiljun and the Catholic Yi Nŭnghwa's thought, and is implied in some statements by reconstruction Protestants, such as that quoted above. However, the question of whether particular ethical items are Confucian or Christian is a red herring in this respect. The real issue was the ethical focus of each system. Here, Yun and An rejected the 'distortion' of the Confucian ethical focus on filial piety and wished to replace it with the Christian focus on love, which meant altruism, philanthropy and self-denial. Further, they regarded Confucianism as 'empty' in a twofold sense. It described ethics but failed to guide people to the source of spiritual power required to practise them; and it was élitist, impracticable by the common people in many respects.[26] Self-reconstruction Protestants claimed they were introducing the Protestant 'everyman's' ethic into everyday life. This perhaps reflects the Protestant designation of all believers as saints and priests, which demands high ethical standards for the rank and file and insists, as it were, that they all join the moral élite. In this sense, Yun Ch'iho's (incompleted) pilot community and An Ch'angho's Hŭngsadan (Tonguhoe) organisations were, despite the neo-Confucian ring of their 'self-cultivation' activities, real innovations. Moreover, the exaltation of commercial and industrial values in these organisations, and in Christian schools such as Osan College, were not inspired by readings of the Confucian Classics.

The insistence, whenever education was encouraged, that a 'learned' person must also be a 'righteous' person appears to reveal a clear Confucian influence, since contemporary Western philosophy, and the Christian, John Newman, allowed that moral inferiority and intellectual excellence could coexist in the same person. It has been argued that Christianity itself encourages the view that apprehension of the 'good' lies outside the scope of rational investigation.[27] The Protestants under discussion were not inclined to allow this. But they did come near it. One Tonguhoe member proposed the formula, 'Know scientifically; act religiously', and claimed that in the West knowledge and faith were regarded as two wheels on the same cart.[28] They also argued the reverse of the Confucian position by teaching that social inferiority and moral excellence could coexist in the same person. There was in any case almost uniform rejection among the Protestants of the *spiritual* ethos of the Chosŏn neo-Confucian tradition. Normally generous to other religious systems, An Ch'angho denounced the Chosŏn dynasty's cultural legacy for corrupting the people's religious outlook. 'Korea is an ancient nation of 4000 years' standing,' he noted. 'Unfortunately, contact with Western civilisation has come late, but Korea's [new] civilisation is one founded on Christianity and nationalism.'[29]

There are Confucian elements in An's description and high evaluation of 'civilisation', however. His definition of civilisation as 'beauty and light' reflects the traditional understanding of *munmyŏng* (*wenming* in Chinese) as brightness and literacy and moral authority.[30] An's system was indeed a very unified one. His doctrine that reality was everywhere concentric and that change therefore commenced at the centre of perception—that is, in the human spirit—working outwards until all else was transformed, was philosophically attractive to intellectuals raised on neo-Confucianism. In fact, almost everything in the Korean tradition—from its high learning in Confucian moral science and Buddhist metaphysics to its popular cosmologies and its nostalgic shamanist epics—earnestly prized, sometimes indeed wistfully sought, universal harmony. But to stop here would be to miss the point. Just as Yun had reinterpreted the universal responsibility of governments and people to manage their nation wisely in terms of the Christian doctrine of 'stewardship', so An grounded the transformation of society and culture on 'repentance'. The iconoclastic flavour of his summons to radical repentance considerably relativises the traditional ideal. Here it does appear that the same terms were used to introduce different notions. It was not merely a case of a rose by any other name. Change was no longer pendular but teleological. Christianity did not simply replace Confucianism as the civilising agency; it constituted a new ideal of civilisation.

It may be that it is premature to attempt such judgments. It is quite possible, especially should Christianity decline in Korea, that future historians will be able to view the Protestant debates of this period as part of a continuing attempt to synthesise the various streams of thought which have divided Korean thinkers from before the beginning of the Chosŏn dynasty in 1392: the metaphysicians, the empiricists, the folk champions and the élitists. And indeed, the traditional, positive evaluation of culture inherited by self-reconstruction Protestants has inhibited debate over the relationship between faith and culture that has occupied Christians from the first centuries AD. This in turn has had its impact on the manner in which Korea's Protestants related to nationalism.

Faith, nationalism and ethnicity

From the end of the nineteenth century Koreans became engaged in a search for a new basis not only for nationhood but also for civilisation in a time of great turmoil. Whereas nationalism in Europe grew out of internal disruptions, in Korea its emergence was stimulated or hastened also by external pressures. Nationalism, the drive to build a strong nation-state, therefore became associated initially with foreign ideas. But as it became clear that these ideas could neither be dismissed as barbaric nor easily absorbed by the traditional ideal of civilisation, the development of serious cultural ambivalence became inevitable. Even so, the nation-state seemed regressive to Korea's Confucian scholars. It was like a return to pre-Confucian Korea, to an age when the cultures of the tribal confederacies were too limited by their local sources and functions to encompass a peninsula, let alone humanity.

But for those who embraced Protestant Christianity, it was Confucianism, or more accurately neo-Confucianism, which lacked the altitude necessary to encompass within its vision the new international order. Christianity was the new universal system, and so arose the Protestants' mission to construct a new nation founded on Christian ideals. For the most part, just as they accepted that government was meant to be secular, self-reconstruction Protestants also adopted the view that the nation-state was a natural secular reality. Few had any argument with the nation-state formula itself.

However, they did have serious disagreements with the definitions and methodologies of nationalism advanced by fellow Koreans. The long-term nature of their approach and especially their principle of political non-resistance came into tension with the more immediate demand to expel Japan, that is, with the normal demands of nationalism under such circumstances. The vacillations of the Tonguhoe movement over its political position reflect the pressures of these demands. But they also reflect the tension between Protestant (and neo-Confucian) universalism and nationalist particularism. In Korea under Japanese occupation, political independence from the Japanese race was an ineluctable element of nationalism. When self-reconstruction nationalists removed this from their (immediate) nationalist agenda, they were accused of removing their nationalism with it. This led in part to the ideological and intellectual crisis examined in Michael Robinson's recent study of Korean cultural nationalism.[31]

There is now some recognition among Korean scholars that Christians were often unable to commit themselves unreservedly to nationalism because of the extreme narrowness of its objectives during the occupation period. The historian and publicist, Song Kŏnho, for example, considered that the lack of universal applicability and relevance of nationalism was 'one of the reasons why Christianity feels a kind of fundamental incompatibility with nationalism'.[32] Although the constant tension in Yun Ch'iho's relation to nationalism was more pronounced than most, Protestants more or less consistently urged that national identity be sought not in ethnic origin but in shared beliefs and values.

This did not mean ethnicity was considered irrelevant to nationality. On the contrary, race was taken for granted. That a nation-state should form around an ethno-linguistic group was viewed as a natural fact, neither surprising nor debatable. Hence Kim Yun'gyŏng related nation-states to the world community as families were to national communities. The extraordinary and spontaneous nature of the nationwide March First Movement had moved even Yun Ch'iho to observe that 'racial instinct is as immortal in the Korean's heart as it is in any other race'.[33] Yi Kwangsu was convinced that race was inescapable, one of the fundamental elements of existence.[34] Yet race was therefore merely a given, a *tabula rasa*: it needed to be moulded into a form and this was where the focus had to be. Amid highly charged emotions, the Protestants hoped to draw fellow Koreans back from the abyss of a nationalism shaped by racial hatred.

In the self-reconstruction nationalists' device of equating healthy nationhood with allegiance to a religious system, the premise of ethnicity was overshadowed but not removed. Their sense of historic mission to unite Christianity and Korean nationality continues unabated to this day. Indeed, it is now the almost universally proclaimed mission among Korea's Christians, who in South Korea account for some 25 per cent of the population. The agenda has, of course, changed. Now it is the unification of their bitterly divided nation which must be attained. And here again the political issue is divisive. Political cleavage between Christians holding different views on reunification may yet prove stronger than their common religious allegiance.

Among South Korea's Evangelical Christians, the identification of the Korean people with the Biblical Israel remains very much alive. But whereas formerly they were too few to unite and mobilise the populace around their religious vision, they now draw confidence from their continuing unusual expansion. And whereas formerly they were humiliated colonial subjects, they are now proud members of a virile church and nation. Moral and spiritual qualities remain the source of true civilisation, but in their view it is not now their own nation but the 'decadent' and spiritually enervated Western nations which need to relearn this lesson. They are the New Israel, the nation God will use to spread renewal throughout the world. For all that, it is unlikely that An Ch'angho would consider the south a 'happy' or 'humane' society; and evidence is still wanting that the renewal promised to the world has yet taken place in the Korean Protestant churches' own social and political relations.

In terms of the relationship between religion and nationalism, this book perhaps raises more questions than it answers. From the cosmological point of view, the reorganisation of the world into nation-states involves an immense loss of altitude. It signifies a descent from the lofty heights of civilisation whence a view of the whole vista of human activity was possible, where all people regardless of race, clime or language belonged to the same Tao, or as in Christianity, to the same great drama. It may be that this 'descent' has brought with it an increase in popular participation in politics, though not a uniform increase in freedom. Even so, the active assent of adherents of universal religious cosmologies to the nation-state formula remains something of an enigma. One can sympathise with Benedict Anderson's call for a Copernican revolution in our understanding of the enduring phenomenon of nationalism, in relation to religion as well as to Marxism.

Notes

Introduction
1 Isaiah Berlin *Against the Current* London: Hogarth Press, 1979, pp. 333–7
2 See Eugene Kamenka 'Political Nationalism—The Evolution of the Idea' in Eugene Kamenka (ed.) *Nationalism: The nature and evolution of an idea* Canberra: Australian National University Press, 1973, pp. 5–7
3 See for instance Nicholai A. Berdyaev *The Meaning of History* Cleveland: Meridian Books, 1962
4 Jacques Ellul 'Politization and Political Solutions' in Kenneth S. Templeton (ed.) *The Politicization of Society* Indianapolis: Liberty Press, 1979
5 Jacques Maritain *Man and the State* Chicago: University of Chicago Press, 1979, p. 7
6 ibid. p. 2
7 ibid. p. 7
8 Quoted in Earnest Gellner *Nations and Nationalism* Oxford: Basil Blackwell, 1983, p. 134
9 ibid. pp. 130–34
10 ibid. pp. 124–30
11 ibid. p. 130
12 Benedict Anderson *Imagined Communities. Reflections on the Origin and Spread of Nationalism* London: Verso Editions and NLB, 1983, pp. 18–19
13 ibid. pp. 11–13
14 See, for example, Reynaldo Ileto *Pasyon and Revolution, Popular Movements in the Philippines, 1840–1910* Manila: Ateneo de Manila University Press, 1979
15 F. R. von der Mehden *Religion and Nationalism in Southeast Asia* Madison: University of Wisconsin Press, 1963, p. 3
16 See Michael Scammell *Solzhenitsyn* New York: W. W. Norton & Co., 1984, p. 992

17 Bruce Kapferer *Legends of People, Myths of State. Violence, Intolerance, and Political Culture in Sri Lanka and Australia* Washington and London: Smithsonian Institution Press, 1988

18 A good introduction to cultural history is supplied in Lynn Hunt (ed.) *The New Cultural History* Berkeley, Los Angeles & London: University of California Press, 1989; other helpful works include Richard Johnson (ed.) *Making Histories* London: Hutchinson, in association with the Centre for Contemporary Cultural Studies, University of Birmingham, 1982; and Hayden White *Metahistory: The Historical Imagination in Nineteenth-Century Europe* Baltimore & London: The Johns Hopkins University Press, 1973

19 See, for example, Gerda Lerna *The Creation of Patriarchy* New York and Oxford: Oxford University Press, 1986; Carroll Smith-Rosenberg *Disorderly Conduct: Visions of Gender in Victorian America* New York and Oxford: Oxford University Press, 1985; and Natalie Zemon Davis *Society and Culture in Early Modern France* Stanford: University of California Press 1975

20 I find that Kapferer (*Legends of People*, p. 6) goes too far when he claims that Christianity and Buddhism have no empirical existence outside their respective Australian and Sri Lankan nationalisms. The nationalist reformulation of religion is by no means hermetically sealed off from the formulations which precede and continue alongside nationalism. Bonhoeffer's efforts did reach into German Protestant nationalism, and Australian 'Christian' nationalism is a target of constant criticism from Christian groups in Australia such as the Zadok and St Mark's centres in Canberra and Middle Earth in Sydney.

21 On Korean cultural nationalism, see Michael Edson Robinson *Cultural Nationalism in Colonial Korea, 1920–1925* Seattle & London: University of Washington Press, 1988

22 Richard Kroner *Culture and Faith* Chicago: University of Chicago Press, 1951, p. 239

23 Needless to say, it is not the only current. See H. Richard Niebuhr *Christ and Culture* London: Faber & Faber, 1952

24 T. S. Eliot *Notes towards the Definition of Culture* London: Faber and Faber, 1962, Ch. 4

25 Karl Mannheim (1893–1947) believed in the possibility of planning a culture and also that culture was transmitted and even created by cultural élites (not the same as class élites). Yi Kwangsu shared this view. See Karl Mannheim *Man and Society in an Age of Reconstruction: studies in modern social structure* 2nd edn, London: Routledge and Kegan Paul, 1951

26 See Wang Gungwu 'The Chinese Urge to Civilize: Reflections on Change' in *Proceedings of the Australian Academy of Humanities 1982–1983* Victoria: The Dominion Press, Hedges and Bell, 1984

27 On neo-Confucian tradition in Korea, see Wm Theodore de Bary and JaHyun Kim Haboush (eds) *The Rise of Neo-Confucianism in Korea* New York: Columbia University Press, 1985

28 For example, Kim Kyuhwan *Ilje ŭi tae han ŏllon, sŏnjŏn chŏngch'aek* Seoul: Iu Publishers, 1978, pp. 257–8

Chapter 1

1 Hong Yi-Sup *Korea's Self-Identity* Seoul: Yonsei University Press, 1973, pp. 123–41

2 Kim Yongsŏp *Han'guk Kŭndae Nongŏpsa Yŏn'gu* Seoul: Ilchogak, 1979, p. 319

3 By 'voluntary' religion is meant religion professed not because of birth or nationality or official patronage, but by conscious decision. The term is used in C. K. Yang *Religion in Chinese Society* Berkeley: University of California Press, 1970

4 Buddhism had flourished during the United Silla and Koryŏ periods (i.e. from the seventh to fourteenth centuries), but was disestablished and severely suppressed under the Chosŏn dynasty despite temporary respite under kings Sejong and Sejo in the mid-fifteenth century. See Lee Ki-baik *A New History of Korea* Cambridge, Massachussets and London: Harvard University Press, 1984, pp. 199–200

5 Charles A. Clark *Religions of Old Korea* Seoul: Christian Literature Society of Korea, 1961 reprint, p. 89. This judgment, stated in different terms, is given also in Han Woo-keun *The History of Korea* Honolulu: University Press of Hawaii, 1974, p. 353; and Hahm Pyong-Choon *The Korean Political Tradition and Law* Seoul: Royal Asiatic Society, Korea Branch, 1971, p. 14

6 Typical of this is a note in *The Independent*, a nationalist newspaper, on 1 August 1896: 'Rumour has it that several hundred priests (Buddhists) from around Seoul have come south, bringing in their kits old fashioned suits of soldier's uniform, which upon occasion they don and proceed to rob and extort money. Rumour has it that an edict has gone forth from Chun Ju to arrest all Seoul priests on sight.'

7 See Yi Songmu 'The Influence of Neo-Confucianism on Education and the Civil Service Examination System in Fourteenth- and Fifteenth-Century Korea' in Wm Theodore de Bary and JaHyun Kim Haboush (eds) *The Rise of Neo-Confucianism in Korea* pp. 134–5

8 See Michael E. Robinson *Cultural Nationalism* pp. 80–81

9 See B. B. Weems *Reform, Rebellion and the Heavenly Way* Tucson: University of Arizona Press, 1964

10 This is particularly true of the new Korean History Research Society (Han'guk yŏksa yŏn'guhoe) organised in Seoul in 1988.

11 For example, Lak-Geoon George Paik *The History of Protestant Missions in Korea, 1932–1910* Seoul: Yonsei University reprint, 1980; R. E. Shearer *Wildfire: Church Growth in Korea* Grand Rapids, Michigan: William B. Eerdmans Publishing Co., 1966; Spencer J. Palmer *Korea and Christianity* Seoul: Hollym Corporation, 1967; Yi Man'yŏl *Hanmal Kidokkyo wa Minjok Undong* Seoul: P'yŏngminsa, 1980; and Donald N. Clark *Christianity in Modern Korea* Lanham: University Press of America, 1986

12 Spencer J. Palmer *Korea and Christianity* p. 89

13 In his recent dissertation, Park Chung-shin questions the idea that Korean religion enjoyed greater affinities with Christianity than any other nation. I also find difficulties with the argument for affinity, but I

confess I find Park's assertion that what they held in common was universal to religion rather superficial. I tend to take an opposite view, that the alleged affinities were not really there. See Park Chung-shin, Protestant Christians and Politics in Korea, 1884–1980s, PhD thesis, University of Washington, 1987

14 Charles A. Clark, p. 143. See also Palmer, pp. 14–18
15 Ch'oe Namson '"Sangddal" kwa kaech'ŏn ch'ŏl ŭi chonggyojŏk ŭiŭi' Tonggwang 7, November 1926, pp. 86–90
16 Il Ung 'Tan'gun shinhwa' Kaebyok 1, June 1920, pp. 61–63
17 Kim Kwang-ok 'Flexibility of Korean Religious Thought' Korea Journal 23, 7, July 1983, p. 65. Dr George L. G. Paik also informed me of the predominance of non-monotheistic belief at this time: Dr George Paik interview, Seoul, 27 August 1981. On this problem, see also Robert N. Bellah 'Religious Evolution' American Sociological Review 29, June 1964, p. 359
18 George A. Lensen Balance of Intrigue. International Rivalry in Korea and Manchuria, 1884–1899 (2 vols) Tallahassee: University Presses of Florida, Vol. 1, p. 11
19 Paik History of Protestant Missions p. 20
20 Quoted in Park Yong-Shin, Protestant Christianity and Social Change in Korea, PhD thesis, University of California, Berkeley, 1975, p. 30
21 Lee Kwangnin 'Kaikaha no kaishinkyō kan' in Kan 7, 11–12, November–December 1978, pp. 10–12. Reformists can be divided into two main groups, the 'moderates' who rejected all Western thought and admitted its material skills only, and the 'radicals' who thought this dichotomy contradictory. It will be noticed that the 'isolationists', the strict neo-Confucianists, agreed with the radical reformists that the moderates' dichotomy was false and thus concluded that the West in its entirety was poison.
22 Park, PhD thesis, pp. 35–6
23 Park, p. 38; Lee Kwangnin 'Kaikaha kaishinkyō kan' p. 29
24 That is, as physician to the American legation. Quoted in F. H. Harrington God, Mammon and the Japanese Madison: University of Wisconson Press, 1966, p. 1
25 Quoted in Park, p. 39
26 Harrington, Ch. 3; Paik, p. 86. In 1897, Dr Allen became Minister Resident and Consul-General, and from 1901–05 was Envoy Extraordinaire and Minister Plenipotentiary. He was decorated by Emperor Kojong on three occasions.
27 Lensen Balance of Intrigue Vol. 1, p. 123
28 Lee Kwangnin, pp. 19–23. The wijŏng chŏksa movement is examined in some detail in Kim Yŏngjak Kanmatsu nashonarizumu no kenkyū Tokyo: Tokyo University Press, 1975
29 Paik, p. 163. On his return from the United States as Royal Envoy, Prince Min Yŏngik reported to Kojong that 'America remains supremely powerful without honouring the military.' [Emphasis added]: Hahm Pyong-Choon 'Korean Perception of America' Sahakji, 7, November 1983, p. 30. Both America and Japan were strong, but the former was so in the 'correct' way. This was an important factor in the gradual

acceptance of the West even among members of the Korean establishment, and in the lapse of the anti-foreign edicts.
30 Paik, p. 135
31 Unpublished diary of J. Henry Davis *Archives of the Presbyterian Church of Victoria, Australia*: 'Korean Mission' Mitchell Library, Public Library of New South Wales, Sydney, 19 and 22 March 1890
32 Quoted in Paik, p. 263
33 C. C. Vinton 'Statistics of the Protestant Churches in Korea' *The Korean Repository* 2, October 1895, p. 383. If non-baptised members are added, the figure for 1895 becomes 1095. For the 1905 figure, see Shearer *Wildfire* pp. 51–2, 167, 176 and Appendix; Yi Man'yŏl *Hanmal Kidokkyo* pp. 67 and 106. Since non-baptised membership was normally greater than full membership, the total number of adherents of Methodist and Presbyterian denominations in 1905 was probably over 28 000.
34 This point was put forcefully by Sŏ Chaep'il in editorials of *The Independent*: 7 April, 16 May, 10 September and 14 November 1896
35 Yun Ch'iho 'Confucianism in Korea' *The Korean Repository* 2 November 1895; G. H. Jones 'The Status of Women in Korea' ibid. 3 June 1896; Annie L. A. Baird *Daybreak in Korea* New York: Fleming H. Revell Co., 1909; editorials in *The Independent* 19 November 1896 and the *Tongnip Sinmun* 21 April, 11 June 1896, 5 January, 20 February, 11 December 1897, 16 November 1898, 5 April, 29–31 May and 7 September 1899. See also Yi Man'yŏl, pp. 33ff. and 74–80
36 Park, pp. 98–100, 129
37 Lee Kwangnin, p. 27
38 *Tongnip Sinmun* 20 August 1896, editorial
39 *Government Gazette* (Kwanbo) 36, 12 May 1895; 117, 22 July 1895; 121, 24 July 1895; 135, 12 August 1895; 138, 15 August 1895 (these dates are by lunar calendar; the following are solar) 257, 25 February 1896; 287, 31 March 1896; *Tongnip Sinmun* 11 and 25 June 1896; *The Korean Repository* 3, June 1896, pp. 248–50
40 *Yun Ch'iho Ilgi* (Hereafter: *Yun Diary*) (8 vols) Seoul: Kuksa p'yŏnch'an wiwŏnhoe, 1973–1986: 31 July and 9 August 1904. Also Yi Man'yŏl, pp. 127–8
41 *Annual Report of the Korea Mission of the Presbyterian Church in the U.S.A.* 1903–1904: 'Seoul Station Report' Seoul, 1904. (H. G. Underwood Collection, Seoul) (Hereafter: *ARPC*)
42 *ARPC* Pyeng Yang and Syen Chyun Reports.
43 Park, p. 225
44 *Kankoku genji ni okeru chihō jinshin jōkyō* 1 November 1909: (2), Jinmin no kakkaikyu o tsūjite sono minshin o shihai suru seiryoku chūshin no idō. (Documents held in Yonsei University Library, Seoul. Hereafter: YUL)
45 ibid. (16), Seisha sono ta no kai no jōkyō: kaiin no kōdō oyobi kanmin no kai ni taisuru kanjō; and (18), Kankokumin no kōdoku suru shinbun mata wa shoseki oyobi sono kanka no jōkyō. Other publications include *Kyoyuk Wŏlbo, Sonyŏn, Taehan Chaganghoe Wŏlbo*, and *Yaso Sinmun*. Shin for his part became president of the Taedong Hakhoe, a conservative study society. Shin died in 1909. Ch'oe Ikhyŏn led a band of

guerillas from the end of 1905 but was captured and died during a hunger strike in 1906.

46 For example, *Kongnip Sinmun* 29 November 1907, editorial.

47 See Shin Ch'aeho 'Taehan ŭi hŭimang' *Taehan Hyŏphoe Wŏlbo* 1, April 1908, pp. 11–20; Na Sōkki 'Minjokjuŭi ron' *Sŏbuk Hakhoe Wŏlbo* 8 January 1906, pp. 38–40; Ku Shinja 'Shinhak kwa kuhak ui kubyol' ibid. p. 41; Yi Posang, 'Hangmushin'gu ro kwŏn'go pulhakja kong' *Kiho Hŭnghakhoe Wŏlbo* 7 February 1909, pp. 5–9

48 *Keimu geppō* 1, 25 July 1910: 'Kankoku tōchū kenpeitai shireibu de kaisaishita kakudō kenpeichō (keimubuchō) kaigi sekijo ni okeru hyōgakubu jikan enzetsu.' (YUL)

49 William Blair and Bruce Hunt *The Korean Pentecost* Edinburgh: Banner of Truth Trust, 1977, p. 63. Part 1 of this book is an edited version of Blair's earlier work of the same title, printed in 1910 by the Board of Foreign Missions of the Presbyterian Church in the United States.

50 Paik, p. 423; Shearer, pp. 48, 60, 167, 176; Yi Manyŏl, pp. 67 and 110–11

51 *Kankoku genji ni okeru chihō jinshin jōkyō* 1 November 1909: (14), Kanmin no Yasokyō ni taisuru hanjō oyobi nyūkyō no dōki narabi ni sakari. (YUL)

52 *ARPC*, 1903–04: Syen Chyun Station Report.

53 Uchida Ryōhei 'Ryūki kaigen himegoto: Heijō no chōsa' 15 April 1907, *Chōsen tōchi shiryō* (10 vols), Tokyo: Kankoku shiryō kenkyūsho, 1970, Vol.4, pp. 120–21 (Hereafter: *CTS*)

54 Blair *The Korean Pentecost* pp. 64–5

55 Yi Man'yŏl, pp. 107–8. Sharp had earlier observed how, during the war, the calmness of the Christians in contrast to non-Christians had attracted membership: *ARPC*, 1903–04: Seoul Station Report.

56 *Keimu geppō* 1, 27 July 1910: loc. cit.

57 *Kankoku genji ni okeru chihō jinshin jōkyō* 1 November 1909, (14)

58 Itō Hirobumi, the Resident-General of Korea, had adopted a more generous attitude toward Christianity in Korea, though with definite political motives. He seems initially to have thought that Christianity would weaken opposition to Japan and, by requesting missionaries to use their moral prestige to keep Koreans in line, he put them in a difficult position.

59 Paik, pp. 370–73

60 Paik, p. 374

61 ibid. p. 370

62 For example, Blair, Ch. 9; *ARPC*, 1907; Min Kyŏngbae *Han'guk Minjok Kyohoe Hyŏngsŏngsa Ron* Seoul: Yonsei University Press, 1974, pp. 38–49; Shearer, pp. 34 and 53

63 Paik, p. 375–8

64 Both Min Kyŏngbae and Yi Man'yŏl suggest this, Min more strongly than Yi. A problem in Min's work is that 'pietism' seems to mean simply anti-intellectualism or even non-intellectualism, as if it did not have a strong intellectual tradition in Christianity.

65 There is evidence that many missionaries who had witnessed the corruption of the Korean administration and its obstruction of reform

considered that Japanese rule might be beneficial. But this attitude began to change once the Residency-General was installed. See Yi Man-'yŏl, pp. 113–18

66 *Kongnip Sinbo* 15 and 22 November 1907
67 Blair, p. 63
68 *ARPC*, 1907, pp. 9–10
69 ibid. Introduction and Seoul, P'yeng Yang and Syen Chyun station reports.
70 *Sinhan Minbo*, 10, 16 and 24 March 1909
71 On the Nevius Method, See Charles A. Clark *The Korean Church and the Nevius Method* New York: Fleming H. Revell, 1930. Also Palmer *Korea and Christianity* pp. 27–8
72 Lillias H. Underwood *Fifteen Years among the Topknots* New York: American Tract Society, 1904, p. 133
73 Park Chung-shin is in error when he claims the Nevius Method was generally applied to all non-Western mission fields. It was not even applied in China, to the chagrin of Dr Nevius who had designed it for that country. Its use in Korea was actually unique. Park seems unaware that the self-governance of the Presbyterian Church in Korea in 1907 was something the missionaries intended on the basis of the Nevius Method and not, as he suggests, something the Koreans wrested from the missionaries at the latter's expense. See his PhD thesis, pp. 27 and 68.
74 Chu Yohan (compiler) *An Tosan Chŏnjip* Seoul: Samjungdang, 1963, p. 28. Chu is careful to make only tentative remarks about An's reported remarks on the revival, whereas Min Kyŏngbae, p. 48, quotes the rumour as solid fact.
75 Yi Kwangsu 'Kŭmil Chosŏn Yaso kyohoe ŭi kyŏlchom' (1917), in *Yi Kwangsu Chŏnjip* (11 vols), Seoul: Ülshinsa, 1979, Vol. 10, pp. 20–24
76 Dr George Paik Interview; *Yun Diary* 8 March 1891
77 This, however, is the claim made in Park Chung-shin, PhD thesis, pp. 65–66
78 Yang Jusam 'Kyŏnggo a Han'guk Yesu kyohoe hyŏngje chamae' *Kongnip Sinbo* 26 February 1908. In 1931 Yang became the first moderator of the United Methodist Church of Korea.
79 *ARPC*, 1903–04, Introduction to the Seoul Report, argues a similar position.
80 *Yun Diary*, 7 December 1890
81 ibid. 13 December 1890
82 ibid. 15 January 1892
83 ibid. 19 January, 9 April and 19 December 1893
84 *Kongnip Sinbo* 25 October 1907
85 ibid. 5 February and 9 September 1908; sermons by Pastor Lee Tŏk ibid. 9 August and 6 September 1907; and his son, Lee Waman ibid. 9 August 1907
86 Palmer, p. 26
87 *Yun Diary* 26 January 1896
88 Collection of manuscripts on 'Modern Missions' *Archives of the Presbyterian Church of Victoria*: Korea Mission. These are four handwritten lectures and they are undated, but internal evidence and the fact that

Australia did not send missionaries to Korea in any numbers until the 1900s suggests that they were probably delivered in the first decade of the twentieth century. The Australian position is supported by writings of American missionaries in Korea. The expected and claimed social impact of missions comes out very clearly in the following works: Annie L. A. Baird *Daybreak in Korea*, and James S. Gale *Korea in Transition* New York: People's Missionary Movement of the United States and Canada, 1909

89 'Christian Missions and Social Progress' *The Korean Repository* February 1898, pp. 64–9

90 Yang Jusam, op. cit.

91 FA McKenzie *The Tragedy of Korea* Seoul: Yonsei University Reprint, 1975 (first published in 1908), p. 151

92 *Collected Letters of Yun Ch'iho* (Hereafter: *Letters*) Seoul: Kuksa p'yŏnch'an wiwŏnhoe 1981: Yun to Dr Y. J. Allen, 25 December 1906

93 ibid. Yun to Dr Candler, 13 October 1907

94 *Kongnip Sinbo* 24 February 1908

95 ibid. 19 February 1908, letter to the editor

96 ibid. 26 February 1908

97 *APRC* 1903–1904, Pyeng Yang Station Report

98 *Kongnip Sinbo* 18 March 1908

99 ibid. 19 February 1908. The newspaper mistakenly calls Ch'oe Sangnyun 'Sŏ Sangyun,' confusing him with one of Korea's first Protestants of that name.

100 *Minjok Undong Ch'ongsŏ* (10 vols) Seoul: Minjok munhwa hyŏphoe, 1980, Vol. 1, pp. 169 and 334–5; also, *Kongnip Sinbo* 8 April 1908

101 *Government-General of Chōsen*: Chōsen no hogo narabi ni heigō, Ch. 1, Section 8 (*CTS*, Vol. 3)

102 Lee Kun Sam *The Christian Confrontation with Shinto Nationalism: A Historical and Critical Study of the Conflict of Christianity and Shinto in Japan during the Period between the Meiji Restoration and the End of World War II (1868–1945)* Philadelphia: Presbyterian and Reformed Publishing Co., 1966, p. 164

103 'Shorter Westminster Catechism' *Westminster Confession of Faith* Glasgow: Free Presbyterian Publications, 1973

Chapter 2

1 Yun Ch'iho 'Kumiin ŭi Chosŏnin'gwan e taehayŏ' *Taep'yo Han'guk Sup'il Munhak Chŏnjip* (2 vols) Seoul: Ŭlsŏ munhwasa, 1975, Vol. 1, p. 117

2 Park Yong-shin, PhD thesis, p. 102

3 The Kapshin Coup, led by Kim Okkyun, Sŏ Kwangbŏm, Hong Yŏngsik, Pak Yŏnghyo and Sŏ Chaep'il on 4 December 1884, lasted barely four days before Ch'ing forces suppressed it. It is one of the best-known events in modern Korean history. There is one study of the coup in English: Harold F. Cook *Korea's 1884 Incident* Seoul: Royal Asiatic Society, Korea Branch, Monograph Series No. 4, 1972

4 For a detailed study of the Independence Club and *Tongnip Sinmun* see Vipan Chandra *Imperialism, Resistance, and Reform in Late Nineteenth-*

Century Korea: Enlightenment and the Independence Club Berkeley: Center for Korean Studies, Institute of East Asian Studies, University of California, 1988

5 *Yun Diary* 18 November 1905

6 Germany, France, Britain and the United States were also involved, but generally had less interest and influence.

7 A more detailed discussion of Yun's pre-conversion activities is given in Kenneth M. Wells 'Yun Ch'i-ho and the Quest for National Integrity' *Korea Journal* 22, 1, January 1982, pp. 42–59

8 *Yun Diary* 2 November 1883

9 Lensen, Vol. 1, p. 23

10 *Letters* Li Hung-chang to Kojong

11 *Yun Diary*, 5 April 1884

12 ibid. 18 January 1884

13 ibid. 6 December 1884

14 ibid. 7, 14, 15, 20 December 1884; 14 February 1885. For the official Japanese response, which was displeasure at the involvement of Japanese liberals, see Hilary Conroy *The Japanese Seizure of Korea, 1968–1910* Philadelphia: University of Pennsylvania Press, 1960, p. 134

15 *Yun Diary* 3 April 1887 and 16 April 1889

16 Yun wrote of the circumstances of his conversion under the heading, 'A Synopsis of What I Was and What I Am,' in June 1887. See Paik *History of Protestant Missions* pp. 166–7

17 *Yun Diary*, 30 March 1889

18 ibid. 14 October 1892. Although Yun mentions reading Gibbon, Macaulay and Carlyle, his diary does not record his having read Spencer. Given his advanced proficiency in Chinese, Japanese and English, it is likely Yun read evolutionary theories of history and nations. In Shanghai, Yun may have read a Chinese translation of T. Huxley's *Evolution and Ethics and Other Essays*, which came into Korea about 1905. (See Lee Kwangnin, op. cit., p. 31)

19 *Yun Diary*, 23 December 1889

20 ibid. 6 May 1890

21 ibid. 20 October 1892

22 ibid. 6 May 1891 and 24 September 1893

23 ibid. 11 October, 14 December 1889

24 A belief held not only by Protestants, of course, nor by all Protestants. However, in America and Great Britain at that time the Protestant link appears to have been strong. Many people go back to the Englishman Richard Baxter as the greatest exponent of this approach. I am not here concerned with applying or testing the theses of Weber and Tawney.

25 *Yun Diary*, 19 February 1893. See also 8 April and 19 December 1893

26 ibid. 20 October 1896

27 ibid. 17 December 1893. 'Ri' is Principle and 'ki' is Essence or Force. There were three schools of thought on this, divided over which should be given priority or whether either took priority over the other. Yun's criticism is of course sweeping and could hardly apply to the Silhak school, but whereas conservative neo-Confucianists pronounced Silhak anathema, reformists admired it.

28 *Yun Diary*, 11 April 1902
29 Here is evidence that the idea that the Korean situation invited foreign
control pre-dates the Japanese 'colonial' interpretation. However, the
idea of moral desert is not the same as the Japanese view. To Yun,
providence meant God's ability to pursue moral ends through the
seemingly amoral processes of history. Korea's fault was not Japan's
justification, but of Korea's fault Yun was certain: ibid. 7 May and 14
November 1902
30 ibid. 6 April 1902
31 Vipan Chandra *Imperialism, Resistance, and Reform* p. 95
32 *Yun Diary* 12 December 1893. Yun does not cite any maxims.
33 ibid. 18 May 1890
34 Hsün Tzu is the philosopher who explicitly claims humans to be basically
evil, but Mo Tzu implies as much when he teaches that humans in their
original, ungoverned state turned necessarily to hate, injury and chaos.
See Vitaly A. Rubin *Individual and State in Ancient China: Essays on
Four Chinese Philosophers* New York: Columbia University Press, 1976,
p. 40
35 *Yun Diary* 17 December 1893. On Buddhism, Yun said very little, which
may reflect the low repute of Buddhism at the time.
36 ibid. 14 December 1900; 25, 26 July 1901; Kim Ŭlhan, *Chwaong Yun
Ch'iho Chŏn* Seoul: Ŭlsŏ munhwasa, 1978, pp. 194–5
37 *Yun Diary* 5 August 1895
38 ibid. 27, 30 November and 24 December 1895, 16 January 1896; *Government Gazette* 9 November 1895 (lunar)
39 *Government Gazette* 12 February (extra edition) and 3 April 1896
40 *Yun Diary*, 31 March 1896
41 *Government Gazette* 25 February and 31 March 1896
42 These reports were titled 'webo'. See *Government Gazette* 20 August to
11 October 1895 (lunar), passim
43 *Yun Diary* 26 February 1896
44 ibid. 25 July 1897. See also Chandra, p. 103
45 ibid. 8, 15 and 29 August 1897
46 *Tongnip Sinmun* (Hereafter: *Tongnip*) 7 May and 12 December 1896; 7
January 1897; 25 July 1899
47 Shin Yongha *Tongnip Hyŏphoe Yŏn'gu* Seoul: Ilchogak, 1981, pp. 34–7.
There is some discrepancy between these figures and those given in
Chandra, p. 109.
48 Quoted in Kim Ŭlhan *Yun Ch'iho* p. 79
49 *Tongnip* 30 April, 4 July, 12 September and 8 December 1896; 5 June
and 27 July 1897; 9 April 1898; 18 January and 18 February 1899
50 ibid. 14 June and 19 September 1898; 9 January, 11 March, 8 August and
18 September 1899
51 ibid. 19 March 1898
52 ibid. 14 June and 19 September 1898; 9 September 1899
53 ibid. loc. cit.
54 *The Independent* 14 November 1896. Also, *Tongnip* 6 August 1896; 16
September 1897; 9 January and 1 March 1899
55 For example, ibid. 11 April 1896; 9 March, 20 April, 5 June and 15 July

1897; 11 January and 15 December 1898; 18 January, 29 May, 16 June and 5 September 1899
56 For example, ibid. 14 May, 11, 30 June and 8 December 1896; 7 January, 23 February and 27 May 1897; 11 January, 11 March, 9, 19 April and 16, 18–21 November 1898; 5 April and 8 August 1899
57 For example, ibid. 16 April, 14 July and 25, 29 August 1896; 18 March, 27 April and 11 December 1897; 19 February, 15, 22 August, 7 September and 30 November 1898; 10 January, 10 April and 12, 14 August 1899
58 For example, *Chosŏn K'ŭrisŭtoin Hoebo* 2 and 24 February, 9 May and 24 November 1897
59 *Yun Diary* 13 February 1898
60 ibid. 27 February 1898
61 *Government Gazette* 14 April 1896; 8, 12, 13 July 1898; 10, 11, 12 (extra), 13, 14 (extra) October 1898
62 A summary in English of these articles is given in Han Woo-keun *The History of Korea* p. 443
63 Yun Ch'iho 'Tongnip Hyŏphoe ŭi hwaldong' *Tonggwang* 26, October 1931, pp. 35–6
64 The manoeuvring of the legations was so blatant that the late Alexander Lensen fittingly titled his two-volume diplomatic history of the period *Balance of Intrigue*. The American diplomat William Sands observed that legation intriguing was open and shameless (*Undiplomatic Memories*, Chs. 3, 5 and 8) and the same theme pervades Harrington, op. cit., Pts 2 and 3. Yun Ch'iho described the conduct of the American Consul-General Greathouse, who replaced the Korean Royal Bodyguard with mercenaries, as 'unconscionable'. (Yun Ch'iho, loc. cit.) The Independence Club succeeded in having the mercenaries removed. The club was anti-Ch'ing from its inception. It maintained good relations with Russia until 1898 when it successfully opposed employment of Russian military and financial advisors. Yun claimed Russia had been guilty of bad faith and accused Japan of 'juggernaut' behaviour. (*Yun Diary* 12 December 1905)
65 *Government Gazette* 14, 22 (extra), 25 November 1898
66 Yun's biographer claims that the bills called for Yun to be the first president (Kim Ŭlhan, pp. 82–3). But Yun's diary says nothing of this and the only quotation of the bill I have come across, in Kim Sehan *Hansŏ-Namgung Ŏk Sŏnsaeng ŭi Saengae* Seoul: Tonga, 1960, pp. 95–6, mentions no names, only the idea.
67 *Yun Diary* 1 and 2 May, 6 November and 27 December 1898; 1 February 1899
68 Chandra, p. 212
69 *Yun Diary* 12 February 1921
70 *Chosŏn K'ŭrisŭtoin Hoebo* 24 November 1897
71 *Tongnip* 5 June 1897
72 ibid. 25 July 1896; 27 May and 1 June 1897; 6 February 1899
73 Kim Yongsŏp *Han'guk Kŭndae Nongŏpsa Yŏn'gu* Seoul: Ilchogak, 1979, pp. 313–19
74 ibid. p. 333
75 ibid. p. 319

76 Yu Kiljun 'Kyŏngjaengnon' *Yu Kiljun Chŏnjip* (5 vols) Seoul: Ilchogak, 1971, Vol. 4, p. 47
77 *Yun Diary* 14 December 1889
78 Carter Joel Eckert, The Colonial Origins of Korean Capitalism: The Koch'ang Kims and the Kyŏngsŏng Spinning and Weaving Company, 1876–1945, PhD thesis, University of Washington, 1986, p. 15
79 ibid. p. 31
80 The Kwangmu reforms, which preceded the Russo-Japanese War, are examined in Kim Yongsŏp, Pt II, Section 3 and Pt III
81 *Yun Diary* 4 May 1904. See also, W. L. Langer *The Diplomacy of Imperialism, 1890–1902* 2nd edn, New York: Alfred A. Knopf, 1951, pp. 168–9; C. A. Fisher 'The Role of Korea in the Far East' *Geographical Journal* 120, 1954, pp. 285ff.; Takeuchi Tatsuji *War and Diplomacy in the Japanese Empire* New York: Doubleday, Doran, 1935, p. 132; Hilary Conroy, p. 328
82 *Government Gazette* 21 August (extra) and 9 September 1904; 6 May 1905 (extra); 'T'ongshin samu insŭng ijŏn ihu sugi kyesan ŭi kubyŏl sinmyŏng': Yun Ch'iho to Acting Japanese Consul, 15 May 1905, *Kuhan-'guk Wegyo Munsŏ* (22 vols) Seoul: Korea University Press, 1965–73, Vol. 7, pp. 563–4
83 *Yun Diary* 8 June 1904
84 ibid. 13 August 1904
85 *Government Gazette* 22, 27, 29 (extra) November, 1, 2, 4 (extra), 5 (extra), 9 (extra) and 21 December 1905
86 This letter is recorded in *Yun Diary* 12 December 1905
87 ibid. 11 March 1893
88 *Letters* Yun to Dr Candler, 22 October 1895
89 ibid. Yun to Dr Candler, 23 January 1896
90 Paik, p. 395
91 Kim Ŭlhan, pp. 115–18
92 Uchida Ryōhei, *Ryūki kaigen himegoto*: 'Heijō no chōsa' 15 April 1907 (*CTS*, Vol. 4, pp. 120–22)
93 *Kongnip Sinbo* 13 September and 22 November 1907
94 Yu Kiljun 'Hŭngsadan ch'wijisŏ' 30 November 1907 *Yu Kiljun Chŏnjip* Vol. 2, pp. 363–7
95 ibid. Vol. 2, p. 264
96 *Kongnip Sinbo* 16 December 1908
97 Quoted in *Sonyŏn* 2, 8, September 1909, pp. 14–16. The compilers of the collected works of Shin Ch'aeho (*Shin Ch'aeho Chŏnjip*, 4 vols), have attributed the Manifesto to Shin (Vol. 3, p. 110). I have checked their source, which is given as the *Taehan Maeil Shinbo*, 7 August 1909, but there is no mention of the Manifesto in that newspaper for that date. In *Sonyŏn*, loc. cit., the Manifesto is published under Yun's name, while Cho Yongman, Song Minho and Pak Pyŏngch'ae *Iljeha ŭi Munhwa Undongsa* Seoul: Minjung sŏgwan, 1973, p. 29 put Yun's name at the head of a list that includes Ch'oe Namsŏn. No mention is made of Shin Ch'aeho.
98 *Sonyŏn*, 2, 9, 1 October 1909, pp. 5ff.; 2, 10, 1 November 1909, pp. 69ff.; 3, 1, 25 January 1910

99 ibid. 1, 2, 1 December 1908, pp. 72–5. See Ken M. Wells 'Civic Morality in the Nationalist Thought of Yun Ch'i-ho' *Papers on Far Eastern History* 28, September 1983, pp. 144–5
100 *Letters* Yun to Dr Candler, 16 April, 1907
101 ibid. Yun to Dr Candler, 3 June 1907
102 William Sands *Undiplomatic Memories* p. 156
103 Chu Yohan *An Tosan Chŏn* Seoul: Samjungdang, 1979, pp. 54–7
104 Marius B. Jansen *The Japanese and Sun Yat-sen* Cambridge, Mass.: Harvard University Press, 1954, p. 105. In 1907, Prime Minister Yi Wan'yong reportedly suggested to Prince Itō that the former leaders of the Independence Club were useful men who could well be employed by the government as district officials. Itō evidently agreed. (*Kongnip Sinbo* 13 September 1907) But An Ch'angho's interview with Itō in 1908 made it clear that the Japanese had no intention of co-operating with nationalists, only of controlling them. When Yi Siyŏng, governor of South P'yŏngan province, began working closely with An and other nationalists, he was simply dismissed. (*Nikkan gaiko shiryō shūsei* [8 vols] Tokyo: Gannando shoten, 1964, Vol. 8, pp. 54–5)
105 *Yun Diary* 16 June 1896
106 *Sonyŏn* 1, 2, 1 December 1908
107 Lin Yü-sheng *The Crisis of Chinese Consciousness: Radical Antitraditionalism in the May Fourth Era* Madison: University of Wisconson Press, 1979, pp. 37–41
108 See Chandra, p. 219
109 See Ch'oe Namsŏn 'Ch'ŏngnyŏn Hakuhoe ŭi chuji' *Sonyŏn* 3, 4, April 1910, pp. 61–5

Chapter 3

1 For a detailed examination of Government-General religious policy, see Wi Jo Kang *Religion and Politics in Korea under the Japanese Rule* New York: Edwin Mellen Press, 1987
2 On Japanese colonial policy, see Ken M. Wells 'Spencer and Mahan in Kimonos: Japanese Colonial Theory' *Journal of East and West Studies* 10, 1, April 1981, pp. 43–58
3 Tatsuji Takeuchi *War and Diplomacy in the Japanese Empire* New York: Doubleday, Doran, 1935, p. 167
4 Dong Wonmo, Japanese Colonial Policy and Practice in Korea, 1905–1945: A Study in Assimilation, PhD thesis, Georgetown University, 1965, p. 25
5 ibid. p. 263
6 Chung Joon-gun, Japanese Colonial Administration in Korea, 1905–19, PhD thesis, Claremont Graduate School and University Center, 1971, p. 125
7 Wells 'Spencer and Mahan' pp. 48–9
8 Dong Wonmo, PhD thesis, pp. 221–2
9 Article III of the Nichi–Rosen Protocol had secured Japan special commercial and industrial interests in Korea. See Lensen, Vol. 2, Ch. 25
10 Sands *Undiplomatic Memories* p. 78

11 Quoted in Henry Chung *The Case of Korea* New York: Fleming H. Revell, 1921, pp. 110–11
12 Dong Wonmo 'Assimilation and Social Mobilization in Korea' in Andrew C. Nahm (ed.) *Korea under Japanese Colonial Rule* Kalamazoo: Center for Korean Studies, Western Michigan University, 1974, p. 155
13 Han Kyo Kim 'An Overview' ibid. p. 50
14 Takayoshi Matsuo 'The Japanese Protestants in Korea, Part One: The Missionary Activity of the Japan Congregational Church in Korea' *Modern Asian Studies* 13, 3, 1979, pp. 403–5
15 ibid. p. 411
16 ibid. pp. 413–14 and 429
17 Hasegawa's *Report* June 1919, Part 2, Section 5: 'Shūkyō ni kansuru ken' (GSC, vol. 1, pp. 499–500).
18 *Sinhan Minbo* 9 November 1916
19 Matsuo, p. 413
20 A. J. Brown to Chosen Mission, 19 October 1915; F. M. Brockman to Dr Mott, 6 September 1915. Presbyterian Church in the United States, Board of Foreign Missions: Korea, religious education controversy. Selected correspondence and documents on microfilm, roll classification No. 762. Presbyterian Historical Society, Philadelphia. (Hereafter USPM)
21 Dr Speer to Dr Brown, date illegible. USPM
22 *APRC* Syen Chyun Station, 1911–12, p. 3
23 *APRC* Syen Chyun Station Report, 1911–12, pp. 61–3
24 E. M. Campbell and A. W. Allen *Korea's Awakening* Melbourne: Brown, Prior and Co. Ltd, 1921, pp. 28–9, say 149 were remanded. Arthur J. Brown *The Conspiracy Case* November 1912, p. 13, says 157. (USPM) Approximately 700 Koreans were detained during the operation.
25 'Statement on the Conspiracy Case' by twelve missionaries under Dr Samuel Moffett, 1912 (*USPM* 762)
26 Rev. J. Jardine 'Statement of the Case' Union Methodist Theological Seminary Report, 25 June 1912; Rev. A. Sharrocks to M. Komatsu, 16 December 1911; 'Letters on the Case' Nos 1–43 (*USPM* 762)
27 Author illegible (Edison?) to Brown, July 1912 (*USPM* 762)
28 Rev. R. Speer to the board, 12 July 1912 (*USPM* 762)
29 Seoul District High Court, Investigation Bureau *Tongnip Undongsa Charyojip* (16 vols) Seoul: Tongnip undongsa p'yŏnch'an wiwŏnhoe, 1972–978, Vol. 14, pp. 760–72
30 Brown *The Conspiracy Case* p. 19; Taegu District Court Records, 1–3 July 1913 (*USPM* 762)
31 Seoul High Court, Criminal Bureau, 9 October 1913 *Chōsen Dokuritsu Undō* (Hereafter: *CDU*) Tokyo: Hara Shobō, 1967, Part 2, Ch. 1, pp. 259–73
32 Mrs A. Sharrocks to Brown, 6 November 1914 (*USPM* 762)
33 Telegram, Governor-General to Minister of Internal Affairs, 15 February 1915; Terauchi to Foreign Minister Katō, Top Secret, 16 February 1915 (*CTS* Vol. 5)
34 *Seoul Press* cuttings (undated) *USPM* 883

35 *Sinhan Minbo* 26 February 1914
36 Cho Tŭngnin 'Han'guk hyŏnshi chŏnghwang' ibid. 16 September 1915.
37 Yi Kwangsu 'Kyumo ŭi in—Yun Ch'iho Ssi' *Tonggwang*, 10, February 1927, p. 8
38 Rev. Jardine 'Statement of the Case' p. 4 (*USPM* 762)
39 *Yun Diary* 29 November 1905
40 Taegu Court of Appeal, Criminal Bureau, 15 July 1913 *Tongnip Undongsa Charyojip* Vol. 14, pp. 772–4
41 *Minjok Undong Ch'ongsŏ* Vol. 6, p. 200
42 *Sinhan Minbo* 23 June 1909
43 Quoted in Henry Chung *The Case of Korea* p. 137. See also the letters printed in *Sinhan Minbo* 13 May 1915 and 13 April 1916
44 See Wells, PhD thesis, pp. 165–7
45 'Results of 3 Years' Administration of Chōsen since Annexation,' Government-General, January 1914. *U.S. Records of the Department of State relating to internal affairs of Korea [Chōsen]*, Doc. 895.00557 (microfilm)
46 ibid.
47 Brown to Komatsu, 16 June 1915 (*USPM* 762)
48 Adams to Guthrie, United States Embassy, Tokyo, 17 August 1915. (*USPM* 762)
49 H. H. Underwood to Brown, 24 July and 13 December 1915; Speer to Brown, 20 September 1915 (*USPM* 762)
50 Komatsu to Brown, 4 November 1915 (*USPM* 762)
51 *Seoul Press* 1 September 1917
52 *Yun Diary* 14 November 1916
53 *Government-General Police Affairs Bureau* (Hereafter: *GGPAB*) Keikō kihatsu, Nos 527 and 553, 13 November and 6 December 1916: Fuonsha hakken shobun no ken *Gendaishi shiryō*: *Chōsen* (Hereafter: *GSC*) (6 Vols) Tokyo: Misuzu shobō, 1966, Vol. 1, pp. 9–13
54 ibid.
55 *Yun Diary* 13 November 1916
56 *GGPAB* keikō kihatsu, Nos 555 and 581, 6 and 22 December 1916: Fuonsha hakken shobun no ken.
57 *Sinhan Minbo* 5 April 1917; Adams to Brown, 9 January 1917 (*USPM* 762)
58 Wasson to Adams, 2 January, 1917 (*USPM* 762)
59 Horace Horton Underwood *Modern Education in Korea* New York: International Press, 1926, p. 162
60 Venable to Brown, 24 October 1916 (*USPM* 762) See also Wells, PhD thesis, pp. 172–4

Chapter 4

1 R. E. Shearer, p. 60; *APRC*, 1913, p. 6; Campell and Allen *Korea's Awakening* p. 28. A Japanese report linked Christian emigration to Siberia, Manchuria, Shanghai, Peking, Hawaii and South America with political circumstances: *Chōsen shireibu chōsei*, 1 June, 1924: Futei Senjin ni kansuru kisoteki kenkyū, Ch. 2, Part 1, pp. 4–5, *Chōsen mondai shiryō*

sōsho (Hereafter: *CMSS*) (10 vols) Tokyo: San'ichi shobō, 1982–83, Vol. 6

2 Shearer, pp. 60 and 167. Baptised members normally comprised one-third of the number of adherents. During this period the proportion of unbaptised members diminished somewhat because of the persecutions.

3 The *kiho p'a* and *sŏbuk p'a* refer to parochial loyalties centred on the central and northwestern provinces respectively.

4 Kim Ku *Paekbŏm Ilchi* Seoul: Paekbŏm Kim Ku sŏnsaeng kinyŏm saŏp hyŏphoe, 1947, pp. 186–7

5 ibid. pp. 196–7

6 *GGPAB* Kōkei kihatsu, No. 422, 3 March 1915: Futei Senjin seinen torishirabe no ken (*GSC* Vol. 1, p. 1)

7 *GGPAB* Kō No. 3094, 18 February 1918: Himitsu kessha hakken shobun no ken. (*GSC* Vol. 1, pp. 35–8)

8 See Kim Ku 'Na ŭi sowŏn' Song Kŏnho (compiler) *Han'guk Kŭndae Sasangga Sŏnjip, 3: Kim Ku* Seoul: Han'gilsa, 1980, pp. 9–18

9 Yi Man'yŏl *Hanmal Kidokkyo* pp. 81–6

10 ibid. p. 116

11 Dr George Paik interview, Seoul, 27 August 1981.

12 An Ch'angho 'Yuk tae saŏp' *Tongnip Sinmun* 8 January 1920

13 Dr George Paik interview. Also Hugh Cynn *The Rebirth of Korea* New York: Abingdon Press, 1920, p. 138

14 Henry Chung *The Case of Korea* p. 159

15 Cynn, pp. 129 and 139–42. Yŏ Unhyŏng ascribed this function to Christianity also: *GGPAB* Kōkei No. 684, 15 January 1920: Kokugai jōkyō: Dokuritsu seigansho teishutsu ni kansuru ken

16 The 'plausibility structure' is a community which gives social and psychological support and credibility to a system of belief. See Peter L. Berger *The Social Construction of Reality* Harmondsworth: Penguin, 1967, pp. 174ff.

17 Hwang Sŏngmo 'P'ŭrot'esŭt'ant'ijŭm kwa Han'guk' *Han'guk Kŭndaehwa ŭi Inyŏm gwa Panghyang* Seoul: Tongguk University Press, 1967, p. 22

18 Yim Louise *My Forty-Year Fight for Korea* Seoul: Chungang University Press, 1964 (1st edn, 1954), pp. 57–61 . Yim became president of Chungang University and a member of the first government of the Republic of Korea.

19 Dr George Paik interview.

20 In Protestant theology there are various traditions on the meaning of the 'Fall'—Lutheran, Reformed, Anglican, Wesleyan, Brethren, Anabaptist and so on. Most, including Reformed and Wesleyan, subscribe to the concept of a remnant of God's image surviving the Fall, the Methodists more unequivocally than the Presbyterians. See Gerrit C. Berkouwer *Man: The Image of God* Grand Rapids, Michigan: William B. Eerdmans, 1969

21 Dr Han T'aedong interview, Seoul, 10 June 1980

22 Yun Ch'iho 'An Old Man's Ruminations (1)' *Letters* 15 October 1945

23 *Kodang Cho Mansik* Seoul: P'yŏngnam minbosa, 1966, pp. 65–9

24 *Sinhan Minbo* 30 June 1913

25 Letters in ibid. 8 and 15 August, 26 September and 3 October 1913. This

was before the education controversy. Observations of church morale by Koreans in Japan af ter 1916 were less positive. See below, p. 96

26 Cho Tŭngnin 'Han'guk hyŏnshi chŏnghwang' *Sinhan Minbo*, 16 September 1915

27 Report of the Bible Society in Korea for 1917, contained in the Rev. Samuel Moffett Collection, Seoul. (Hereafter: Moffett Collection.)

28 Yim Louise *My Forty-Year Fight* pp. 93 and 100

29 'Koguk ch'in'gu haru chŏnyŏk niyagi' Parts 6 and 7; *Sinhan Minbo* 22 and 29 June 1916

30 *GGPAB* Keikō kishu No. 23727–1, 20 November 1915: Yōchūi Senjin no kikan (*GSC* Vol. 1, p. 5)

31 *GGPAB* Kō No. 23808, 16 August 1918: Kokken kaifuku o hyōbō seru futei Senjin kenkyo no ken. (*GSC* Vol. 1, pp. 58–62)

32 An Ch'angho 'Chaemi Hanin ŭi chesil ch'aeg'im' *Sinhan Minbo* 23 June 1913

33 An Ch'angho 'Illyu ŭi haengbok' ibid. 13 August 1914

34 ibid. 26 March 1914, editorial

35 Kang Yŏngso 'Happyŏng ŭi wŏnin' ibid. 10 September 1914

36 Kil Ch'ŏnu 'Minjok kaeryang non (1)' ibid. 6 April 1916

37 This and the previous quotation are taken from J. S. Mill *A System of Logic* Book VI, Ch. 9, Section 2. Mill did, however, state that there were different kinds of causes, and he insisted that individual phenomena and their causes 'must be studied apart'—ibid., loc. cit. Section 3. Kil Ch'ŏn'u's article seems to follow Mill here, but there was a tendency amongst some of the Christians to think that all causes were spiritual.

38 Kil Ch'ŏn'u 'Minjok kaeryang non (2)' *Sinhan Minbo* 4 May 1916

39 ibid. 8 July 1915

40 An Ch'angho 'Uri kungmin ŭi chinhwa ŭi shunsho' ibid. 22 January 1916

41 An Ch'angho, speeches delivered in Los Angeles in June 1916 ibid. 15 and 22 June 1916

42 ibid. 15 June 1916

43 Richard H. Mitchell *The Korean Minority in Japan* Berkeley and Los Angeles: University of California Press, 1967, pp. 15–18

44 See Peter Duus *Party Rivalry and Political Change in Taishō Japan* Cambridge, Mass.: Harvard University Press, 1968, Ch. 5; Kim Sŏngsik *Ilcheha Han'guk Haksaeng Tongnip Undongsa* Seoul: Chŏngŭmsa, 1974, p. 26; Mitchell, p. 18

45 Chŏn Yŏngt'aek 'Chōsen Yasokyō no kako oyobi genjō' speech at Kanda YMCA, 30 October 1917. This and the following speeches are in *GSC* Vol. 2, pp. 1–18

46 Kim Nokjun, farewell speech, Tokyo YMCA, 5 November 1917

47 Sŏ Ch'un 'Chōsen to Yaso kyōkai' Tokyo YMCA, 29 December 1917

48 Welcome speeches, Tokyo YMCA, 26 September and 26 October 1918

49 Sŏ Ch'un 'Kamisama no shintai nansho o ronjite seibutsu tetsugaku ni oyobu' Hakuhoe oratorical meeting, Tokyo YMCA, 22 November 1918

50 Yi Kwangsu 'Yasokyo ŭi Chosŏn e chun ŭnhye' July 1917 *Yi Kwangsu Chŏnjip* (Hereafter: *Yi Works*) (11 vols) Seoul: Ushinsa, 1979, Vol. 10, pp. 17–19. Yi praised Christianity as a light-bearer, the source of the Silhak scholar Tasan's enlightenment and the inspirer of high morality,

194   NEW GOD, NEW NATION

democratic values and respect for women. But certain tendencies dis-
turbed him, and these he outlined in December 1917. Yi's discussion of
the 'faults' of Korean Christianity concerned the survival of traditional
religious habits which he called 'superstitions', and in the main indicate
that he expected Christianity to serve the interests of liberal democracy
and high culture: 'Kŭm'il Chosŏn Yaso kyohoe ŭi kyŏlchŏm' ibid. Vol.
10, pp. 20–24
51 For a discussion of this question, see Kenneth M. Wells 'Background to
the March First Movement: Koreans in Japan, 1905–1919' pp. 5–21
52 Yi Kwangsu 'Kyumo ŭi in—Yun Ch'iho Ssi' *Tonggwang* 10, February
1927, p. 9
53 Quoted in ibid. loc. cit.
54 ibid. loc. cit.
55 Kim Hyŏn'gu 'Uri nara Yesukyo paltal e taehan kippŭm kwa kŏkjŏng'
Sinhan Minbo 7 January 1915. Uchimura Kanzō, a Protestant and political activist in his earlier life, later reacted against the view that Christianity
was to be valued primarily as an instrument of socio-political change.
56 *Sinhan Minbo* 18 July 1913
57 ibid. loc. cit.
58 Yang Jusam 'Kyŏngo a Han'guk Yesu kyohoe hyŏngje chamae' *Kongnip
Sinbo* 26 February 1908
59 *Sinhan Minbo* 5 September 1913, editorial; ibid. 29 April 1914, letter to
the editor
60 Yi Tonghwi, letter to compatriots, ibid. 19 February 1914
61 Kim Yŏngsŏp, speech at the Tokyo YMCA, 5 November 1917 (*GSC* Vol.
2, p. 5)
62 Yim Louise, pp. 55–6
63 'Koguk ch'in'gu haru chŏnyŏk niyagi' Part 6 *Sinhan Minbo* 22 June 1916

Chapter 5
1 Joungwon A. Kim *Divided Korea. The Politics of Development, 1945–
1972* Cambridge, Mass.: Harvard University Press, 1976, p. 27
2 Chōsen shireibu chōsei, 1 June 1924: Futei Senjin ni kansuru kisoteki
kenkyū, Ch. 6, Part 1, p. 41 (*CMSS* Vol. 6)
3 Henry Chung *The Case of Korea* p. 301
4 Dae-sook Suh *The Korean Communist Movement* pp. 55–6
5 See Wells, PhD thesis, p. 215
6 For example, this statement by Vasili Andreivich Mun: 'Christianity in
Korea has been recognised as the national religion, from which we have
learned the meaning of democracy and the value of liberty.' Declaration
of the Korean National Council in Nikolsk–Ussurisk. *Records of the Department of State relating to internal affairs of Korea (Chōsen) 1910–1929*
Doc. No. 895.00/606, microfilm reel 2
7 Yi Kwangsu 'Na ŭi kobaek' Sŏ Kŏnsŏk (compiler) *Yi Kwangsu Chŏnjip*
2nd edn, Seoul Samjungdang, 1974, p. 259
8 See Lee Chong-sik *The Politics of Korean Nationalism* Berkeley and Los
Angeles: University of California Press, 1963, pp. 149–50
9 Henry Chung, p. 190

10 *GGPAB* Kōkei No. 1581, 23 May 1922: Kokumin daihyōkai no keika ni kansuru ken (*CDU* Part 3, Ch. 1, pp. 178–80)

11 See R. A. Scalapino and Lee Chong-sik 'The Origins of the Korean Communist Movement I' *Journal of Asian Studies* 20, 1, November 1960, p. 16. Stephen Bonsal's published diary *Suitors and Suppliants: The Little Nations at Versailles* New York: Prentice-Hall Inc., 1946, contains a first-hand account of Kim's disillusionment on pp. 220–26. See also Young-won Kim, p. 29, and Chōsen shireibu chōsei, 1 June 1924: Futei Senjin ni kansuru kisoteki kenkyū, Ch. 2, Part 4, p. 7

12 Yŏ Unhyŏng, speech delivered at the National Delegates' Conference, 12 May 1921, printed in *Tongnip Sinmun* 14 May 1921

13 ibid. 31 May 1921

14 See Kenneth M. Wells 'Spencer and Mahan in Kimonos' pp. 46–8

15 *Nihon rekishi daijiten* Tokyo: Kawade shobō 1970, Vol. 6, p. 60

16 Dong Wonmo, PhD thesis, pp. 155–6

17 Henry Chung, p. 270

18 *Yun Diary* 13 September 1919

19 See, for example, the following *GGPAB* documents: Kōkei No. 34939, 9 December 1919: Keijō ni okeru fuon jōkyō tsuibō; No. 36043, 23 December 1919: Futei Senjin kenkyo no ken; No. 36611, 26 December 1919: Fuon bunsho hakken ni kansuru ken; No. 983, 22 January 1920: Himitsu kessha kokuminkaien boshūsha oyobi fuon bunsho seifusha kenkyo ni kansuru ken; Kōkei No. 2917, 6 February 1920: Kitoku shinkōkai soshiki keikaku ni kansuru ken. (*CDU* Part 2, Ch. 3, pp. 230–78)

20 On the Presbyterian and Methodist Assemblies' debates see *GGPAB* Kōkei No. 32746, 18 November 1919: Hokkanrikyō dai jūni kai nenkai ni kansuru ken; No. 33687, 28 November 1919: Yasokyōto oyobi kari seifuen no kokuzai renmeikaigi ni taisuru undō keikaku no ken; No. 32779, 19 November 1919, Keijō minjō ihō: Senjin bokushi no gendō. (*GSC* Vol. 1, pp. 576ff.)

21 *GGPAB* Kōkei No. 28470, 6 October 1919, Chihō minjō ihō: Nankanriha Yasokyō nenkai nite sōjō hannin no kazoku ni taisuru gienkin boshū no ketsugi.

22 *GGPAB* Kōkei No. 34850, 9 December 1919: Himitsu kessha Daikan kokuminkai oyobi Daikan dokuritsu seinendan no kenkyo ni kansuru ken. (*CDU* part 2, Ch. 3, pp. 225–30)

23 *GGPAB* Kōkei No. 32779, 19 November 1919, Keijō minjō ihō: Kitokukyō seinenkai kōen no jōkyō. (*GSC* Vol. 1, p. 582)

24 Taegu District Court, Records of the trial of the Youth Diplomatic Corps and Patriotic Women's Society, 29 June 1920 (*CTS* Vol. 5, pp. 739ff.); *GGPAB* Kōkei No. 33497, 5 December 1919: Daikan minkoku aikoku fujinkai kenkyo no ken; No. 1536, 22 January 1920: Daikan aikoku fujinkai ni kansuru ken. (*CDU* Part 2, Ch. 3, pp. 221–4, 265–6); Bansai sōjō jiken (san'ichi undō) (3): Eibun shiryō *Chōsen Kindai Shiryō (11)* Tokyo: Gannandō shoten, 1964, pp. 70–74; and Saitō Makoto's policy statements in *Seoul Press*, 3 and 18 January 1920 and *Japan Advertiser*, 14 January 1920

25 See Robinson *Cultural Nationalism* Ch. 2

26 'Shōwa rokunen ni okeru shakai undō no jōkyō. Zairyū Chōsenjin no

undō: 5. Minzokushugi undō' *Naimushō keihōkyoku hen* (Hereafter: *NHK*) (16 vols) Tokyo: San'ichi shobō, 1971, Vol. 3

27 *CMSS* Vol. 6, p. 53

28 *GGPAB* Kōkei No. 13004, 7 May 1921: Yasokyō seinen rengōkai ni kansuru ken. (*CDU* Part 2, Ch. 3, pp. 584–7)

29 *Yun Diary* 29 January, 5, 23, 24, 26 February, 1 and 2 March 1919

30 Yi Kwangsu 'Na ŭi kobaek' in Sŏ Kŏnsŏk *Yi Kwangsu Chŏnjip* pp. 236–7. See also Ku Ch'anghwan 'Ch'unwŏn munhak e nat'anan Kidokkyo sasang' Shin Tonguk (ed.) *Ch'oe Namsŏn kwa Yi Kwangsu ŭi Munhak* Seoul: Saemunsa, 1981, pp. 118–32

31 Yi Kwangsu 'Uri ŭi sasang' *Yi Works* Vol. 10, pp. 244–9

32 Yi Kwangsu 'Na ŭi Kobaek' p. 264

33 *Yi Works* Vol. 10, pp. 116–48

34 ibid. loc. cit.

35 *The Presbyterian* 11 October 1922 (Archives of the Presbyterian Church of Victoria: Korea Mission)

36 ibid. 11 October 1922

37 Chin Tŏkkyu '1920 nyŏndae kungnae minjok e kwanhan koch'al' Song Kŏnho and Kang Man'gil (eds) *Han'guk Minjokjuŭi Ron* Seoul: Ch'angjak kwa pip'yŏngsa, 1982, pp. 140–59; Michael E. Robinson, The Origins and Development of Korean Nationalist Ideology, 1920–1926: Culture, Identity, National Development and Political Schism, PhD thesis, University of Washington, 1979, pp. 270ff.

38 *Minjok Undong Ch'ongsŏ* Vol. 6, p. 244

39 The Manifesto is printed in ibid. pp. 244–6

40 Pak Talsŏng 'Sigŭp'i haegyŏl hal Chosŏn ŭi tae munje' *Kaebyŏk* 1, 25 June 1920, pp. 23–9. *Kaebyŏk* was managed largely by Ch'ŏndogyo adherents.

41 *The Presbyterian* 11 October 1922

42 That is, Aoyanagi Nanmei. See Dong Wonmo, PhD thesis, p. 21

43 Lee Chong-sik *Politics of Korean Nationalism* p. 241

44 Dong Wonmo, PhD thesis, p. 410

45 See Michael Robinson *Cultural Nationalism* Ch. 4

46 Yi Kwangsu 'Chungch'u kyegŭp gwa sahoe' *Yi Works* Vol. 10, pp. 104–9

47 Naimushō keihōkyoku, genmitsu: Shōwa gonen ni okeru shakai undō no jōkyō: 2, Minzokushugi undō no jōkyō. (*CDU* Part 3, Ch. 6, p. 573)

48 *GGPAB* Tōkyō shutchōben, May 1924: Zaikyō Chōsenjin jōkyō; Dr George Paik interview

49 Government-General Justice Bureau, 1938: Chōsen dokuritsu shisō undō no hensen. (*CDU*, Part 2, Ch. 3). There are discrepancies between the dates given in this document and those that appear in the Jubilee History of the Hŭngsadan (*Hŭngsadan Oship Junyŏnsa* Seoul: Hŭngsadan oship junyŏnsa p'yŏnch'an wiwŏnhoe, 1963, p. 40), but I have followed the dates in the former document. The differences are not great.

50 *Tonga Daily* 2 January 1924

51 ibid. 3 January 1924

52 ibid. 5 and 6 January 1924

53 Yi Kwangsu 'Ŭigi ron' *Chosŏn Mundan* 3, December 1924

54 Ch'oe Tugo 'Amhŭkki kaehwain ŭi sunansa—Yun Ch'iho' *Yŏksa ŭi*

Inmul Seoul: Ilsin'gak, 1979, Vol. 8, pp. 213–20
55 *Yun Diary* 12 June 1893
56 See Wells, PhD thesis, pp. 14–15; Dae-sook Suh *Korean Communist Movement* pp. 55–6
57 *Yun Diary* 4 August 1894
58 ibid. 19 December 1919
59 ibid. 19 February and 21 December 1920; 17 April 1921
60 ibid. 4 March 1921
61 ibid. 27 September 1921
62 ibid. 17 May 1920
63 ibid. 31 July 1919

Chapter 6
1 *Minjok Undong Ch'ongsŏ* Vol. 7, p. 94
2 See Dae-sook Suh *The Korean Communist Movement* pp. 82–4
3 *Tonga Daily* 12, 17, 19 and 20 November 1925
4 Kim Pyŏngno 'Sin'ganhoe ŭi haesoron i taeduham e chehayŏ' *Tonggwang* 8, February 1931, pp. 7–8
5 Chu Yohan 'Muŏt poda do' ibid. 1, May 1926, p. 19
6 Changbaek Sanin 'Kaein ilsang saenghwal ŭi hyŏksin i minjok palhŭng ŭi kŭnbon' ibid. 1, May 1926, pp. 29–33
7 An Ch'angho 'Tongp'o ege kohanŭn kŭl' Peking, 1924, and 'Tongjidŭl kke chunŭn kul' 1926(?), in Chu Yohan (compiler) *An Tosan Chŏnjip* (Hereafter: *An Works*) Seoul: Samjungdang, 1963. The contents of these pieces were printed in *Tonggwang*, from May to December 1926 and January and February 1927.
8 An Ch'angho, letter to Hŭngsadan members, 7 July 1921, ibid. loc. cit.
9 An Ch'angho 'Kaejo' 1919(?) ibid.
10 An Ch'angho 'Sarang' 1920 ibid.
11 ibid. loc. cit.
12 An Ch'angho 'Mujŏnghan sahoe wa yujŏnghan sahoe' *Tonggwang* 2, June 1926, pp. 29–33 (under pseudonym: Som'me)
13 An Ch'angho op. cit and 'Tongjidŭl kke chunŭn kŭl'
14 See Arthur Leslie Gardner, The Korean Nationalist Movement and An Ch'ang-ho, Advocate of Gradualism, PhD thesis, University of Hawaii, 1979, pp. 183–184
15 An Ch'angho 'Tongp'o ege kohanŭn kŭl'
16 Records of the Provisional Government Legislature, 9 July, 1919, in *An Works*
17 An Ch'angho 'Sarang'
18 See the concluding remarks of 'Two Concepts of Liberty' in Isaiah Berlin *Four Essays on Liberty* New York: Oxford University Press, 1970
19 An Ch'angho 'Tongp'o ege kohanŭn kŭl'; 'Tongnip undong pangch'im'; 'Mul panghwang'; and 'Chŏngbu esŏ sat'oe hamyŏnsŏ' in *An Works*
20 An Ch'angho 'Tongp'o ege kohanŭn kŭl'
21 Benjamin Schwartz *In Search of Wealth and Power: Yen Fu and the West* Cambridge, Mass: the Belknap Press of Harvard University Press, 1964, pp. 116–17

22 L. T. Hobhouse *Liberalism* London: Williams and Norgate, 1911, p. 26
23 ibid. p. 123
24 An Ch'angho 'Onŭl ŭi Chosŏn haksaeng' and 'Tongjidŭl gge chunŭn kŭl'
25 Kim Yun'gyŏng 'Kaein kwa sahoe' *Tonggwang* 9, January 1927, pp. 20–31. Kim became a teacher at the Methodist Paehwa College.
26 Kim Yun'gyŏng 'In'gyŏk kwa tan'gyŏl' ibid. 6, October 1926, p. 6
27 See also Paul Tillich *Love, Power and Justice* Oxford: Oxford University Press, 1960, Ch. 2
28 An Ch'angho 'Hapdong kwa pulli' *Tonggwang* 1, May 1926, pp. 14–18 (under pseudonym: Sanong)
29 Kim Yun'gyŏng 'In'gyŏk ŭi hangnijŏk haeŭi' ibid. 4, August 1926, pp. 6–10
30 *GGPAB* Kōkei 37234, 24 November 1920: Kokugai jōhō, Shanhai futei Senjin no soshiki seru kakushu dantai. (*CDU* Part 3, Ch. 2, pp. 418–20)
31 The concurrence of the Ch'ŏndogyo and Buddhist nationalist leadership was clearer in relation to economic movements, and is mentioned in Chapter 7. Yun Ch'iho and Yi Chongnin worked well together, establishing the Yŏnnonghoe in the early 1930s. See Kim Kyuhwan *Ilche ŭi tae Han ŏllon sŏnjŏn chŏngch'aek* Seoul: Iu, 1978, p. 258
32 *Tonga Daily* 12 December 1922
33 R. W. Macaulay 'The Key to the Far East' 1934, pp. 12–13, in the *Archives of the Presbyterian Church of Victoria: Korea Mission*, and R. H. Baird 'Present Day Religious Problems' 50th Anniversary of the Korea Mission (Presbyterian), June–July 1934 (Moffett Collection)
34 *Seoul Press* 8 March 1919
35 Kim Kyuhwan, p. 176
36 See Shin Ch'aeho 'Chosŏn hyŏngmyŏng sŏnŏn' *Tanjae Shin Ch'aeho Chŏnjip* Vol. 3, pp. 35–6
37 Shin Ch'aeho 'Yong gwa Yong ŭi tae kyŏkjŏn' ibid. Supplementary Volume, p. 283
38 ibid. p. 286
39 ibid. p. 286
40 ibid. p. 296
41 *Hŭngsadan Oship Junyŏn Sa* p. 69
42 Chōsen Sōtokufu hōmukyoku, 1938: Chōsen dokuritsu shisō undō no hensen: Koshidan. (*CDU* Part 2, Ch. 3, pp. 333–8)
43 An Ch'angho, letter to Han Sŭnggon and Chang Rido, 2 August 1927, *An Works*
44 Chōsen sōtokufu hōmukyoku, 1938, loc.cit.
45 ibid.
46 An Ch'angho op. cit.
47 Chu Yohan 'Suyang tanch'e ŭi nagal kil' *Tonggwang* 15, July 1927, p. 2
48 Chu Yohan 'Nalgŭn todŏk ŭi sae yongch'ŏ' ibid. 15, July 1927, p. 3
49 Chu Yohan op. cit.
50 See pp. 156–157
51 Chōsen sōtokufu hōmukyoku, 1938, loc. cit.
52 ibid.
53 An Ch'angho 'Ch'ŏngnyŏn ege hosoham' *Tonggwang* 18, February 1931, pp. 12–13 (under pseudonym: San'ong)

54 An Ch'angho 'Hŏnshinjŏk chŏngshin ŭi paeyang' ibid. 21, May 1931, p.42 (under pseudonym: Sanong)
55 Chu Yohan 'Tonguhoe nŭn muŏshin'ga?' ibid. 36, August 1932, pp. 36–7
56 Yi Kwangsu 'Sihwa' and 'Inyŏk' ibid. 17, January 1931, pp. 2 and 40–41
57 Yi Kwangsu 'Kŭrisŭto ŭi hyŏngmyŏng sasang' Ch'ŏngnyŏn 11, 1, January 1931
58 ibid.
59 GGPAB 1939: Saikin ni okeru Chōsen chian jōkyō. (CDU Part 2, Ch. 3, p. 345)
60 A Japanese report claims Shin's Positive Faith Corps was modelled on the Hitler Youth Movement, with the idea of creating a 'positive Christianity': CDU Part 2, Ch. 3, p. 343. However, in 1934 Shin lamented that 'in these days of dictatorships and Fascisms, liberalism seems to have suffered a serious setback', and claimed that Christian thought was the 'soul of liberalism'. (Hugh Cynn 'Laymen and the Church' Within the Gate, Northern Methodist Mission in Korea, 1934, p. 119)
61 Cho Mansik 'Chungsim kigwan ŭi chaejojik' Shin Tonga January 1936
62 Cho Mansik 'Ch'ŏngnyŏn iyŏ apkil ŭl parabora' Samch'ŏlli January 1936
63 Yun Ch'iho 'Ilch'i tan'gyŏl hagi rŭl' ibid. January 1936
64 Interview with Yi Chongnin, 23 January 1936, recorded by the monk, Ch'on An, in An Works. Ch'unwŏn is Yi Kwangsu's pen name.
65 Kim Pyŏngno, Chang Rido and Kim Yangsu 'Tosan ŭl mal handa' Saebyŏk November 1960 (An Works)
66 Cho Mansik 'Uri ŭi cheil chuŭi nŭn?'—Chungshim tanch'e chojik' Samch'ŏlli February 1936
67 Cho Mansik 'Saengsan kwa sobi wa uri kago' Ch'ŏngnyŏn April 1936
68 Cho Mansik 'Kidok ch'ŏngnyŏn ŭi isang' ibid. January 1937
69 ibid.
70 Cho Mansik 'Sŏ, In, Kŭn' Cho Kwang May 1937
71 Cho Mansik 'Kidok ch'ŏngnyŏn ŭi isang'

Chapter 7

1 Lee Kwangnin 'Kaikaki no Kansei chihō to Kaishinkyō' Kan 8, 2, February 1979, pp. 9–10 and 20
2 Ch'oe Hojin Han'guk Kyŏngjesa Seoul: rev. edn, Pag'yŏngsa, 1981, pp. 220–21
3 Carter Eckert, The Colonial Origins of Korean Capitalism, PhD thesis, p. 34
4 Y. Hayami 'Rice Policy in Japan's Economic Development' American Journal of Agricultural Economics 54, 1, February 1972, pp. 24–5
5 Charles A. Fisher 'The Role of Korea in the Far East' Geographical Journal 120, 1954, pp. 289–90; Andrew J. Grajdanzev Modern Korea New York: John Day Co., 1944, pp. 118ff.
6 Seoul Press 30 April 1913
7 Ch'oe Hojin, p. 223
8 ibid. p.224. Also see Shōwa hachinen ni okeru shakai undō no jōkyō: Zairyū Chōsenjin no undō. (NKH Vol. 5)
9 Chul Won Kang 'An Analysis of Japanese Policy and Economic Change

in Korea' Nahm (ed.) *Korea under Japanese Rule* p. 80
10 Daniel S. Juhn 'Nationalism and Korean Businessmen' ibid. pp. 49ff.
11 Chung Joong-gun, Japanese Colonial Administration, PhD thesis p. 164
12 Fisher, p. 289
13 Eckert, p. 412
14 ibid. p. 86
15 ibid. pp. 88–9 and 104
16 See Michael Robinson *Cultural Nationalism* Ch. 4
17 *Sinhan Minbo* 28 July 1909
18 *Tonga Daily* 22 August 1920, p. 4 and 23 August 1920, p. 4
19 Han Kǔnjo *Kodang Cho Mansik* Seoul: T'aegǔk, 1979, p. 156
20 *Minjok Undong Ch'ongsǒ* Vol. 9, p. 245
21 O Kiyǒng 'Cho Mansik Ssi ǔi ikkǒl chǒkkǒl' *Tonggwang* 17, January 1931, p. 43
22 *Tonga Daily* 17 December 1922
23 Cho Kijun *Han'guk Chabonjuǔi Sǒngnip Saron* Seoul: Korea University Press, 1973, p. 505
24 *Tonga Daily* 26 December 1922
25 Cho Kijun p. 505
26 *Tonga Daily* 11, 22 and 23 January 1923
27 Shōwa rokunen ni okeru shakai undō no jōkyō: Zairyū Chōsenjin no undō. Minzokushugi undǒ. (*NKH* Vol. 3)
28 *Tonga Daily* 3 and 5 February 1923
29 ibid. 9 February 1923
30 ibid 5, 8, 13, 14, 16, 19, 21 and 23 February 1923
31 Cho Kijun p. 511
32 *Tonga Daily* 13 February 1923
33 ibid. 5 and 14 February 1923
34 ibid. 15 February 1923
35 ibid. 16 and 18 February 1923
36 ibid. 16–18 February 1923
37 ibid. 16 February 1923
38 ibid. 22 February 1923
39 Cho Kijun, p. 513
40 ibid. p. 514; *Chosǒn Mulsan Changnyǒhoe Hoebo* (Hereafter: *Mulsan*) 1, 2, February 1930, p. 65
41 *Tonga Daily* 1 January 1925
42 Cho Kijun p. 523
43 *Tonga Daily* 3, 5, 7 and 8 February 1924
44 Quoted in Chin Tǒkkyu '1920 nyǒndae kungnae minjok undong e kwanhan koch'al' Song Kǒnho and Kang Man'gil (eds), p. 148
45 *Tonga Daily* 18 February 1923
46 ibid. 20–21 February 1923
47 ibid. 1 January 1925
48 Cho Kijun, p. 521
49 *Mulsan* 1, 3, March 1930, p. 47
50 Cho Kijun, p. 522
51 *Chosǒn Daily* 6 April 1928
52 Cho Kijun, p. 523

53 *Mulsan* 1, 5, May 1930, pp. 28–31
54 ibid. 1, 3, March 1930, p. 50; *Tonga Daily* 6 June 1928
55 For example, Han Sŭngin 'Hyŏpdong chohap iron muŏsin'ga?' serialised in *Tonggwang* from July 1932 to February 1933, consisted of an historical overview of co-operatives, their economic, political, social and international aspects, strengths, pitfalls and rules of development.
56 Of the 97 major, mainly consumer, co-operatives formed between 1920 and 1932, 83 were established in the final four years (from a survey in ibid. 33, May 1932, pp. 170–171).
57 Han Yongun 'Yŏngjŏk pinp'ip ŭro kot'ong' *Tonga Daily* 9 January 1923; Kim T'aehyŏp 'Chahwal ŭi chŏngsin' *Changsan* 2, 3, March 1931, pp. 8–12. (*Changsan* is the successor to *Mulsan*, renamed in 1931.)
58 *Tonga Daily* 26 January 1922
59 ibid. 12 January 1923
60 *Mulsan* 1, 2, February 1930, p. 55
61 ibid. p. 57
62 Yi Kŭngno 'Chajak chagŭp ŭi ponŭi' ibid. loc. cit. pp. 12–14. It is not unimportant that Yi later became an official in the DPRK (North Korea), since his description of 'self-sufficiency' here is similar to the North Korean *juch'e* principle. Recently, *juch'e* has been branded 'primitive' by a North Korean critic of Kim Il-Sŏng: Lim Un (pseudonym) *The Founding of a Dynasty in North Korea* Tokyo: Jiyūsha, 1982, pp. 286–90
63 For example, A Reporter 'Saengsan t'onggye ro pon Chosŏnin ŭi hyŏnhwang (3)'; Ch'oe Hyŏnbae 'Chosŏn mulsan changnyŏhoe ŭi immu'; and Sŏl T'aehŭi 'Chosŏnin sanggongŏpjadŏl ege' *Mulsan* 1, 3, March 1930, pp. 27–33; 1, 12, December 1930, pp. 2–4; and *Changsan* 2, 3, March 1931, pp. 2–4
64 Sŏl T'aehui op. cit.
65 Kim T'aehyŏp op. cit.
66 See note 47.
67 Unless otherwise acknowledged, these details are gleaned from nationalist journals such as *Tonggwang* and the society journal, *Mulsan*, from *Han'guk Inmyŏng Taesajŏn* Seoul: Sin'gu munhwasa, 1980, from Cho Kijun, pp. 506–7, and from Chin Tŏkkyu op. cit. p. 147
68 Dae-sook Suh, p. 120
69 See, for example, Sŏl T'aehŭi 'Hŏnbŏp sŏ-ŏn,' in *Taehan Hyŏphoe Hoebo* 3, 25 June 1908, pp. 28–31, and 'Kyŏngjehak ch'ongnon' *Taehan Chaganghoe Wŏlbo* 8, February 1907, pp. 29–31
70 Yi Man'yŏl *Hanmal Kidokkyo* p. 128; Lee Kwangnin, 'Kaikaha no kaishinkyō kan' *Kan* 7, 11–12, November–December 1978, p. 38
71 *Kongnip Sinbo* 5 July 1907
72 *Seoul Press* 7 October 1910
73 *Yun Diary* 5 April 1921
74 *Tonggwang* 2, 7, July 1927, p. 24
75 Na had made this assurance in *Tonga Daily* 13 March 1923. Chu's articles, titled 'Musan kyegŭp kwa mulsan changnyŏ,' were printed on page 1 of the newspaper, 6–23 April 1923.
76 Quoted in Robinson, PhD thesis, pp. 243–4

202

NEW GOD, NEW NATION

77 ibid. p. 245

78 *Kodang Cho Mansik* p. 106

79 Dr George Paik interview

80 Yun Yŏngnam 'Cham'yŏl in'ga, tosaeng in'ga?' *Tonga Daily* 26 April 1923, p. 4

81 This does seem to conform with Marx's own words: 'When a society has discovered the natural law that determines its own movement . . . even then it can neither overleap the natural phases of its evolution, nor shuffle them out of the world by a stroke of the pen.' (Quoted in K. R. Popper *The Open Society and its Enemies* [2 vols] London: Routledge and Kegan Paul, 1980, Vol. 2, p. 86)

82 Na Kongmin 'Sahoe munje wa mulsan changnyŏ' *Tonga Daily* 26–29 April 1923, p. 1

83 Namely: 1. real material capacity for class struggle among the proletariat; 2. the morale and determination necessary to persevere in the struggle; and 3. an internationally favourable climate. The absence of this final condition was blamed for the failure of 1919, and Na believed no improvement was in sight.

84 There is, of course, the very important factor of the Japanese economic superstructure, but treatment of this is outside the purpose of this study. Nationalists did consider this factor when planning their movements, as in, for example, *Tonggwang* 31, March 1932, pp. 57–61

85 *Tonga Daily* 26 February 1923, p. 1

86 Shin Ch'aeho 'Chosŏn hyŏngmyŏng sŏnŏn' *Shin Ch'aeho Chŏnjip* Vol. 3, pp. 43–4

87 See 'Hŏmu Tang' 1 January 1926, *Tae-Il Minjok Sŏnŏn* Seoul: Ilu mun'go, 1972, pp. 122–4. This Nihilist Party was an offshoot of the Ŭiryŏl Dan, a group founded in Kirin in November 1919 which adopted terrorism in the 1920s and whose Manifesto was composed by Shin in 1923. The Nihilist Party's Manifesto began, 'We of this present age have neither hope, nor goal, nor future, nor anything at all . . . ' and made 'self-immolation of this utterly meaningless and valueless, wretched existence for the sake of the masses' its ideal.

88 Yun Yŏngnam *Tonga Daily* 26 April 1923, p. 4

89 Na Kongmin ibid. 26 April 1923, p. 1. Needless to say, the radical left did not consider themselves to be advocates of quite this position, but the charge of despair and escapism was a major element in the society's counter-attack.

90 Questionnaire in *Tonggwang* 29, January 1932, p. 58

91 One must allow for the fact that in citing these persons, Cho was answering a *Tonggwang* questionnaire and was given no space to explain what he meant. It is clear from his 1937 comments on Marxism, which are quoted on p. 137, that Cho did not agree with historical materialism or economic determinism. Probably it was Marx's vision of a just society that appealed to Cho rather than his political program, and this reminds one that Marx did not of course invent socialism, nor did he claim to have done so.

92 *Yun Diary* 7 October 1919

93 ibid. 15 October 1919

94 ibid. 16 May 1921 and 13 December 1923
95 ibid. 11 December 1920 and 23 March 1921
96 ibid. 22 January 1921
97 ibid. 1 December 1921
98 ibid. 21 February 1923 and 25 January 1924
99 *GGPAB* Kei kō hi No. 8036, 27 October 1928: Himitsu kessha Chōsen Kyōsantō narabi ni Kōrai Seinenkai jiken kensha no ken. (*GSC* Vol. 5, p. 94)
100 ibid. loc. cit.
101 Kim Ildae 'Ch'ŏndogyo nongmin undong ŭi iron kwa silche' *Tonggwang* 20, April 1931, p. 41
102 Shearer *Wildfrire* p. 142
103 Henry George *Social Problems* London: New Popular Edition, United Committee for Taxation of Land Values Ltd, 1928 (first published 1883), p. 74
104 'Sahoe kaejo ŭi chesasang' *Tonggwang* 22, June 1931, p. 73
105 See Eckert, PhD thesis, pp. 437ff.
106 See for example Pak Hŭido's contributions to the leftist journal *Sin Saenghwal* in 1922.
107 Seoul High Court, Investigation Bureau: Shisō ihō No. 18, March 1939, pp. 12–14 (*CMSS* Vol. 8)
108 Sōtokufu hōmukyoku, 1938: Chōsen dokuritsu shisō undō no hensen. (*CDU* Part 2, Ch. 3, pp. 334–8)
109 *Minjok Undong Ch'ongsŏ* Vol. 6, pp. 263–4
110 *Tongnip Undongsa Charyojip* Vol. 12, pp. 1365–1433. Yi Kwangsu, Chu Yohan, Kim Yun'gyŏng and others were initially sentenced to three to five years' imprisonment. Yun Ch'iho, Shin Hŭngu and Yu Ŏkkyŏm had not been brought to trial before the Japanese Government ordered a political solution.
111 *GGPAB* 1939: Saikin ni okeru Chōsen chian jōkyō. (*CDU* Part 2, Ch. 3, pp. 346–7)

Conclusion
1 This claim is made in *Han'guk Inmyŏng Taesajŏn* p. 574, and by Ch'oe Tugo 'Amhŭkki kaehwain ŭi Sunansa—Yun Ch'iho' *Yŏksa ŭi Inmul* Vol. 8, p. 219, among others.
2 Some Korean scholars seem to take this as a commentary on Yi's whole position. See, for instance, Lee See-jae 'A Study on Korean Rumours during Wartime Japanese Colonial Occupation' *Korea Journal* 27, 8, August 1987, p. 5
3 Michael Bommes and Patrick Wright, in '"Charms of Residence": the public and the past' Richard Johnson (ed.) *Making Histories: Studies in history writing and politics* London: Hutchinson, in association with the Centre for Contemporary Cultural Studies, University of Birmingham, 1982, make this point very clearly in relation to 'official' nationalist histories. The same would seem to apply to any history informed and inspired by a sectional national interest, including the 'people'.
4 *Han'guk Ilbo* 28 July 1981, p. 6; 1, 5 and 6 August 1981, p. 6

5 Kim Junyŏp 'Sae Tongnip Undongsa' *Han'guk Tongnip Undongsa* Vol. 1
   Seoul: Han'guk Ilbo sa, 1987, pp. 25–6
6 Chin Tŏkkyu '1920 nyŏndae kungnae minjok undong'
7 In support of his position, Chin cites (p. 148) a Government-General
   Police Affairs Bureau summary of reports from 1933–38, which deal with
   the Japanese divide-and-rule policy against nationalism at that time. Such
   reports do refer back to earlier periods and, while they note a decline in
   nationalist movements in the mid-1920s, the decline is *relative to socialist
   movements*. Since socialists were still nationalistic, a rise in socialism did
   not mean nationalist sentiment was discarded. Japanese reports also note
   a decline in radicalism by the early 1930s and the resurgence of what they
   termed 'pure nationalism.' See Shakai undō no jōkyō: Minzokushugi
   undō no jōkyō, 1931, 1935 and 1937. (*CDU* Part 3, Ch. 6)
8 See 'Chŏngch'i ron'gang,' Ko Junsŏk (compiler) *Chōsen kakumei tēze*
   Tokyo: Tsuge shobō, 1979, pp. 81–8
9 Carter Eckert, PhD thesis, p. 15
10 ibid. pp. 98 and 438ff.
11 As does Carter: ibid. p. 466
12 Megan Cook *The Constitutionalist party in Cochinchina: The Years of
   Decline, 1930–1942* Victoria: Monash Papers on Southeast Asia, No. 6,
   Centre of Southeast Asian Studies, Monash University, 1977, p. 8
13 ibid. pp. 27–33
14 Susan Abeyasekere *One Hand Clapping: Indonesian Nationalists and the
   Dutch, 1939–1942* Victoria: Monash Papers on Southeast Asia, No. 5,
   Centre of Southeast Asian Studies, Monash University, 1976, p. 2
15 ibid. pp. 8–9
16 *Collected Works of Mahatma Gandhi* New Delhi: Publications Division,
   Navajivan Press, 2nd edn, 1969, Vol. 12, Article 505
17 See Christopher Read *Religion, Revolution & the Russian Intelligentsia,
   1900–1912* London: Macmillan, 1979
18 Jacques Ellul 'Politization and Political Solutions' p. 218
19 Yi Kwangsu 'Ŭigi ron' *Chosŏn Mundan*, 3, December 1924
20 Wang Gungwu indicates the difficulties in his 'Nationalism in Asia'
   Eugene Kamenka (ed.) *Nationalism. The Nature and Evolution of an Idea*
   pp. 82–98. See also Lin Yü-sheng *The Crisis of Chinese Consciousness*,
   and the works of Joseph Levenson on Liang Ch'i-ch'ao and Chinese Confucianism.
21 For instance, Henry George wrote that social reform 'is not to be secured
   by noise and shouting; by complaints and denunciation; by the formation
   of parties, or the making of revolutions; but by the awakening of thought
   and the progress of ideas. Until there be correct thought, there cannot be
   right action . . . Power is always in the hands of the masses of men. What
   oppresses the masses is their own ignorance, their own short-sighted
   selfishness' (*Social Problems* p. 209)
22 Quoted in Michael Robinson, PhD thesis, pp. 234–5
23 Peter Clarke *Liberals and Social Democrats* Cambridge: Cambridge University Press, 1978, p. 6
24 Schwartz *In Search of Wealth and Power* p. 85. See also pp. 72–3 and
   86–7

25 *Sinhan Minbo* 26 March 1914, editorial
26 See the discussion on this in Chapter 2
27 Stanley Rosen *Nihilism, A Philosophical Essay* New Haven and London: Yale University Press, 1969, pp. xiv–xv and 140–97. Also, Allan Megill *Prophets of Extremity* Berkeley and Los Angeles: University of California Press, 1985. See also John Henry Newman *The Idea of a University* Oxford: Clarendon Press, 1976, Discourse V, 9, pp. 110 and 112, where he argues that 'knowledge is one thing, virtue another', and that refinement of the mind by education is 'absolutely distinct' from 'cultivation of virtue'.
28 Kim Ch'angse 'Kwahak kwa chonggyo' *Tonggwang* 12, April 1927, pp. 53–61
29 Interview with Western journalists, Shanghai, 9 September 1919, *An Works*
30 Wang Gungwu 'The Chinese Urge to Civilize: Reflections on Change' pp. 22–4
31 Robinson *Cultural Nationalism* Ch. 5
32 Quoted in Kang Man'gil 'Han'guk minjokjuŭiron ŭi ihae' Yi Yŏnghŭi and Kang Man'gil *Han'guk ŭi Minjokjuŭi Undong kwa Minjung* Seoul: Ture, 1987, p. 19
33 *Yun Diary* 27 February 1919
34 Yi Kwangsu 'Chosŏn minjok undong ŭi sam kich'o saŏp' *Tonggwang* 30, February 1932, pp. 13–15

Select Bibliography

Primary materials

Korean and Sino-Korean

(a) Documents and Collections

An Tosan Chŏnjip (Complete Works of An Ch'angho), Seoul: Samjungdang, 1963.

Han'guk Kŭndae Sasangga Sŏnjip, 3: Kim Ku (Anthology of modern Korean thinkers, 3 Kim Ku) Seoul Han'gilsa, 1980, compiled by Song Kŏnho

Kim Ku. *Paekbŏm Ilchi* Seoul: Paekbŏm Kim Ku Sŏnsaeng kinyŏm saŏp hyŏphoe, 1947

Ku Han'guk Wegyo Munsŏ (Diplomatic documents of Old Korea [i.e. 1876–1905]) 22 vols Seoul: Asiatic Research Centre, Korea University Press, 1965–1973

Kwanbo (Government Gazette) 1894–1910, 17 vols, Seoul: Asea munhwasa, 1973–1974

Minjok Undong Ch'ongsŏ (National movements series) 10 vols Seoul: Minjok munhwa hyŏphoe, 1980–1981

Tae Il Minjok Sŏnŏn (Anti-Japanese national declarations) Seoul: Ilu mun'-go, 1972

Taep'yo Han'guk Sup'il Munhak Chŏnjip (Anthology of Korean literary essays) 2 vols, Seoul: Ŭlsŏ munhwasa, 1975

Tanjae Shin Ch'aeho Chŏnjip (Complete Works of Tanjae Shin Ch'aeho) 4 vols, Seoul: Tanjae Shin Ch'aeho Sŏnsaeng kinyŏm saŏphoe, Hyŏngsŏl, 1979

Tongnip Undongsa Charyojip (Source materials on independence movements) 16 vols, Seoul: Tongnip yugongja saŏp kigŭm unyŏng wiwŏnhoe, 1972–1978

Yi Kwangsu Chŏnjip (Complete works of Yi Kwangsu) 11 vols, Seoul: Ŭlshinsa, 1979

Yu Kiljun Chŏnjip (Complete works of Yu Kiljun) 5 vols, Seoul: Ilchogak, 1971
Yun Ch'iho Ilgi (Diary of Yun Ch'iho) 8 vols, Seoul: Kuksa p'yŏnch'an wiwŏnhoe, 1973–1986, Vol. 1

(b) Journals

Changsan
Cho Kwang
Ch'ŏngnyŏn
Chosŏn K'ŭrisŭtoin Hoebo
Chosŏn Mulsan Changnyŏhoe Hoebo
Chosŏn Mundan
Kaebyŏk
Samch'ŏlli
Shin Saenghwal
Shin Tonga
Sŏbuk Hakhoe Wŏlbo
Sonyŏn
Taehan Chaganghoe Wŏlbo
Taehan Hyŏphoe Hoebo
Tonggwang

Japanese

Chōsen dokuritsu undō 5 vols, Tokyo: Hara shobō, 1967, compiled by Kim Chŏngmyŏng
Chōsen mondai shiryō sōsho 10 vols, Tokyo: San'ichi shobō, 1982–1983, compiled by Pak Kyŏngsik
Chōsen tōchi shiryō 10 vols, Tokyo: Kankoku shiryō kenkyūsho, 1970–1972, compiled by Kim Chŏngju
Gendaishi shiryō: Chōsen 6 vols (Vols 25–30 in *Gendaishi shiryō* series), Tokyo: Misuzu shobō, 1966, compiled by Kang Tŏksang
Naimushō keihōkyoku hen: Shakai undō no jōkyō 14 vols, Tokyo: San'ichi shobō, 1971–1972
Nikkan gaikō shiryō 8 vols, Tokyo: Hara shobō, 1980, compiled by Ishikawa Masaaki (Kim Chŏngmyŏng)

English

Archives of the Presbyterian Church of Victoria: Korea Mission Mitchell Library, Public Library of New South Wales, Sydney
Chōsen kindai shiryō, Chōsen sōtokufu kankei jūyō bunsho senshū 11 vols, Tokyo: Gannandō shobō, 1964, Vol. 11: Bansai Sōjō jiken (San'ichi undō: 3), (Eibun shiryō). Compiled by Kondō Ken'ichi
The Collected Letters of Yun Ch'iho Seoul: Kuksa p'yŏnch'an wiwŏnhoe, 1981.
Horace G. Underwood Collection, Seoul
Records of the Department of State relating to internal affairs of Korea (Chōsen) 1910–1929 National Archives of the United States of America

Presbyterian Church in the U.S.A., Board of Foreign Missions Korea, religious education controversy, Japanese colonial government, 1915. Selected correspondence, reports and miscellaneous papers. Photoduplication of original manuscripts by the Presbyterian Historical Society, Philadelphia, 1972
Samuel Moffett Collection, Seoul
Yun Ch'iho Ilgi (The Diary of Yun Ch'iho) 8 vols, Seoul: Kuksa p'yŏnch'an wiwŏnhoe, 1973–1986, Vols 2–8

Newspapers

Chosŏn Ilbo Seoul: 1920–1940
Tonga Ilbo Seoul: 1920–1940
Independent, The, Seoul: 1896–1899
Kongnip Sinbo San Francisco: 1907–1909
Seoul Press, The Seoul: 1907–1945
Sinhan Minbo San Francisco: 1909–
Tongnip Sinmun Seoul: 1896–1899
Tongnip Sinmun Shanghai: 1919–1928

Interviews

Han T'aedong, Professor of Church History, Yonsei University, Seoul: 10 June 1980
Paik, Lak-Geoon George, President Emeritus, Yonsei University, Seoul: 27 August 1981
Pak Chaech'ang, President of the Kodang Cho Mansik Memorial Society, Seoul: 15 September 1981

Secondary materials

Books

(a) Korean and Japanese

Cho Kijun *Han'guk Chabonjuŭi Sŏngnipsa Ron* (History of the establishment of Korean capitalism) Seoul: Asiatic Research Center, Korea University Press, 1973
Cho Yongman, Song Minho and Pak Pyŏngch'ae *Iljcheha ŭi Munhwa Undongsa* (History of cultural movements under Imperial Japan) Seoul: Minjung sŏgwan, 1970
Ch'oe Hojin *Han'guk Kyŏngjesa* (Economic history of Korea) rev. edn Seoul: Pag'yŏngsa, 1981
Han Kunjo *Kodang Cho Mansik* Seoul: T'aeguk Press, 1976
Hŭngsadan Oship Junyŏnsa (Jubilee history of the Hŭngsadan), Seoul: Hŭngsadan oship junyŏn p'yŏnch'an wiwŏnhoe, 1963
Kidokkyo Sasang editorial division: *Han'guk Kyohoe wa ideollogi* (The Korean Church and ideology) Seoul: *Kidokkyo Sasang* 300 ho kinyŏm nonmunjip 3, Taehan Kidokkyo sŏhoe, 1983
Han'guk ŭi Chongch'i Sinhak (Korean political theology) Seoul: *Kidokkyo Sasang* 300 ho kinyŏm nonmunjip 4, Taehan Kidokkyo sŏhoe, 1984

Kim Kyuhwan *Ilche ŭi Tae Han Ŏllon, Sŏnjŏn Chŏngch'aek* (Japanese speech and propaganda policies towards Korea) Seoul: Iu press, 1978

Kim Sehan *Hansŏ Namgung Ŏk Sŏnsaeng ŭi Saengae* (Life of Hansŏ Namgung Ŏk) Seoul: Donga, 1960

Kim Sŏngsik *Ilcheha Han'guk Haksaeng Tongnip Undongsa* (History of Korean student independence movements under Japan) Seoul: Chŏngŭmsa, 1974

Kim Ŭlhan *Chwaong Yun Ch'iho Chŏn* (Biography of Yun Ch'iho) Seoul: Ŭlso munhwasa, 1978

Kim Yŏngjak *Kanmatsu nashonarizumu no kenkyū* (Study of nationalism at the end of the Chosŏn dynasty), Tokyo: Tokyo University Press, 1975

Kim Yongsŏp *Han'guk Kŭndae Nongŏpsa Yŏn'gu* (History of modern Korean agriculture) Seoul: Ilchogak, 1979

Ko Junsŏk (compiler) *Chōsen kakumei tēze* (Korean revolutionary theses) Tokyo: Tsuge shobō, 1979

Kodang Cho Mansik Seoul: P'yŏngyangji kanhaenghoe, P'yŏngnam minbosa, 1966

Lee Kwangnin *Han'guk Kaehwasa Yŏn'gu* (History of the Korean reform movement) Seoul: Ilchogak, 1969

Min Kyŏngbae *Han'guk Minjok Kyohoe Hyŏngsŏngsa Ron* (History of the formation of the Korean national church), Seoul: Yonsei University Press, 1974

Shin Tonguk (ed) *Ch'oe Namsŏn kwa Yi Kwangsu ŭi Munhak* (Literature of Ch'oe Namsŏn and Yi Kwangsu) Seoul: Saemunsa, 1981

Shin Yongha *Tongnip Hyŏphoe Yŏn'gu* (Study of the Independence Club) Seoul: Ilchogak, 1976

Song Kŏnho and Kang Man'gil (eds) *Han'guk Minjokjuŭi ron* (Studies on Korean nationalism) Seoul: Changjak kwa pip'yŏngsa, 1982

Yi Man'yŏl *Han'guk Kidokkyo Munhwa Undongsa* (History of Korean Christian cultural movements) Seoul: Han'guk Kidokkyo paengnyŏnsa series 3, Taehan Kidokkyo Press, 1987

——*Han'guk Kidokkyo wa Yŏksa Ŭisik* (Korean Christianity and historical consciousness) Seoul: Chisik sanŏpsa, 1981

——*Hanmal Kidokkyo wa Minjok Undong* (Christianity and national movements at the end of the Chosŏn dynasty) Seoul: P'yŏngminsa, 1980

Yi Yŏnghŭi and Kang Man'gil (eds) *Han'guk ŭi Minjokjuŭi undong kwa Minjung* (Korean nationalist movements and the masses) Seoul: Ture sinsŏ 23, Ture, 1987

Yu Tongsik *Han'guk Chonggyo wa Kidokkyo* (Korean religion and Christianity) Seoul: Taehan Kidokkyo sŏhoe, 1983

Yun Pyŏngsŏk, Shin Yongha and An Pyŏngjik *Han'guk Kŭndaesa Ron II: Ilche singminji shidae ŭi minjok undong* (Studies in modern Korean history: II National movements during the Japanese colonial period) Seoul: Chisik sanŏpsa, 1977

(b) English

Abeyasekere, Susan *One Hand Clapping: Indonesian Nationalists and the Dutch, 1939–1942* Melbourne: Monash Papers on Southeast Asia 5, Centre of Southeast Asian Studies, Monash University, Victoria, 1976

Anderson, Benedict *Imagined Communities Reflections on the Origin and Spread of Nationalism* London: Verso edns and NLB, 1983
Baird, Annie L. A. *Daybreak in Korea* New York: Fleming H. Revell, 1909
Berdyaev, Nicholai A. *Dream and Reality* London: Geoffrey Bles, 1950
——*The Meaning of History* Cleveland: Meridian Books, 1962
Berlin, Isaiah *Against the Current* London: Hogarth Press, 1979
——*Four Essays on Liberty* Oxford: Oxford University Press, 1969
Blair, William N. and Hunt, Bruce F. *The Korean Pentecost and the Sufferings which Followed* Edinburgh: Banner of Truth Trust, 1977
Campbell, E. M. and Allen, A. W. *Korea's Awakening* Melbourne: Brown, Prior & Co., 1921
Chandra, Vipan *Imperialism, Resistance, and Reform in Late Nineteenth-Century Korea* Berkeley: University of California Press, 1988
Chung, Chong-Shik and Ro, Jae-Bong *Nationalism in Korea* Seoul: Research Center for Peace and Unification, 1979
Chung, Henry *The Case of Korea* New York: Fleming H. Revell, 1921
Clark, Charles Allen *Religions of Old Korea* New York: Fleming H. Revell, 1932
——*The Korean Church and the Nevius Method* New York: Fleming H. Revell, 1930
Clark, Donald N. *Christianity in Modern Korea* Lanham: University Press of America, 1986
Clarke, Peter *Liberals and Social Democrats* Cambridge: Cambridge University Press, 1978
Conroy, Hilary *The Japanese Seizure of Korea 1868–1910* Philadelphia: University of Pennsylvania Press, 1960
Cook, Megan *The Constitutionalist Party in Cochinchina: The Years of Decline, 1930–1942* Melbourne: Monash Papers on Southeast Asia, 6, Centre of Southeast Asian Studies, Monash University, Victoria, 1977
Cynn, Hugh Heung-wo *The Rebirth of Korea* New York: Abingdon Press, 1920
Deutsch, Karl W. *Nationalism and its Alternatives* New York Alfred A. Knopf, 1969
Eliot, T. S. *Notes Towards the Definition of Culture* London: Faber and Faber, 1962
Gale, James S. *Korea in Transition* New York: People's Missionary Movement in the United States and Canada, 1909
Gellner, Ernest *Nations and Nationalism* Oxford: Basil Blackwell, 1983
Grajdanzev, Andrew J. *Modern Korea* New York: John Day, 1944
Hahm Pyong-Choon *The Korean Political Tradition and Law*, Seoul: Royal Asiatic Society, Korea Branch, 1971
Harrington, F. H. *God, Mammon, and the Japanese* Madison: University of Wisconsin Press, 1966
Hobhouse, L. T. *Liberalism* London: Williams and Norgate, 1911
Hunt, Lynn (ed.) *The New Cultural History* Berkeley, Los Angeles and London: University of California Press, 1989
Jansen, Marius B. *The Japanese and Sun Yat-sen* Cambridge, Mass.: Harvard University Press, 1967
Johnson, Richard (ed.) *Making Histories: Studies in history writing and poli-*

tics London: Hutchinson, in association with the Centre for Contemporary Cultural Studies, University of Birmingham, 1982

Kang Wi Jo *Religion and Politics in Korea under the Japanese Rule* New York: Edwin Mellen Press, 1987

Kamenka, Eugene (ed.) *Nationalism: The Evolution of an Idea* Canberra: Australian National University Press, 1975

Kim, C. I. and Doretha E. Mortimore (eds) *Korea's Response to Japan: The Colonial Period, 1910–1945* Kalamazoo: Center for Korean Studies, Western Michigan University, 1977

Kohn, Hans *The Idea of Nationalism* New York: Macmillan, 1945

Kroner, Richard, *Culture and Faith* Chicago: University of Chicago Press, 1951

Lamont, William L. *Richard Baxter and the Millennium* London: Croom Helm, 1979

Lee Chong-sik *The Politics of Korean Nationalism* Berkeley and Los Angeles: University of California Press, 1963

Lensen, George Alexander *Balance of Intrigue: International Rivalry in Korea and Manchuria, 1884–1899* 2 vols, Tallahassee: University Presses of Florida, 1982

Lerner, Gerder *The Creation of Patriarchy* New York: Oxford University Press, 1986

Levenson, Joseph R. *Confucian China and its Modern Fate* 3 vols, London: Routledge and Kegan Paul, 1965

—— *Revolution and Cosmopolitanism: The Western Stage and the Chinese Stages* Berkeley: University of California Press, 1971

Lim Ŭn (pseudonym) *The Founding of a Dynasty in North Korea: An Authentic Biography of Kim Il-sung* Tokyo: Jiyūsha, 1982

Lin Yü-sheng *The Crisis of Chinese Consciousness: Radical Antitraditionalism in the May Fourth Era* Madison: University of Wisconson Press, 1979

McKenzie, Frederick A. *Korea's Fight for Freedom* Seoul: Yonsei University Reprints, 1969

—— *The Tragedy of Korea* Seoul: Yonsei University Reprints, 1975

Maritain, Jacques *Man and the State* Chicago: University of Chicago Press, 1951

von der Mehden, F. R. *Religion and Nationalism in Southeast Asia* Madison: University of Wisconsin Press, 1963

Mitchell, Richard Hank *The Korean Minority in Japan* Berkeley and Los Angeles: University of California Press, 1967

Nahm, Andrew C. (ed.) *Korea under Japanese Colonial Rule* Kalamazoo: Center for Korean Studies, Western Michigan University, 1974

Niebuhr, Helmut Richard *Christ and Culture* London: Faber and Faber, 1952

Paik, Lak-Geoon George *The History of Protestant Missions in Korea, 1832–1910* Seoul: Yonsei University Reprints, 1971

Palmer, Spencer J. *Korea and Christianity* Seoul: Hollym Corporation, 1967

Palumbo, Michael and Shanahan William O. (eds) *Nationalism: Essays in Honour of Louis L Snyder* Westport: Connecticut: Greenwood Press, 1981

Read, Christopher *Religion. Revolution and the Russian Intelligentsia, 1900–1912* London: Macmillan, 1979

Robinson, Michael Edson *Cultural Nationalism in Colonial Korea, 1920–*

1925 Seattle and London: University of Washington Press, 1988

Sandeen, Ernest R. *The Roots of Fundamentalism: British and American Millenarianism, 1800–1930* Chicago: University of Chicago Press, 1970

Sands, William *Undiplomatic Memories: The Far East, 1896–1904* Seoul: Royal Asiatic Society, Korea Branch, Reprint, 1975

Schwartz, Benjamin *In Search of Wealth and Power: Yen Fu and the West* Cambridge, Mass.: Belknap Press of Harvard University Press, 1964

Shearer, Roy E. *Wildfire: Church Growth in Korea* Grand Rapids, Michigan: William B Eerdmans, 1966

Snyder, Louis L. *The Meaning of Nationalism* New Brunswick, New Jersey: Rutgers University Press, 1954

Suh Dae-sook *The Korean Communist Movement, 1918–1948* New Jersey: Princeton University Press, 1967

Tivey, Leonard (ed.) *The Nation-State: the formation of modern politics* New York: St Martin's Press, 1981

Underwood, Horace Horton *Modern Education in Korea* New York: International Press, 1926

Weems, B. B. *Reform, Rebellion and the Heavenly Way* Tucson: University of Arizona Press, 1964

Yim Louise *My Forty-Year Fight for Korea* Seoul: Chungang University Press, 1964

Articles

(a) Korean and Japanese

Ch'oe Tuko 'Amhŭkki kaehwain ŭi sunansa' *Yŏksa ŭi Inmul* 10 vols, Seoul: Ilshinsa, 1979, 8

Lee Kwangnin 'Kaikaha no Kaishinkyūkan' *Kan* 7, 11–12 (November–December 1978)

—— 'Kaikaki no Kansei chihō to Kaishinkyō' *Kan* 8, 2 (February 1979)

Yi Man'yŏl 'Iljche kwanhakjadŭl ŭi Han'guksa sŏsul' *Han'guk Saron*, 6 (1979)

(b) English

Fisher, Charles A. 'The Role of Korea in the Far East' *Geographical Journal* 120 (1954)

Hahm Pyong-Choon 'Korean Perception of America' (Posthumous article) *Sahakji* 17 (November 1983)

—— 'Shamanism: Foundation of the Korean World-view Part Two: Society and Social Life' *Korean Culture*, 2:1 (February 1981)

Kim Kwang-ok 'Flexibility of Korean Religious Thought' *Korea Journal* 23:7 (July 1983)

Lee Ki-baik 'Nationalism in Tanjae's Historical Study' *Korea Journal* 19:9 (September 1979)

Matsuo Takayoshi 'The Japanese Protestants in Korea, Part One: The Missionary Activity of the Japan Congregational Church in Korea' *Modern Asian Studies* 13:3 (1979)

—— 'The Japanese Protestants in Korea, Part Two: The 1st March Movement and the Japanese Protestants' *Modern Asian Studies*, 13:4 (1979)

Wang Gungwu 'The Chinese Urge to Civilize: Reflections on Change' *Proceedings of The Australian Academy of the Humanities, 1982–1983* Victoria: The Dominion Press-Hedges and Bell, 1984

Wells, Kenneth M. 'Background to the March First Movement: Koreans in Japan, 1905–1919' *Korean Studies* 13 (1989)

—— 'Civic Morality in the Nationalist Thought of Yun Ch'i-ho, 1881–1911' *Papers on Far Eastern History* 28 (September 1983)

—— 'The Rationale of Korean Economic Nationalism under Japanese Colonial Rule, 1922–1932: The Case of Cho Man-sik's Products Promotion Society' *Modern Asian Studies* 19:4 (November 1985)

——'Spencer and Mahan in Kimonos: Japanese Colonial Theory,' *Journal of East and West Studies* 10:1 (April 1981)

——'Yun Ch'i-ho and the Quest for National Integrity' *Korea Journal* 22:1 (January 1982)

Unpublished doctoral dissertations

Chung Joong-gun, Japanese Colonial Administration in Korea, 1905–1919, Claremont Graduate School and University Center, 1971

Dong Wonmo, Japanese Colonial Policy and Practice in Korea, 1905–1945: A Study in Assimilation, Georgetown University, 1965

Eckert, Carter J., The Colonial Origins of Korean Capitalism: The Koch'ang Kims and the Kyongsong Spinning and Weaving Company, 1876–1945, University of Washington, 1986

Gardner, Arthur Leslie, The Korean Nationalist Movement and An Ch'ang-ho, Advocate of Gradualism, University of Hawaii, 1979

Park Chung-shin, Protestant Christians and Politics in Korea, 1884–1980s, University of Washington, 1987

Park Yong-Shin, Protestant Christianity and Social Change in Korea, University of California, Berkeley, 1975

Robinson, Michael E., The Origins and Development of Korean Nationalist Ideology, 1920–1926: Culture, Identity, National Development, and Political Schism, University of Washington, 1979

Wells, Kenneth M., Protestants and the Formation of Korean Self-Reconstruction Nationalism, 1896–1937, Australian National University, 1985

Index